BEYOND NATIONALIST FRAMES

Postmodernism,
Hindu Fundamentalism, History

Beyond
Nationalist Frames
Postmodernism,
Hindu Fundamentalism, History

SUMIT SARKAR

INDIANA
University Press
Bloomington & Indianapolis

This book is a publication of

Indiana University Press
601 North Morton Street
Bloomington, Indiana 47404-3797 USA

http://iupress.indiana.edu

Telephone orders	800-842-6796
Fax orders	812-855-7931
Orders by e-mail	iuporder@indiana.edu

Published in South Asia by Permanent Black
D-28 Oxford Apts, 11 IP Extension, New Delhi 110092

This edition is for sale outside South Asia
by arrangement with Permanent Black

Printed in India

Cataloging information is available from the Library of Congress.

ISBN 0-253-34203-1 (cloth)

1 2 3 4 5 07 06 05 04 03 02

Contents

Acknowledgements

THE IDEA of this book came from Aditya, who has helped also through criticisms and suggestions. To Tanika, as always, I remain grateful for trenchant criticism, abundant help, and inspiration from her own work. It will be obvious how much many parts of the book owe to Pradip Datta's findings and stimulating ideas.

The specific occasions for which earlier versions of several chapters were prepared have been mentioned at the appropriate places. In addition, I have been trying out some of the material and interpretations presented here with many different audiences and locations: in Delhi University and several of its colleges; at Jadavpur, Pune, and Mumbai Universities; at the School of Oriental and African Studies (London), on more than one occasion; at Toronto, Ottawa, Johannesburg, Cape Town, and in lectures to the University of Hawaii at Manoa; and at research institutes and universities in Berlin, Heidelberg, Pavia, Bologna, and Rome. I have benefited much from the responses and criticisms everywhere.

The chapter on nuclearisation is heavily indebted to Praful Bidwai and Achin Vanaik. Among the very many who have helped, through comments, conversations, work on conjoint themes, I want to mention particularly Jasodhara Bagchi, Himani Bannerji, Neeladri Bhattacharya, Sekhar Bandopadhyay, Amiya Sen, and Radhika Singha. Rukun Advani has been the most patient and helpful of editors. The responsibility for omissions and errors remains mine alone.

And a very special word of thanks for all who came forward, in friendship and solidarity, during the attack on the *Towards Freedom* volumes.

Introduction

THE CHAPTERS of this volume were originally written between 1996 and 2001. Chapters VI, VII, and VIII are substantially revised; the others are published here for the first time. Though written for varied occasions, without any thought, till quite recently, of incorporation into a single format, I think they do have a certain unity. As in my earlier collection of long essays, *Writing Social History* (1997), this has emerged from an unity of contexts: the vicissitudes of our times, at once political and academic

I had defined such contexts in 1997 in terms of the advance of the Hindu Right and of 'globalised' forms of capitalism; a worldwide marginalisation of Marxisms, whether 'orthodox' or 'revisionist', after the sudden demise of most 'actually existing' socialist regimes; and the academic shift from social history towards cultural studies and varied 'postmodernistic' moods. The challenges such developments have posed evidently continue, often in aggravated form, and are in some ways particularly acute for a historian who retains an unfashionable commitment to socialist-feminist values and a vision of democratic and humane forms of socialism, and who therefore finds any simple, nostalgic return to the orthodoxies of yesteryears as unpalatable as swimming with the current tides of history and politics.

As in the earlier volume, I have tried here to explore the possibilities of a renewal of radical, flexibly Marxian social history, in part through a series of research-based articles on late-colonial Bengal. These are followed by one explicitly theoretical essay which seeks to explicate a complicated position about postmodernism, refusing both total rejection and uncritical acceptance of the dominant postmodernist positions. The book ends with three political interventions about current Hindutva policies and values.

Re-reading and revising the essays for publication, I have been struck by another unifying theme more directly linked to my professional concerns as a historian working on colonial India. The dominant historiographical assumption here—one that has cut across many widely-varied approaches—has been of a single, overwhelmingly predominant, colonial/anti-colonial binary. This is at its most obvious in conventional nationalist histories and textbooks, where quite often virtually nothing seems to have happened between the 1880s and 1947 except the 'freedom struggle', colonial repression, and sundry 'separatist' tendencies acting in tandem with British divide-and-rule to tarnish the coming of freedom with a tragic Partition. Left-nationalist, Marxist, and, above all, early Subaltern Studies and other attempts at 'histories from below' considerably complicated and improved this model. The initiatives and mentalities of peasants, adivasis, and workers, previously marginalised or assumed to have been capable of being mobilised from 'above' alone, came to be highlighted, and there was a search for elements of subaltern autonomy having complicated relations, of simultaneous impetus and constraint, with 'mainstream' nationalism. But the implicit standard for the evaluation of such movements remained the degree of their 'contribution', or otherwise, to anti-colonialism.[1] Today, of course, critiques of nationalism have become extremely influential among many intellectuals. Yet I think there remains a paradoxical continuity through rejection, for denunciations of the 'nation-state project' are based primarily on the grounds of its origin in the modern West. They

---

[1] In an earlier essay I drew attention to such an 'unnoticed drift' in Ranajit Guha's initial formulation of the Subaltern Studies project in the first volume of that series. His essay was entitled 'On Some Aspects of the Historiography of Colonial India': it dealt almost exclusively with the historiography of Indian nationalism and described as its fundamental lacuna the failure 'to acknowledge the contribution made by the people on their own to the making and development of this nationalism.' *Subaltern Studies I* (Delhi, 1982), pp. 2–3; Sumit Sarkar, 'The Decline of the Subaltern in Subaltern Studies', in *Writing Social History* (Delhi, 1997), p. 92.

commonly take the form of a colonial discourse/indigenous authenticity binary which often seems a 'culturalist' variant of that earlier dichotomy.

But not everything in late-colonial subcontinental history can or should be reduced to a single colonial/anti-colonial frame. Evaluation in terms of contribution to anti-colonial politics or degree of cultural authenticity can be particularly constrictive for histories of gender and women's rights, as well as of subordinate-caste movements. For such affirmations by the underprivileged among the colonised often used as important resources, ideas derived from Western-colonial modernity, and sought assistance from the institutions of the colonial state. Similar complications arise with some tribal, peasant or labour protests, as well as concerning many communities sought to be constructed around particular languages, ethnicities, or religions. We need to be open to the possibility of many histories and trajectories, in need of evaluation by multiple criteria, and here some aspects of postmodernistic scepticism about homogenised, unilinear models do provide helpful warnings.

Yet there can be no question, obviously, of any denial of the crucialness of colonialism and of anti-colonial struggles in modern South Asian history, least of all when so many forms of imperialist domination are staging a massive, worldwide comeback camouflaged by the anodyne rhetoric of 'globalisation'. There remains a need to make distinctions between different kinds of 'nation-state' projects, with specific contours and locations in time. Homogenisation quite often operates nowadays through homogenised rejections. Nor do I find at all helpful efforts to push rejection of unilinearity towards an assumption that only 'fragments' or non-processual fleeting moments can be studied. The search for interconnections must not be abandoned, but made much more complicated and freed from all forms of reductionism. The imposition of a single frame, and values derived from it, on an entire immensely varied subcontinental history is harmful and indeed impossible, but it remains vital to explore the multitude of interrelations and crosscurrents. We may take a cue from the development of the more fruitful kinds of feminist history in the West, in recent decades. It could not have emerged without a rejection of tendencies towards collapsing gender into class and production relations in reductive manner (characteristic of much orthodox Marxism) but—at its best—does not abstract gender studies from histories of evolving capitalist social forms.

'Colonial Times: Clocks and Kaliyuga', the earliest of the essays (1996), is less connected with the problematic just outlined and indicated through the title of the present volume. Nationalist frames, however, have often shared with the more aggressive kinds of 'civilising-mission' writings an assumption of an over-sharp pre-colonial/colonial disjunction, with of course the value judgements inverted. I argue that this may have contributed to the strange neglect in historiography so far both of the advent of mechanical clock-time in South Asia, as well as of the persistence-through-change of the motif of Kali-yuga. My essay speculates about possible reasons for the delayed entry, despite no lack of contacts with the West from at least the sixteenth century onwards, and explores some of the complicated responses through a study of nineteenth-century printed vernacular material.

Like clock-time, the late entry of mechanical print has been inadequately problematised. Both, I feel, have been somewhat occluded by the specific form which the current focus on colonial cultural domination has tended to adopt—a concentration on 'English education', once widely hailed as the harbinger of a 'renaissance', nowadays denounced as a mere instrument of alien hegemony. Predominantly vernacular print-culture had, however, a much wider social range, and, arguably, greater historical significance. Delayed entry—attributable in both cases not to technological non-availability, but social conditions stimulating, or hindering, demands for deployment—seems to have meant a telescoping of phases of change that had been much more spread out temporally in the West, and consequently, perhaps, a greater impact at times. Thus print-culture in nineteenth-century Bengal came to be quickly associated not just with the stimulus to vernacular publication via reductions in price and exact reproduction inseparable from its entry everywhere, but also with insertion of punctuation, vastly enhanced portability, and a great expansion in prose genres. Some of these developments had taken place at times within scribal culture in the West, as for instance the shift from *volumina* to a much more portable *codex* manuscript form in later Roman-Imperial times, or the coming of Latin punctuation in the early middle ages.[2] In Bengal, punctuation is generally associated with Vidyasagar, and the typical manuscript even in the nineteenth century seems to have been far from readily portable, or conducive to easy reading.[3] But then the whole vital subject of the physical, formal aspects of reading matter, manuscript or print, remains grossly under-explored by historians in South Asia.[4] I am aware that, with some partial exception in relation to lower-caste writings, my own analysis of the vernacular tracts that constitute the bulk of the new empirical data I present in these essays remains at the level of content, and has failed to explore questions of form or of possible ways of reading.

Chapters I to V use a large number of little-known vernacular tracts, occasional archival material, and one major text of high-culture—Rabindranath's *Ghare-Baire* (1915–16)—in efforts to enter the social worlds of lower-middle-class *bhadralok*, lower castes, Muslim peasants and rural literati, and gender images and relationships. The temporal focus—clock-time chapter apart—is on the ten years or so following the decline of the Swadeshi movement in Bengal. Except for the saga of revolutionary terrorism, standard nationalist frames have naturally found little space for this decade, which came as a trough between two peak points of anti-colonial struggle, Swadeshi and Non-Cooperation–Khilafat. I am indebted to Pradip Datta for first drawing my attention to its importance as seed-time for a large number of alternative and crosscutting possibilities and identity formations: communalisms both Hindu and Muslim, castes, peasants, women.[5]

Feminist history and cultural studies have stimulated a major revival of interest in nineteenth-century middle class 'social reform', with its predominant focus on women's issues. The era of high

[2] Guglielmo Cavallo and Roger Chartier, eds, *A History of Reading in the West* (Oxford, 1999), chapters 2–3, and *passim*.
[3] Tanika Sarkar, *Words to Win: The Making of Amar Jivan: A Modern Autobiography* (Delhi, 1999), p. 64.
[4] See, however, for a brief but helpful overview of changing South Asian manuscript forms, Jeremiah P. Losly, *The Art of the Book in India* (London, 1982).
[5] Pradip Kumar Datta, *Carving Blocs: Communal Ideology in Early Twentieth-century Bengal* (Delhi, 1999), as well as numerous personal conversations.

nationalism, in sharp contrast, has been relatively neglected, and an impression prevails that the 'women's question' was marginalised in the early twentieth century through a nationalist ideological 'resolution'. Chapter V argues, on a combination of conceptual and empirical grounds—once again drawing on post-Swadeshi data—that some debilitating simplifications have been at work here. The thrust of this chapter, however, is not polemical, but a reading of *Ghare-Baire* that seeks to highlight the importance and abiding value of that novel—as critique of nationalism, of course, but even more as a sensitive portrayal of alternative conceptions of masculinity and womanhood embodied in the personal interrelationships of Sandip, Nikhilesh, and Bimala. Simultaneously, I try to relate the novel, along with the series of remarkable short stories which Tagore published just around that time in *Sabuj Patra*, to a largely unnoticed renewal-cum-extension of nonconformist thinking on women's issues in the post-Swadeshi years. This was stimulated particularly by contrasting responses to a *cause celebre* of early 1914, the Snehalata Case.

Chapters II and III seek to build upon the pioneering work of Sekhar Bandopadhyay on Namasudras.[6] The interrelationships between identity formations and imaginings of history are explored through a close reading of seven Namasudra texts, juxtaposed with available data about changing agrarian relationships of bhadralok gentry and Namasudra peasants and sharecroppers in the Bakargunj-Faridpur region of East Bengal.[7] Throughout the research-based chapters, I have tried to combine empirical analysis with the raising of some more general issues—among which I will mention at this point the one closest to the overall tenor of my argument. There was a close concordance, in location, time, and probable social composition, between the Namasudra caste movement, a dissident religious sect (the Matuas) and agrarian unrest during the Swadeshi and immediate post-Swadeshi years. Yet certain disjunctions are also apparent, manifested for instance in the fact that we learn about the sharecropper agitation mainly from official documents: Namasudra

[6] Sekhar Bandopadhyay, *Caste, Protest, and Identity: The Namasudras of Bengal, 1872–1947* (Richmond, 1997).

[7] I have benefited considerably here from the work of Nariaki Nakazato, *Agrarian System in Eastern Bengal, c. 1870–1910* (Calcutta, 1994).

caste-pamphlets remain silent about it. The theoretical question that emerges concerns the relationships/distinctions between formations of class and of identity—in today's terms, the articulations (or, more often perhaps, their absence) between a politics of redistribution or equality, and one of recognition.[8]

Late-colonial South Asia was marked by the invention and/or consolidation of a large number of putative, inevitably crosscutting, identities. Organisations claiming to speak on behalf of anti-colonial 'nationalist', language-based 'regional', religious, ethnic, caste, labour, peasant, and gender solidarities all emerged between the 1870s and 1920s. That identities were hardening in this era is very widely recognised today, though explanations as to why that was happening might differ. It is less often noted that synchronous alternative emergence also produced fragility, and that one response tended to be the fostering of enemy images of one or several Others. The post-Swadeshi decade in Bengal seems to offer particularly rich illustrations of these processes. Chapter III traces the genesis of a kind of 'Hindutva' ideology among some high-caste elements. This emerged in the vortex of a felt threat posed by lower-caste upthrust and peasant unrest, along with the much better-known simultaneous development of Muslim identity politics. Datta and Bandopadhyay provide considerable evidence that communalised Hindu unity projects did gain significant support at times also from lower-caste groups, though the tensions here were never completely overcome. Chapter IV, a conjoint reading of two mutually-contrasting Muslim tracts of 1909–10 directed towards peasants, indicates the occasional possibility of a trajectory of an opposite kind, where a felt need for class unity could undercut calls for communal solidarity.

Chapter VI (which in its initial incarnation was a presentation to a philosophy seminar) is an essay of a different, more 'global' kind, not primarily geared to questions of South Asian historiography or history. Postmodernist critiques of history have taken two main forms. From a relativistic angle, refurbished by deconstructionist questioning of genre distinctions in language-use, the truth-claims of

[8] For a recent formulation—one of many, of course—that I have found helpful, see Nancy Fraser, 'Rethinking Recognition', in *New Left Review*, May–June 2000.

history are condemned as unreconstructed positivism. Simultaneously, history-writing is convicted for an allegedly indissoluble contami-
nation by post-Enlightenment forms of statist power. I attempt a
nuanced response that acknowledges elements of value in some of this
critique, but argue that the benefits can be obtained only through a
simultaneous struggle against many of the built-in thrusts within
postmodernism itself. The historiographical data I deploy for my
argument is taken in significant part from recent work on British and
European social and cultural history. But links with many of the
general themes emerging from the earlier chapters will also be evident.
Thus I suggest that the current appeal of postmodernistic ways for
a significant number of South Asian scholars—historians within or
influenced by late Subaltern Studies, students of literature drawn into
the burgeoning field of 'postcoloniality', many feminists—often has
had a paradoxical, largely unrecognised, cultural-nationalistic ambience that is helping to refurbish the binary mode of thinking that I
am arguing against. Paradoxical, because there is much in postmodernism that can help to undermine precisely such assumptions.

The three chapters that make up the concluding part of the volume
confront directly the current onslaughts of the Hindu Right. The
issues I take up are nuclearisation, the anti-Christian campaign centred around the issue of conversions, and Hindutva versions of
history—where I also touch on the recent official blocking of some
volumes of the 'Towards Freedom' project. A general question that
emerges from these chapters concerns the complicated pattern of
simultaneous disjunctions and affinities between Hindutva and other
kinds of South Asian nationalisms. We cannot afford to downplay
the distinctions: no other cultural-political formation has so consistently and systematically advocated the bomb, inculcated hatred of
Muslims and Christians, propagated and sought to impose utterly
outdated, crudely chauvinist notions of history. The Hindu Right is
much more than just another, particularly unpleasant, 'nation-state'
project, and I have little patience with efforts to collapse critiques of
it into a generalised rejection of 'Western modernity'. The tinges of
cultural nationalism often present in such positions make chauvinistic appropriation by no means impossible.

Yet, as I argue in these three chapters, affinities operate in other directions, too. Being more conventionally 'secular', in the predominant Indian sense of non- or anti-communal, has often involved immersion in a language of 'national' unity as the supreme value, 'integration', independent development along technocratic-statist lines. Initial reactions to Pokhran, and unexpected hesitations on the conversions issue, indicate how such values can spill over into quasi-Hindutva positions. The Hindutva version of Indian history, again, is obviously grounded on certain kinds of 'nationalist' readings that had once predominated, had been overcome at sophisticated levels through research over the past generation, but are now being sought to be reimposed by state action. As perhaps also in the concomitant defence of national sovereignty against globalised imperialism, secular political nationalism might be at times an indispensable fall-back position. There remains a need, simultaneously, to seek beyond the parameters of 'statist' and 'culturalist' nationalisms alike, whether in history-writing or political activism—to move towards socially radical and internationalist values appropriate to our vastly transformed times.

CHAPTER I

Colonial Times
Clocks and Kali-yuga[1]

THE TITLE of this essay seeks to play on an ambiguity. 'Colonial times': the reference, primarily, is to a familiar yet surprisingly little-explored fact. Despite fairly high levels of contact with Europe from at least the late fifteenth century, clocks and watches entered India on a significant scale very late—only under colonial rule, around the turn of the eighteenth-nineteenth century. This belated entry produced a remarkable yet little-noticed telescoping of phases. The transition from late medieval stationary clocks (showing hours alone), to watches (portable and increasingly ubiquitous, ticking off minutes and seconds), to bureaucratic-industrial structures of time took some five hundred years in Western Europe. Belatedness in the oriental context meant that clocks, watches, and time-discipline were brought to colonial India more or less simultaneously, across a couple of generations, starting *c.* 1800. Elements of tension, conflict and pain in the Western transition to clock-time have often been emphasised: one could expect these to have been present in South Asia too, aggravated by the fact that the abrupt shift was a foreign imposition.

Indological scholarship is copious on 'cyclical' notions of time in high-Hindu Sanskrit texts: Satya, always followed by ever-more

[1] This is a revised version of a paper presented at a conference on notions of time at the Maison des sciences de l'homme, Paris, June 1996. I have been greatly helped by comments and criticisms made at the conference.

degenerate Treta- Dwapar- and Kali-yugas, succeeding each other in
endless cycles. High-Hindu notions of time embedded in Sanskrit
religious texts provided, in fact, a principal foundation for Mircea
Eliade's influential study of the 'myth of the eternal return'. For
Eliade, Hindu cyclicity represented the polar opposite of the allegedly
unique Judaeo-Christian notion of linearity from which alone the
modern conception of time could have emerged.[2] One could expect
a transition from such presumed notions to commonsensically modern, 'linear' assumptions about time to have been exceptionally sharp,
perhaps painful.

Most crucially of all, perhaps, scholars as different as Jacques Le
Goff, E.P. Thompson, Michel Foucault, David Landes, and many
others have directed attention to the disciplinary aspects of modern
clock-time in the West.[3] It should surely be interesting to explore
whether similar processes were unleashed by the coming of clocks to
India, as well as the extent and the ways in which colonial rule may
have made things different. 'Colonial times', then, also in a second,
conjoint sense—that of context, overall conditions.

I am concerned here with interconnections between shifts in notions of time and in technologies for its measurement, on the one
hand, and evolving colonial society on the other. My focus will be
on Bengal, on account of my familiarity with its language and sources,
as well as the early and deep colonial penetration of that region.

My theme is a little-explored one, I have said, so far as historians
of modern India are concerned—and one might begin by briefly con-
sidering why. One barrier to historical exploration might have been
over-sharp notions of a fundamental cyclical/linear binary, which

[2] Mircea Eliade, *The Myth of the Eternal Return* (Paris, 1949; trans. London,
1955), *passim.*

[3] Jacques Le Goff, 'Labour Time in the Crisis of the Fourteenth Century: From
Medieval Time to Modern Time', *Le Moyen Age*, 1963; translated in Le Goff,
Time, Work, and Culture in the Middle Ages (Chicago, 1980); E.P. Thompson,
'Time, Work-Discipline, and Industrial Capitalism', *Past and Present* 38, De-
cember 1967, reprinted in Thompson, *Customs in Common* (Penguin 1993);
Michel Foucault, *Discipline and Punish* (Paris, 1975; Peregrine, 1977); David
Landes, *Revolution in Time: Clocks and the Making of the Modern World* (Cam-
bridge, Mass., 1983); David Harvey, *The Condition of Postmodernity* (Cambridge
Mass., and Oxford, 1990), Part III.

now, happily, is in the main discarded.[4] Cyclical time, as construed in much Indological scholarship, tended to have an exotic, strongly 'Orientalising' flavour, far removed from today's commonsense, and not obviously present in the sorts of sources with which most historians of nineteenth- or twentieth-century India have worked till fairly recently: colonial archives, plus Indian writings in English. (I shall argue, though, that Indian-language sources might sometimes make a partial difference.) It was easy to assume, therefore, a quick, total, unproblematic transition from cyclical to linear with the advent of the clock. This assumption has been strengthened by the further postulate—common to a wide range of otherwise very different, even mutually conflicting, historiographical traditions—of a virtually total rupture between the pre-colonial and the colonial. Aggressively colonialist writings confident of Britain's civilising mission, nationalist theories of absolute decline under foreign rule, Marxist explorations of transitions from 'Asiatic' or 'feudal' society, and recent theories of all-pervasive colonial power-knowledge—all have tended to share such an assumption. Dissident views emphasising continuities across pre-colonial and colonial have been widely suspected (not entirely without basis, at times) of a degree of affinity with that other kind of neo-colonial apologetics which, failing to establish the case for effective progress or modernisation under British rule, blames not colonial exploitation but persistent natural, social or cultural barriers to growth and prosperity.

My interest in colonial times was first aroused by evidence of the persistence, even proliferation, of the Kali-yuga motif in some kinds of Bengali-language writings of the late nineteenth century, well after

[4] Many recent anthropological and historical writings on time in non-Western societies begin with repudiations of the cyclical/linear binary, for it is now widely recognised that combinations have been common, and perceptions of duration or sequentiality are common to both. For evidence from places and times as far apart as pre-colonial Yucatan and present-day Bali, see Nancy M. Farris, 'Remembering the Future, Anticipating the Past: History, Time and Cosmology among the Mayas of Yucatan', *Comparative Studies in Society and History*, 29, iii, July 1987, and L.E.A. Howe, 'The Social Determination of Knowledge: Maurice Bloch and Balinese Time', *Man*, New Series, 19, 1981. There are also elements of linearity within classical Hindu cyclical time, for Treta, Dwapar, and Kali come successively after Satya in an invariable order.

the introduction of clock-time. What appeared important was not so much mere persistence or survival, but modulations of old stereotypes of Kali-yuga in ways that indicated a response to the new pressures of colonial time-discipline. Before studying these responses, however, there is a need to probe three questions. If the cyclical/linear binary is unhelpful, where precisely did pre-colonial notions of time differ from the commonsensically modern? Dare one speculate about why the coming of clocks and watches was so delayed in South Asia? And finally, what were the specific sites of colonial time-discipline, and which were the social groups initially affected by it? Answers to these would help contextualise and better understand the vernacular plays and tracts in which references to Kali-yuga are so abundant.

II

The high-Hindu, Brahmanical notion of time emphasised moral deterioration both within the successive Satya, Treta, Dwapar, and Kali-yugas, and across them, each being worse than its predecessor. The present, invariably described as Kali, was the worst of all. It would last no less than 432,000 years and end in apocalyptic manner with universal fire, flood, or martial intervention by Kalki, the last incarnation of Vishnu, after which another identical four-yuga cycle would commence. The emphasis upon aeons of time, very different from the biblical idea of Creation as an event 4000-odd years before Christ, in effect reduced the importance of cyclicity, since the new cycle would begin only in a very distant future. Much more crucial was the stress upon retrogressively linear moral decline. Time, in other words, was not abstract, empty duration, but relevant primarily for moral qualities inseparable from its cyclical phases.

A few details about standard notions of Kali-yuga need to be presented here in order to appreciate the nineteenth-century modulations which comprise one of my themes. A recurrent and powerful format for voicing high-caste male anxieties for some two thousand years, the evils of Kali-yuga include disorders in nature, oppressive alien kings, Brahmans corrupted by too much rationalistic debate, overmighty Shudras no longer serving their caste superiors, and women choosing their own partners, disobeying and deceiving husbands, and having intercourse with menials, slaves, and even animals.

The principal role of the yuga-cycle in Brahmanical discourses was thus to suggest through dystopia the indispensability of correct caste and gender hierarchy. The two have been necessarily imagined as interdependent, for purity of caste descent could be ensured only through male control over the reproductive capacities of women, keeping marriage restricted within permitted boundaries. The central message was one of resignation: the evils of Kali-yuga were inevitable and the apocalypse lay so far in the future as to be largely irrelevant. The evils could, however, be made more endurable by modifications in ritual practices: the Kali-varjya, things allowed earlier but now declared impermissible by Brahman ritual experts. Caste and gender discipline was tightened through these from the twelfth-thirteenth century. The endless cycles themselves sometimes came to be considered part of the world of maya (illusion; or, more precisely, an inferior order of reality), and the high-Hindu ideal came to be not so much the restoration of Satya-yuga, which would degenerate anyway, but purely individual escape, moksha, through the alternative paths of asceticism, intellectual contemplation, ritual, or bhakti.[5]

Kali-yuga notions came to be modified in a significant way in the medieval centuries, when powerful bhakti movements developed with the considerable participation, and even occasional leadership, of lower castes and women. Shudras and women, normally the primary sources of Kali-yuga evil, were now sometimes even exalted as ideal devotees, for whom deliverance would be easiest through simple recitation of the divine name and by the performance of appropriate duties towards high-caste men and husbands. A richly ambiguous space, of the order of a safety-valve, was thus created for subordinate groups: attractive, at times almost encouraging rebelliousness, but always open to ultimate recuperation by dominant caste and gender

[5] A principal *locus classicus* of the classic Kali-yuga myth is in the *Mahabharata*, 'Vanaparva', Sections 187–90 of the 'Markandya-Samasya'. I am using an English prose translation by Pratapchandra Roy (Calcutta, n.d.), as well as the authoritative nineteenth-century Bengali translation by Kaliprasanna Sinha in the Gopal Haldar edition (Calcutta, 1974). I have also consulted P.V. Kane, *History of the Dharmashastras*, volume III (Pune, 1973), chapter XXXIV; R.C. Hazra, *Studies in the Upapuranas*, volume I (Calcutta, 1963), pp. 140, 324–5; and Mircea Eliade, op. cit., chapters I, II, IV.

hierarchies. Subalternity could be privileged, provided it remained properly subaltern.[6]

The standard Indological assumption of a single, cyclical notion of time in pre-colonial India has been much questioned in recent years. Classical Indology tended to ignore Indo-Islamic notions entirely, and scholars have noted the presence of not one but several layers even in pre-Islamic Indian conceptions of time. Dynastic eras and chronicles of rulers often had little to do with yuga cycles except in prefatory or moralising passages. They could be perfectly precise about dates and clearly operated within quite linear frames. One needs to be open also to the possibility of work or task-oriented times, where the degree of exactitude could vary according to specific requirements. Ritual experts and astrologers needed a precise fix on certain time-points to determine auspicious moments for ceremonies, or when making predictions. Rural labour processes, in contrast, demanded little more than a grasp over general daily and seasonal rhythms.[7] It is necessary to emphasise also that our virtually total ignorance of notions of time among pre-colonial peasants or lower-caste people in general provides no grounds for assuming that they must have invariably internalised the hierarchised values inseparable from formulations of the four-yuga cycle that have come down to us.[8]

[6] For analysis of the paradoxes of bhakti, in general as well as in relation to Kali-yuga, I have found helpful Kumkum Sangari, 'Mirabai and the Spiritual Economy of Bhakti', *Economic and Political Weekly*, xxv, 27–8, 14 July 1990; W.C. Beane, *Myth, Cult and Symbol in Shakta Hinduism* (London, 1977), pp. 237–9; and Madeleine Biardeau, *Hinduism: The Anthropology of a Civilisation* (Delhi, 1989), p. 105.

[7] For studies emphasising such variations, see Raymondo Panikkar, 'Time and History in the Tradition of India: Kala and Karma', in L. Gardet *et al.*, *Cultures and Time* (Paris, 1976); L. Gardet's essay on Islamic notions of time in the same volume; and Romila Thapar, *Time as a Metaphor of History: Early India* (Delhi, 1996).

[8] A late but still striking example: Balaram Hadi (*c.* 1780–1850), founder of an entirely plebeian low-caste sect in central Bengal (Nadia district), postulated a Divya-yuga (divine era) superior and prior to the four yugas of Brahmanical orthodoxy. Balarami oral traditions invariably express bitter hostility towards high-caste landlords. Sudhir Chakrabarti, *Balarami Sampraday Tader Gan* (Calcutta, 1988).

Are generalisations about pre-colonial or pre-modern times permissible at all, then, amidst such variety? I find very helpful here Moishe Postone's suggestion that a concrete/abstract distinction would be more relevant than the conventional cyclical/linear binary. Exploring the wider implications of the basic Marxist concept of abstract labour time, Postone argues that a characteristic and fundamental feature of the capitalist era is its universalisation of 'temporality as a measure of activity'. The main function of time becomes the measurement and synchronisation of labour through the application of 'commensurable, interchangeable and invariable' work-units. Such time is 'empty', 'abstract', 'an independent variable; it constitutes an independent framework within which motion, events and action occur.'[9] Pre-capitalist notions of time, despite their immense variety, were in contrast qualitative or concrete, 'functions of events', characterised less by direction than by being a dependent variable: 'time was not an autonomous category, independent of events, hence, it could be determined qualitatively, as good or bad, sacred or profane.'[10]

Postone's conception of concrete time is broad enough to cover an immense range of time-notions: 'task' or 'job-oriented' times which could differ very widely in precision; time dominated by moral quality, as in the Brahmanical four-yuga cycle; ritual time-points as in astrology or medieval European monasteries, which had to be fixed with great precision and yet could manage with hours varying with seasons, because the fixing of points was needed much more than exact measurements of duration. Linear times, Christian or Islamic, were also concrete, in the sense of being dependent on crucial sacred events (for Christianity: the Fall, Crucifixion, the Second Coming).

Helpful as it is, one needs to be careful not to press the concrete/abstract distinction too far, and to avoid erecting it into yet another rigid binary. For the abstract time of modern societies is also often experienced and responded to in varying and different ways, as notably in class struggles over the length of the working day. Periods of time, a sociologist reminds us, can 'acquire qualities by virtue of

[9] Moishe Postone, *Time, Labor, and Social Domination: A Reinterpretation of Marx's Critical Theory* (Cambridge, 1993), p. 202.
[10] Ibid., p. 201, and *passim*.

association with the activities peculiar to them, and this as much in traditional as in industrial societies.'[11] This might help us understand how moods associated with Kali-yuga and its notions could flourish well after the penetration of clock-time linearity.

Besides being *abstract*, in the sense of being conceptually removed from both specific tasks or events as well as moral qualities, the linear time measured by clocks—which has become the commonsense of modern societies[12]—is marked by three other interrelated features. It is, first, time that is *measurable*, with ever-increasing precision and minuteness. Second, and crucially from the social-historical point of view, time has become *individualised*, made immediately and personally knowable through portable watches: these, much more than the stationary clocks invented several centuries earlier, have been key agents of change in technological terms. (Sun-dials and water-clocks or clepsydra could be almost as accurate as early mechanical clocks, but only watches allow the real individualisation of time.) Third, such individualisation has enabled the enforcement and internalisation of modern *time-discipline*. Both internalisation and a varying degree of partially autonomous management, it should be added—as when trade unions struggle to reduce the length of the working day, or when watches allow students to efficiently manage the writing of answers in examinations.

The transformations in notions of time that today make this set of assumptions appear so 'natural' would have been impossible without the development of mechanical clocks and portable watches. There remains the need to avoid technological determinism, for the changes have not been automatic responses to innovation. Rather, innovations became generalised only in areas and situations where broader social processes created specific needs for the precise and abstract measurement of time.[13] It is in terms of such specific contexts

---

[11] Gilles Pronovost, 'Sociology of Time', in *Current Sociology*, 37, iii, Winter 1989.

[12] Commonsense—as distinct from philosophical and scientific thinking (where other notions of time are often seriously debated).

[13] As Landes puts it in his fine study, 'The clock did not create an interest in time measurement; the interest in time measurement led to the invention of the clock.' He reminds us also that a process of denaturalising is needed for the posing

and demands, or rather their absence, that we can perhaps tentatively indulge in some guesswork as to why clock-time took so long to come to South Asia. Despite the widespread consensus that medieval Indian machine-making technology was generally below the levels attained by China, and from around the fourteenth century below those of parts of Western Europe, a narrowly technological explanation will not do. There was a flourishing maritime trade with Western Europe from the sixteenth century and a probable import of some mechanical clocks for use by Europeans, and as novelties in court circles.[14] The problem is why this did not lead to adaptation or significant import and use for several centuries.

III

Landes's study of the evolution of clocks and watches in the West pinpoints two specific areas of demand for the precise measurement and synchronisation of time which lay at levels beyond the reach of sun-dials, clepsydra using water, and sand-clocks. Both kinds of demand seem to have had significantly less relevance for South Asia.

From the sixteenth century down till the late eighteenth, one basic European quest in horological technique was for an effective combination of precision and portability in calculating time on ships crossing oceans. Long-distance oceanic commerce, across the Atlantic above all (the famous triangular trade in African slaves, West Indian sugar and American tobacco or cotton, and British manufactures), was of course a key dimension of 'primitive accumulation'— the story written in 'letters of blood and fire' to which Marx had

---

of the right questions here. The dissociation of time from human events, which appears so natural to us today, was anything but that when it first started happening: 'Where and how did so strange, so *unnatural* a need develop?' Landes, op. cit., pp. 58, 66.

[14] The Jesuit missionary Matteo Ricci had taken some 'self-ringing bells'— mechanical clocks—with him to the Chinese court in 1577. The Manchu emperors 'purchased or accepted as gifts an extraordinary array of timekeepers', which, however, remained decorative curiosities in the imperial palace. It might be interesting to explore if similar things happened with the Mughal and other Indian courts: one sees no reason why it should not have. Landes, op. cit., pp. 38–43.

devoted a famous and eloquent section in his *Capital*.[15] Precision in time-measurement was necessary when crossing the oceans because, while latitude could be calculated through the altitude above the horizon of the Pole Star, or of the sun at noon, the other space co-ordinate, longitude, required a comparison of local time on board ship with the time at a place of known longitude. Thus north–south passages, as well as of course routes that did not need to move too far from coasts, were not a problem, particularly after the compass had come into general use; but crossing oceans laterally along roughly the same latitude was. Keeping a second clock on board precisely set according to time at a place of known longitude could solve the problem—but the accurate pendulum clocks that had been developed by the 1650s needed stable grounding and so could not work aboard ships on sea. Spain, France, England, all announced lavish prizes for more precise marine chronometers, stimulating intensive and competitive search. This finally proved successful around the 1780s.[16] Precise calculation of time, in possibly significant contrast, was a less pressing requirement for the flourishing Indian Ocean-centred South Asian overseas trade, which could follow coasts or cross the Arabian Sea using regular monsoon winds. Here Asian merchants survived in strength, often competing successfully with European companies and private traders till at least the late eighteenth century. Western domination had to be established primarily through force.

Clear correlations can be observed, in the second place, between spurts in the development of clocks and watches and critical points in the transition to capitalist production relations. Mechanical clocks put up on towers first arose and proliferated in the towns of mid-fourteenth-century north Italy, northern France and Flanders—these being areas of textile manufacture hit by economic crisis and marked by sharp class struggles over the measurement and length of the working day. In 1963 Jacques Le Goff, in a pioneering essay, analysed this fourteenth-century struggle over work bells, the Werkglocken.[17] The

[15] Karl Marx, *Capital*, volume I (1867; New York, 1975), chapters XXVI, XXXI.
[16] Landes, op. cit., chapters 6–11.
[17] Thus, at Amiens in April 1335, Philip VI granted the mayor and aldermen the power 'to issue an ordinance concerning the time when the workers of the said city and its suburbs should go each morning to work and . . . when they

shift from the precocious urban manufactures of some parts of high-medieval Italy and Flanders to more dispersed, largely rural, putting-out forms of merchant domination of production may have reduced somewhat the pressure for more precisely calculable disciplinary time. The second crucial period came only with the early industrial revolution in late-eighteenth- and early-nineteenth-century Britain, when the rapid spread of watches coincided with the leap from manufacture to large-scale factory production. This is the story illumined in E.P. Thompson's famous article, with its focus upon pressures for the internalisation of time-discipline and the simultaneous and continuing resistance to the 'deadly statistical clock' so liked by Dickens' Gradgrind.[18]

One has to avoid, though, any impression of unilinear determinism or teleology. The transition to large-scale industrial production has been slow and incomplete everywhere, as well as subject to reversals—as is particularly evident today, with highly developed global capitalism often spawning new forms of putting-out and scattered, home-located production. The point about time-discipline requirements concerns not so much concentration or otherwise in big factories, but the extent and efficacy of capitalist control at the points of production, the precise forms of which might vary very widely. And production apart, the spread of clock-time is connected with the density and universalisation of commodity production: the latter is intimately bound up with the intensified division of labour, which in turn demands the synchronisation of work, transportation and exchange.

The old model of the self-sufficient Indian village and the marginality of trade has long been abandoned, for it is obvious that there

---

should quit work for the day: and that by the issuance of said ordinance, they might ring a bell which has been installed in the Belfry of the same city . . .' Workers hit back through efforts to destroy or silence work bells. The conflict—and the putting up of the new mechanical clocks on turrets—was principally in the centres of textile manufacture. Jacques Le Goff, 'Labour Time in the "Crisis" of the Fourteenth Century: From Medieval Time to Modern Time', in his *Time, Work and Culture in the Middle Ages*, op. cit., pp. 45–7.

[18] E.P. Thompson, 'Time, Work-Discipline and Industrial Capitalism', op. cit.

was no lack of either commodity production or forms of putting-out in some parts of pre-colonial South Asia. Gujarat, the Coromandal, and Bengal together constituted till the late eighteenth century the world's biggest centre of cotton textile production. The relevant questions for any (so far non-existent) research on the lag in the entry of clock-time even in such areas, open to intensive European commerce from the sixteenth century, would have to probe these two aspects— the degree of entrepreneurial control over production, and the density of commodity production.

IV

What could be called the 'material' history of clocks in colonial India remains unwritten, and is beyond my reach in this essay. Diligent investigations of trade figures should be able to unearth statistics about variations in the import, sale, and prices of clocks and watches into India: these seem not so crucial in an essay that focuses primarily upon sites of time-discipline and shifts in perceptions. One need only note that indigenous manufacture came very late and is, in fact, a post-Independence phenomenon (e.g. the Hindustan Machine Tool watches). This is hardly surprising, given the virtual absence of a machine-tools industry throughout the colonial era—even much of the textile machinery for the Bombay and Ahmedabad mills had to be imported—and given the global domination of clock and watch production by a succession of select countries: Britain in the eighteenth century, followed by Switzerland, the USA, and more recently Japan.[19]

Some inferences are possible, however, about the areas in which the discipline of clock-time would have had its initial sites in the specific conditions of colonial India: more precisely, for the purposes of this essay, of Bengal. Fortunately, from the point of view of a study of perceptions, a certain coincidence is noticeable between these sites and the reach of that other belated entrant into South Asia, print-culture, which too came only with colonialism. The varied strata of the colonial educated middle class of Bengal, therefore, will assume a

[19] Landes, chapters 14–21.

certain centrality in the remaining part of this essay, for here considerable contemporary evidence about clock-time perceptions and
responses is available through the democratising impact of printing.[20]

Factory production, in the shape of British-owned jute mills, came
rather late to colonial Bengal, and the fact that the jute-mill labourers
were largely non-Bengali-speaking meant that their experiences were
for long of little concern for the middle-class literati. There was little
sign of any capitalistic transformation in agriculture, and few Bengalis
were recruited for that other potential site for the imposition of time-
discipline, the colonial army. For my purposes, the three key areas
were the railways; the new 'modern' or 'Western' schools and colleges;
and—above all, I shall argue—government and mercantile offices.[21]
Some interesting patterns of partially differentiated responses to
clock-time emerge through a study of the available material on these
three areas.

As elsewhere, the construction of railways in India from the 1850s,
along with telegraph lines, quickly made the standardisation of time
across space both necessary and possible in the interests of a synchronisation of traffic. The move towards a single uniform clock-time
across the subcontinent—what came to be called Indian Standard
Time—began within a decade of the first railway. The crucial role
of trains in inculcating time-discipline and stimulating the purchase
of watches is quite obvious—particularly, it needs to be stressed, for
suburban commuters travelling to offices in metropolitan cities
on a daily basis. The point is important because, as we shall see, the

[20] The spread of literacy in both colonial and postcolonial India has remained
slow and highly skewed in terms of caste, class, and gender. But printing did
become associated with the development of vernacular prose, and thus enabled
the circulation of writing on a much wider variety of themes than had been
feasible under conditions of scribal culture. Printing helped constitute a literary
public sphere, initially overwhelmingly confined to high-caste (or elite-Muslim)
male literati, but opening out over time to include a growing number of women
and people of lower-caste origin. For recent work on this subject on parts of India
other than Bengal, see Veena Naregal, *Language Politics, Elites, and the Public
Sphere: Western India Under Colonialism* (Delhi, 2001); and Francesca Orsini,
Hindi and the Public Sphere (Delhi, 2002).

[21] Another possible area, which I am not exploring at this point, is the modern
hospital.

Calcutta office clerk (in Bengali, *kerani*), quite often a commuter, will play a rather central role in this story of the imposition of time-discipline in Bengal. As for responses, the railways did arouse some criticism and hostility. The more conservative were initially shocked by the inevitable mingling of castes and sexes in crowded compartments and station platforms.[22] Racist categorisation aboard trains quickly became a major grievance, with first-class berths generally reserved for whites and the vast majority of Indian passengers herded into third-class compartments with very few amenities. The funding of railway investments—in large part by Indian tax-payers, British entrepreneurs being given a guarantee of minimum profit by the colonial state—the choice of routes and the overall economic impact of railways all became in course of time the subject matter for nationalist critiques. In all this the aspect of time-discipline hardly figured. It was quickly accepted and internalised, so far as the railways were concerned, as both obviously necessary and helpful. What came to be resented soon enough by passengers was unpunctuality, not—as in some other areas—its reverse.

The second key site for clock-time discipline was constituted from the early nineteenth century by 'modern' schools and colleges, and here there is a symbolic appropriateness in the fact that one of the pioneers of English education in Calcutta was a watchmaker from Scotland, David Hare. For one of the distinguishing features of the colonial school was its attempt to impose strict time-discipline. Traditional village pathshalas had been without 'fixed class-routine, time-table, or school-calendar'. From the early nineteenth century onwards, though only with partial success, missionaries, colonial officials, and increasingly, Western-educated Indians all strove to introduce order, regularity, and 'proper' time schedules into education. In

---

[22] See for instance the images of social-cum-sexual chaos in a Bengali satire dated 1873: 'the *hari* [member of an untouchable caste] on top of the babu, the woman on top of the man, the man on top of the woman, the bum against the mouth, and the mouth behind the bum.' Kalidas Mukhopadhyay, *Kalir Nabaranga* (Calcutta, 1873), cited in Tanika Sarkar, 'Talking About Scandals: Religion, Law and Love in Late Nineteenth-century Bengal', *Studies in History*, New Series, XIII, 1, January–June 1997, p. 85. Reprinted in her *Hindu Wife, Hindu Nation: Community, Religion and Cultural Nationalism* (Delhi, 2001).

the 1850s, to cite a specific instance, an attempt was made in Bengal to start normal school training for village headmasters, where the 'gurumahashaya' would be taught the virtues of strict time schedules, attendance registers, and regular examinations.[23] Those who have seen Satyajit Ray's famous trilogy might recall the contrast between the village school attended by the boy Apu in *Pather Panchali*, run by an irascible but easily distracted grocer who alternates teaching with running his shop, and the high school to which the hero comes in *Aparajito*, where the headmaster is patrolling the corridor with a watch, periodically reminding teachers and students exactly how many minutes still remain before the arrival of the Inspector of Schools. Another example, this time from higher education, is provided by a biography of Iswarchandra Vidyasagar which admiringly relates the efforts of the famous educationist and social reformer, as Principal of the Sanskrit College in Calcutta in the 1850s, to impose regular attendance times and classroom discipline within his institution.[24]

Little is known about what school pupils might have felt about the new time-discipline, though one can guess that the response would not have been particularly enthusiastic. Grown-up commentators could also be occasionally critical, as when in 1874 Rajnarayan Basu, himself a distinguished product of Hindu (later Presidency) College, listed among the principal evils of contemporary times an alleged physical decline of Bengalis caused by 'excessive work' without the earlier afternoon break, and long hours cooped up in enclosed schoolrooms in childhood.[25] On the whole, however, clock-time discipline in education was generally accepted as conducive to improvement

---

[23] Kazi Shahidullah, 'Purpose and Impact of Government Policy on Pathshala Gurumahashayas in Nineteenth-century Bengal', in N. Crook, ed., *The Transmission of Knowledge in South Asia* (Delhi, 1996). Some of the changes were quite unimaginative and unsuited to local conditions—for instance the insistence on a 10 a.m.–4 p.m. schedule, as against the earlier practice of having classes from early morning till 10 a.m. and then again from 3 p.m. till sunset—which is much more sensible in a hot country.

[24] Chandicharan Bandopadhyay, *Vidyasagar* [in Bengali] (Calcutta, 1895), pp. 92, 103.

[25] Rajnarayan Basu, *Sekal-ar-Ekal* [Then and Now] (Calcutta, 1874).

and progress. Many aspects of 'English' education—the foreign med-
ium at the higher levels, and much of its content—did come under
criticism with the rise of anti-colonial nationalism. But time-discipline figured little in such critiques, and seems to have been accepted
as a matter of course in alternative schemes of 'national education.'[26]

Formal education, leading on to a professional career, became in
colonial times the principal avenue for social advance and middle-
class respectability. This was particularly so in regions like Bengal,
where the weight of British capital for long hindered the development
of indigenous commerce and industry, and restricted alternative
career options.[27] For the higher, and very much better documented,
strata of the nineteenth-century educated middle class—successful
writers, lawyers, doctors, teachers, socio-religious reformers or reviv-
alists, journalists, politicians—clocks and watches quickly became
both necessary for the efficient pursuit of careers and important in-
dices of status, respectability, and an upwardly mobile life. Another
tale about Vidyasagar, who imposed on himself an unusually austere
and simple lifestyle, points to this aspect of the appeal of the still-novel
mechanical time-piece (through a negative example). A biography
published in 1895 relates how in the 1850s a village woman, waiting
to see Vidyasagar, had refused to believe that the great man had just
walked past her, as he had had 'no carriage, watch, good clothes.' A
paraphrase of the same story made in a biographical account of 1969
omitted, probably unconsciously, the reference to the watch—which
by then had become a commonplace for a much larger number.[28] It
should be possible some day to trace the filtration downwards of

[26] In more general terms: Gandhi is known to have been a great stickler for
punctuality.

[27] Higher education had not been an indispensable prerequisite for top-
ranking military or political positions in pre-colonial times. As in the medieval
West, even kings could be illiterate. The British made administrative recruitment
dependent on examinations, while simultaneously restricting middle-class Indian
job opportunities by virtually reserving top army and bureaucratic posts for
whites. The 'liberal' professions for the more successful, clerical employment for
the rest, became therefore the two paths that remained open for the Bengali middle class.

[28] Chandicharan Bandopadhyay, op. cit.; Indramitra, *Karunansagar Vidyasagar*
(Calcutta, 1969).

clocks and watches, motivated as much, if not more, by status aspirations[29] as by more 'material' pressures or needs. This may be through indirect evidence such as passages in contemporary literature, early photographs, etc.

For the more successful among the middle class, clock-time could thus get associated with some sense of linear improvement or progress, distinct from the earlier widespread assumption of the present, as Kali-yuga, being necessarily decadent. Yet, as already indicated, the Kali-yuga motif was very far from being dead in the mid- or late-nineteenth century. It seems to have enjoyed a kind of revival, in fact, precisely alongside the spread of clock-time and print-culture. Moods of alienation, pessimism, and the moral decline traditionally associated with that term can often be discerned even in texts that do not explicitly use the motif, as for instance in the essay by Rajnarayan Basu (op. cit.) where *ekal*, 'now', is repeatedly declared as inferior to *sekal*, 'then'.

Printing made the old texts on Kali-yuga much more widely accessible, particularly through vernacular translations.[30] But the real explanation for the persistence of the theme must be in terms of some resonance with contemporary needs and sensibilities, and here, as I have suggested in a number of recent essays, a partial distinction

[29] An interesting essay on the spread of clocks and watches in the Catskill Mountains area of interior New York state in the early nineteenth century argues that, initially, this was related not to any requirement of factory discipline, but to a combination of other factors: to the vast enhancement of supply, from *c.* 1808, through mass production via standardised interchangeable parts, and the status-appeal of time-pieces for upwardly mobile farmers. By 1836, however, the industrial—or, more precisely, class-struggle—aspect had also become important. The Catskill labour struggle that year was against employer manipulation of the factory bell. Workers protested that their own watches indicated how the boss was trying to trick them: an excellent example of resistance through internalisation. Martin Bruegel, 'Time that can be relied on': The Evolution of Time-consciousness in the mid-Hudson Valley, 1790–1860', *Journal of Social History*, 28 iii, Spring 1995.

[30] Thus the late-medieval Sanskrit text *Kalki-purana*, which described in great detail both Kali-yuga, and its ending through the coming of Kalki, the tenth and last incarnation of Vishnu, was translated into Bengali in 1886, 1899, and 1908. The 1899 version I have used had gone into its tenth edition by 1962.

between two 'levels' or 'layers' in educated middle-class society might be helpful.[31] If the more successful of the (still overwhelmingly high-caste, and male) educated could get into the 'liberal' professions, the less fortunate or more indigent of the 'bhadralok'[32] had little other recourse than to crowd into clerical posts in government or mercantile firms in which their bosses were overwhelmingly whites. Along with groups of traditional literati unwilling or unable to make the switch into Western education, these came to constitute a 'lower middle class' that was distinct from its Western counterparts in being set apart from artisanal production via a high-caste status that was usually sought to be jealously preserved. We need to grasp, further, both distinction, and permeability within middle-class society: the most eminent of the bhadralok could have kinsmen eking out a living from humble clerical posts, or among the ranks of the educated unemployed. The experience of the kerani thus came to have a symbolic importance much in excess of the number of people actually holding, or trying to obtain, clerical jobs.

Office work was far from being entirely new: the Mughals, for their time, had had a formidable bureaucracy. But for reasons already suggested,[33] the office did come to acquire a novel centrality in colonial times, and it became the key site for attempts to enforce tighter discipline through clock-time routine and Victorian notions of the virtues of punctuality.[34] What added to the burdens of *chakri* (office-job) was the combination of this new time-discipline with the direct experience—not that common in other kinds of employment or

[31] Sumit Sarkar, *Writing Social History* (Delhi, 1997), chapters V–VIII; 'Renaissance and Kali-yuga: Time, Myth and History in Colonial Bengal', in Gerald Sider and Gavin Smith, eds, *Between History and Histories: The Making of Silences and Commemorations* (University of Toronto, 1997).

[32] 'Bhadralok', genteel folk—a Bengali term which has come to be widely used in South Asian historiography to denote a social group characterised in colonial times by high-caste (Brahman, Vaidya or Kayastha) status, education, and usually some connection with land in the form of middling or petty rentier incomes.

[33] See f.n. 27 above.

[34] An example: two circulars issued by the Government of Bengal, in May 1873 and June 1877, instructed judges to insist upon strict punctuality in law courts. Such circulars, it added, should 'nowhere be ignored'. Bengal Government Judicial Proceedings, June 1877, n.67–8 (West Bengal State Archives).

professions—of having to work under white, quite often highly racist, bosses who conveyed orders in an often imperfectly understood foreign language of command. Railway journeys, schools, professions, all had come under the sway of clock-time. But in contrast to such areas of experience, clerical employment under foreign bosses was perceived as peculiarly alienating, meaningless, marked by a daily round of humiliation and insults.

The most striking feature of the late-nineteenth-century proliferation of the Kali-yuga theme, in a mass of cheap tracts, plays and farces, as well as in some religious discourses, was precisely this sharply negative response to the rigours of time-discipline associated with office work. It normally appeared in combination with a reiteration of traditional evils, some of which also came to be modulated by contemporary pressures. Of the two standard founts of Kali-yuga degeneration—overmighty Shudras and insubordinate women—the first figured rarely in nineteenth-century writings using that trope, probably because, in contrast to regions like Maharashtra, lower-caste protest or affirmations did not yet worry the Bengali bhadralok very much.[35] The insubordinate and disorderly woman remained a prime target, but there was a new emphasis on the harm being done by the 'modern', educated wife, who was simultaneously portrayed as having expensive, 'Western', tastes and as preferring to read books rather than do housework. The new woman often became a symbol not so much of sexual immorality as of a commodification which was presented as threatening traditional family values. And this in turn got linked to the theme of oppressive, time-bound office work: for the wife-on-top, with her craving for luxury, was allegedly pushing her husband into this sort of degrading occupation.

Perhaps the most striking—and certainly the most influential—instance of these linkages is to be found in the discourses of Ramakrishna, as recorded and published later by his disciple Mahendranath Gupta, in a very widely read Bengali text, the *Ramakrishna-Kathamrita*. Ramakrishna's conversations repeatedly harped on a

---

[35] This changed significantly around the turn of the century, as I have tried to explore in a preliminary manner in my *Writing Social History*, chapter IX. In a late example of use of the Kali-yuga format, *Kalir Bamun* (1926), the target of ridicule is the attempt by lower castes to rise to high-caste status.

trinity of evils, *kamini, kanchan,* and *chakri*: lust, money, office work. The framing of this text itself is quite relevant for our theme. Its highly educated chronicler took great care to state exact dates and times, against which are made to stand out the discourses of Ramakrishna—a rustic, poor Brahman with little formal education and hardly any English, whose words conveyed an impression of timeless truths, with few direct references, for instance, to British rule. The effect—the product of a quite deliberate authorial strategy—is of a clock- and time-bound universe, an unhappy and degenerate world reaching out towards the eternal verities of devotion. Among urban life situations, the one that emerges most vividly is that of clerical office work, with Ramakrishna once going so far as to tell a disciple that it would be better to jump into the river than 'become a slave by taking a job.' Two examples will have to suffice for the very many references in Ramakrishna's conversations to the *dasatya* of *chakri* (the bondage of office work), and it will be noticed that disciplinary time and subordination to foreign bosses merge in this entirely negative assessment of the life of the clerk:

> 'Look, how many educated people trained in English, with so many degrees, accept chakri, and receive kicks from their master's boots every day. Kamini is the sole reason for this.'
>
> . . .
>
> 'Your face seems to have a dark shadow upon it. That's because you are working in an office. In the office, you have to handle money, keep accounts, do so much other work. You have to be alert all the time.'[36]

Let me move now to a text of a very different kind.

Durgacharan Roy's *Debganer Marte Agaman* [The Coming of the Gods to Earth] (Calcutta, 1889) is a long serio-comic account of the misadventures of epic Hindu gods who have come down to visit British India. They travel by train, but get thrown out of a first-class, whites-only waiting-room, while one of them buys a watch—only to

[36] 'M', *Ramakrishna-Kathamrita,* volume II (Calcutta, 1904, 1982), p. 201 [1 March 1885]; volume III (Calcutta, 1908, 1982), p. 143 [12 April 1885]; volume I (Calcutta, 1901, 1980), p. 121 [15 June 1884]. I have attempted a detailed study of Ramakrishna in relation to changing nineteenth-century notions of *Kali-yuga, chakri,* and *bhakti* in my *Writing Social History,* chapter 8.

have it stolen. The author, though writing in the 1880s—when Ramakrishna had won many devotees among Calcutta's English-educated middle class—shows no awareness of the saint, and even mentions the temple where he lived, at Dakshineswar, without any reference to him. All the more striking, therefore, is the convergence on the question of clerical life. The gods see clerks everywhere: 'clerks . . . dozing as they return home from office. Their faces are worn out after the whole day's work . . . The sahib's kicks and blows the whole day, and when they return . . . the nagging of wives.'[37] They see the clerks driven into degrading *chakri* by wives nagging them for ornaments, get deeply depressed, and then fall asleep, with one of them telling the others the tale of Kali-yuga.

Kali-yuga surfaces repeatedly in the themes, and sometimes even the titles, of a large number of late-nineteenth-century Bengali plays and farces,[38] and in such references the kamini-kanchan-chakri triad is almost ubiquitous. And gradually the theme starts getting modulated in a patriotic direction. In Harishchandra Bandopadhyay's *Kaler Bau* (A Wife for the Times) (1880), for instance, the kerani complains: 'Slaves to government officials, we spend our time at home as slaves to wives.' The modern wife ill-treats her mother-in-law, the husband goes along with her—and the son's neglect of his mother, it is suggested, is analogous to the way Bangamata (Mother Bengal) has become the '*dasi* [slave/servant] of the London queen.'[39] Incipient anti-colonial nationalism is thus interwoven with reassertions of patriarchy.

Where the discipline of clock-time is given absolute centrality, however, is in the two plays I have come across that are directly focused on clerical life: the anonymous *Kerani-darpan* (A Mirror for Clerks, 1874),[40] and Prankrishna Gangopadhyay's *Kerani-carit* (A

---

[37] Durgacharan Roy, *Debganer Marte Agaman* (Calcutta, 1889), pp. 520, 523.

[38] Thus in a massive catalogue of 505 plays printed between 1858 and 1905, thirty-one have Kali in their titles, and content analysis reveals many more references. Jayanta Goswami, *Samajchitre Unabingsha Shatabdir Bangla Prahasan* (Calcutta, 1974).

[39] Goswami, p. 1031.

[40] I am grateful to Anamitra Das for getting me a xerox copy of this very rare play from an obscure district library in West Bengal. The playwright is described on the title page as the author of *Mohanter Ei Ki Kaj*, a farce about a contemporary

Clerk's Life, 1885). The two deserve a closer look, which might also reveal signs of some slight but interesting changes over time.

Kerani-darpan opens with a scene of great bustle and hurry in the home of its clerk-hero, Gokul Banerji, with wife, daughter, and maid-servant all trying desperately to prepare the morning meal for him. The master of the household, of course, takes no part in these preparations, but hurries on the others by frequently looking at his watch. The emphasis on women's labour is interesting, for it goes along with a certain openness or ambivalence about women in relation to the new education and other aspects of colonial modernity. There are references, to be sure, to extravagant Westernised wives pushing husbands into clerical subservience, but also some praise of the possible virtues of modern education, as well as a scene where women talking among themselves hail Bentinck's ban on sati. Such ambivalences are missing in the 1885 play, where the Kali-yuga stereotype reigns unchallenged.[41] Gokul's family has to hurry because clerks coming late to office are humiliated, fined, and made to obtain a medical certificate which can be quite expensive. The office is like a prison, surrounded by walls and guards; the white superintendent is arbitrary as well as brutal in trying to impose time-discipline, but not particularly successful.[42]

Kerani-carit, published a decade later, is equally dominated by the theme of clock-time, but one gets an impression of a move from arbitrariness towards more effective, bureaucratised regularity:

'Our routine has no gap across 24 hours . . . We have to wait at the boss's bungalow for orders from 6 to 9 A.M.; 9 to 10 is spent in bathing and

scandal, concerning the religious head of the Tarakeswar temple, which became a roaring success and established the nascent public stage of Calcutta as a permanent part of city life. *Mohanter Ei Ki Kaj* was written by Lakshminarayan Das. For a detailed study of the Tarakeswar affair, see Tanika Sarkar, 'Talking About Scandals', in *Hindu Wife, Hindu Nation*, op. cit.

[41] The shift provides some confirmation of Tanika Sarkar's argument, in 'Talking About Scandals', that an initial relative openness and debate on the women's question was giving place to a hardening of patriarchal conservatism by the 1880s.

[42] Act III.i of *Kerani-darpan* has a rather bold, wish-fulfilment kind of scene where Bengali and Eurasian employees combine to blacken the face of the tyrannical superintendent and go off early from the office.

dressing for office; from 10 to 6 is donkey-work at the office; returning home takes from 6 to 7 P.M.; 7 to 10 goes on more paperwork at home; dinner and going to bed takes care of 10 to 11; then sleep from 11 P.M. to 6 A.M., often interrupted by nightmares about the dreaded white boss.'[43]

Not that possibilities of resistance are denied or ignored in the later play, however: there are a few signs, rather, of a passage from a purely sporadic outburst like the blackening of the superintendent's face in *Kerani-darpan* to efforts at more self-conscious and organised nationalism. A schoolteacher tries to organise a meeting of clerks, calling on them to give up their demeaning office jobs and take to independent professions.[44] Muslim subordinate staff are shown teaching bhadralok clerks the value of united struggle, and in the last scene the hero, Jnanendranath Mukhopadhyay, dismissed for protesting against racist abuse by white overseers, comes on stage singing a patriotic song.[45]

V

The responses of the colonised to clock-time and its disciplines were thus highly differentiated, with railways, school and college timetables, and clerical office work all evoking quite distinct reactions. One would guess that the attitudes of the same person could vary, too, depending on specific situations. The clerk complaining about the rigours of clock-time in office could be seriously inconvenienced by an unpunctual train if he happened to be a suburban commuter. At home, meanwhile, he might be simultaneously trying to urge the virtues of punctuality and diligence upon his wife, servants, and children. Gokul Banerji does precisely that in *Kerani-darpan*, hurrying on the preparations of his meal by repeatedly looking at his watch. Kaliyuga tracts and farces, so eloquent about the bondage of disciplinary time in offices, denounce with equal vehemence the educated wife who wastes her time on novels instead of performing her household chores with proper time-bound diligence. A spate of late-nineteenth-century domestic manuals, mostly written by men, endlessly reiterate

[43] *Kerani-carit,* i.iv, p. 37.
[44] Ibid., ii.iii, p. 45.
[45] Ibid., ii.iv, ii.vi, pp. 54, 63.

the virtues of systematic household management. Imported clock-time has become helpful in the refurbishing of indigenous patriarchal discipline.

The voices we hear are mostly of middle- or lower-middle-class high-caste men. An overwhelming majority of the authors of the plays woven around Kali-yuga and chakri, along with their clerical protagonists, have high-caste surnames. But the spread of print culture had begun to permit the entry of some women and lower-caste men into the emerging literary public sphere of late-colonial Bengal, and here we get occasional glimpses of alternative perceptions of time.

A recent analysis has highlighted the subtle ways through which the first published autobiography in Bengali, Rashsundari Debi's *Amar Jivan* (1868/1875), undercut assumptions—still very widespread today—of the housewife's domestic space as a domain of beauty, grace, and bounteousness. But the burden of daily chores was of course nothing new, and *Amar Jivan*, in significant contrast to the kind of male literature I have been surveying, rejects the view that the present is any retrogression: rather, 'Blessed, blessed, is the Kali-yuga.' For, some lucky girls were now getting a chance to go to schools and colleges, and Rashsundari herself, who as a young housewife had mastered letters in secrecy and fear, had been able as a mature widow to get a publisher for her autobiography.[46]

This optimism about current times was strikingly shared also by many of the lower-caste writings that started getting more numerous from around the 1900s. A verse biography of Harichand Thakur, founder of a lower-caste (predominantly Namasudra) dissident Vaishnava sect (the Matuas), also found Kali-yuga blessed, for in it divine incarnations emerge in Shudra households. Its author, Tarakchandra Sarkar, like Rashsundari a generation earlier, drew upon the well-known bhakti modulation of Kali-yuga that emphasised the prospect it brought of easy, indeed privileged, access to salvation for low castes and women.[47] But, like Rashsundari again, there was a simultaneous and growing stress upon new possibilities. For some lower-caste men,

[46] Tanika Sarkar, *Words to Win: The Making of Amar Jivan, A Modern Autobiography* (Delhi, 1999), *passim*.

[47] Tarakchandra Sarkar's *Sri Sri Harileelamrita* (Olpur, Faridpur, 1916; 2nd edition, Rampal, Khulna, 1924) pointed out that Vishnu has incarnated himself

this involved both education and a degree of agrarian or commercial enterprise: themes that become important in the biography of Guruchand Thakur, the second Matua leader.[48] The Matua creed, as reformulated under him, was projected as a combination of this-worldly activity and piety—*hate kam mukhe nam*—an improvement ethic very similar to the moods that suffuse tracts produced by or for upwardly mobile Muslim peasant groups in early-twentieth-century Bengal.[49]

Indigenous responses to disciplinary clock-time, then, were extremely varied, conditioned by the specifics of institutional sites and social and gender location. The major determinant of attitudes seems to have been perceived prospects, or their absence, of a degree of autonomous use and improvement. These appeared well-nigh non-existent for clerical chakri, and here complaints about time-discipline acquired a certain centrality in so far as it became an input into emerging nationalism: a stimulus, however, that was also inextricably bound up with reaffirmations of patriarchy through a shifting of guilt to the 'modern' wife.[50]

The theme of clock-time thus provides a valuable entry point for an important but generally neglected area of modern Indian social history—the relatively indigent yet predominantly high-caste clerical lower middle class. The clerk as a sign of colonial domination, constituted through an amalgam of sympathy and contempt,[51] had,

---

lower and lower down the social scale, from Ram the Kshatriya through Krishna reared in a Gop (Vaishya) family to today's avatar, the Namasudra Harichand.

[48] Mahananda Haldar, *Sri Sri Guruchand Charit* (Khulna, 1943).

[49] For a fuller account of these and other Namasudra writings, see chapter II below. Pradip Kumar Datta's *Carving Blocs: Communal Ideology in Early Twentieth-century Bengal* (Delhi, 1999), chapter II, provides a perceptive analysis of the evolving Muslim peasant improvement theme.

[50] A centrality with limits, however. I have come to feel increasingly that there is a need to move towards conceptions of many histories and multiple times. The unitary colonial/anti-colonial mould into which all colonial Indian history still tends to get cast can also be quite constrictive. I intend to elaborate this problem in several of the essays that follow.

[51] This amalgam is very noticeable in the two plays directly about clerical life. *Kerani-darpan* repeatedly draws attention to the paradox of clerical work involving humiliation and yet being much sought after. In *Kerani-carit,* Jnanendranath

however, an emotive potential that could extend much beyond lower-middle-class confines. In course of time it came to be linked, for instance, with the central nationalist theme of deindustrialisation. The surfeit of clerks could be plausibly attributed to the closing of other opportunities for gainful employment under colonialism. To take one striking instance of the reach of this sign, Rabindranath Tagore, a poet of aristocratic origin who had no social connections whatsoever with the lowly world of clerks, could still, in an essay dated 1902, counterpose the modern clerk to the ideal of the ancient Brahman. Today, he argued, 'the Brahman has to work with lowered head in the office of the sahib', and there is a danger that all Brahmans will degenerate into 'a vast society of tired clerks worn out by excessive labour.'[52]

But let me end with another set of linkages which could highlight yet another variable—that of shifts across time. In September 1905, just twenty years after the publication of *Kerani-carit*, and as the Swadeshi movement against Curzon's Partition of Bengal was getting into its stride, middle-class sentiments were deeply stirred by a strike of 300 clerks of the Burn Iron Works, Howrah. The issue, apart from racist insults, was a new mechanical system of recording attendance times. The sympathy wave evoked by the Burn strike led to a series of pioneering middle-class nationalist efforts to set up trade unions and help organise strikes among (mainly, though not entirely) white-collar employees of British-owned firms and offices. More generally, strikes during the Swadeshi era, as well as later, indicate a considerable centrality of the issue of the length of the working day and employers' efforts at 'cribbing' time. The Factory Labour Commission Report of 1908 gave considerable space to this question of time in its analysis of the principal causes of labour unrest among blue—as well as white-collar workers.[53] The clerical world of Calcutta, it needs to be added, far from remaining in the conditions of subservience implied in most

has been forced to become a clerk by his father, a lazy, servile Brahman zamindar who thinks independent business is demeaning, fit only for the lower castes.

[52] 'Brahman' (Asar 1309/1902), *Rabindra-Rachanabali*, volume IV (Calcutta, 1940, 1975), pp. 393, 395.

[53] For some details, see my *Swadeshi Movement in Bengal 1903–1908* (New Delhi, 1973), chapter V.

of the plays and discourses around the chakri of the late nineteenth century, became in course of time, and still largely remains, a bastion of the Left in Bengal.

By the early twentieth century, then, there are signs of transitions towards the familiar capitalist world of simultaneous internalisation of time-discipline, and trade union struggles over the length of the working day, disciplinary regulations of time, and conditions of work. These are not just, or quite often even primarily, organised labour movements, however. Complaints and perceptions abound about Indian office employees being almost proverbially unpunctual and lacking in 'work ethic', adept at 'wasting time'. Drives to enforce time-discipline, whether colonial or postcolonial, have clearly been far from brilliantly successful, and perhaps the picture of Ramakrishna that hangs over many State Bank and other offices in Calcutta might be a rather appropriate symbol. Nor should these be regarded as just indicators of inadequate capitalist development, bound to diminish over time. Alf Ludtke's studies of everyday life within factories in highly industrialised Nazi Germany, marked by forms of *eigensinn* or 'distancing', can provide a valuable corrective to such teleological perspectives.[54]

Excessive romanticisations, I feel, can be rather dangerous here. We need to keep away from bland affirmations of teleologies of 'modernisation', but one has to recognise, simultaneously, that resistance to time-discipline can also, at times, be fairly problematic. The burden of unpunctuality and distancing from work processes might often fall on the more lowly and oppressed, as much, perhaps more, than on employers—as when in West Bengal today, the payment of pensions gets inordinately delayed because files fail to move on time in government offices; or when industrial workers complain about clerical inefficiency in handling employees' state insurance claims. And yet perhaps there remains a need, particularly in our highly managerial, grossly market-dominated times, to hold on to a dream,

[54] Alf Ludtke, 'What Happened to the "Fiery Red Glow"? Workers' Experiences and German Fascism', in Ludtke, ed., *The History of Everyday Life* (Princeton, 1995). See also Geoff Eley, 'Labour History, Social History, Alltagsgeschichte: Experience, Culture, and the Politics of the Everyday— A New Direction for German Social History?', in *Journal of Modern History*, 61, June 1989.

at once utopian and relevant, of a world set free from totally rigid time schedules and insurmountable divisions of labour, where human beings could hunt and farm and work in factories and still write books or philosophise.

CHAPTER II

Identities and Histories
Some Lower-caste Narratives from Early Twentieth-century Bengal*

A TRACT ENTITLED *Namasudra Darpan* (A Mirror for Namasud-ras) was published from Calcutta in 1909, the first, chronolo-gically, of the seven Namasudra texts which will constitute the core source-material of this essay.[1] In an appendix, its author, Rash-bihari Roy Pandit, a villager from Tarali in the south-central Bengal district of Khulna, describes the considerable difficulties he had in getting his book published from a Calcutta press. Printing costs had been met by small donations, mostly of one or two rupees, collected by the author by personally visiting a large number of places scattered over Khulna, 24 Parganas, Jessore, and Hooghly districts, as well as Calcutta. He carefully provides lists of contributors and places, claims that visiting Namasudra settlements has become for him now a life-long 'pilgrimage', and goes on to regret that 'we have so long been ignorant even of where, in which districts, people of our lineage have been living.' But now there is the Census, and Roy Pandit goes on to cite extensively from the 1901 statistics, giving the total number

---

*Revised version of a paper presented at an international conference at the National Museum of Ethnology, Osaka, January 1999, and published in the Japan Centre for Area Studies, Symposium Series ii, 2000.

[1] Rashbihari Roy Pandit, *Namasudra Darpan I* (Calcutta, 1316/1909), 176 pp., Re. 1.00.

(over two million) and district-wise distribution of Namasudras in Bengal.[2]

The autobiographical note with which the text begins—which, we are told, the printer had demanded from the Tarali villager—unwittingly reveals that, despite its claim to be a 'mirror',[3] Roy Pandit's book was not so much an expression of an already given identity as part of an ongoing effort at its constitution. Not only had Namasudras of different places been largely ignorant of each other's existence, their surnames often had occupational rather than caste associations. Thus the author's father, a goldsmith, had taken the surname Swarnakar, but Rashbihari, a schoolteacher, was a Pandit. Two years later, another pamphlet described Namasudras as being 'principally agriculturists, as prescribed by Aryadharma', but including also some engaged in the occupations of 'manufacturing and trade, jotedari, talukdari, haoladari [different forms of intermediate tenures], teaching, law, western and indigenous medicine, administrative jobs . . .'[4] There were clearly possibilities, therefore, of alternative solidarities and fissures.

What made the unifying Namasudra project important for Roy Pandit and many others, however, was a common sense of discrimination and injustice. Specifically, as these and other pamphlets emphasise, there was the habit among many 'Brahmans, Vaidyas, and

[2] Ibid., pp. 160–76. Roy Pandit exaggerated the number slightly: the 1901 Bengal Census Report estimated the population of the people it described as 'Namasudras or Chandals' as 1.86 million. In Bengal proper, they were the third biggest caste grouping, after the Mahishyas (c. 2.5 million) and Rajbansis (around 2 million). *Census 1901, Volume VI (Bengal)*, pp. 391, 395–6. Located in the south-central, south-western, and northern parts of the province, respectively, Namasudras, Mahishyas, and Rajbansis developed the three major caste-movements of early twentieth-century Bengal.

[3] There had been quite a vogue for a 'darpan' literature in Bengal in the 1860s and 1870s, stimulated by Dinabandhu Mitra's famous play *Neel-darpan* (1860). The authors then had all been high caste. Roy Pandit's tract, and numerous other similarly titled lower-caste pamphlets in the early twentieth century, represented a subordinate-caste entry into a bhadralok literary genre.

[4] Kaviraj Sashikumar Baroibiswas, *Namasudra-Dwijatattva* (Namasudras as Twice-Born; Village Maluhar, Post Office Iluhar, Swarupkhati, Barisal, April 1911; 104pp., Re. 1.00), p.71.

Kayasthas . . . who did not deserve the title of "bhadralok" '[5] of using the derogatory epithet 'Chandal' to refer to people of diverse occupations and endogamous groups but a roughly similar, despised, social position.[6] Such contempt could stimulate a sense of solidarity among 'Chandals' or 'Namasudras' of otherwise very different socio-economic levels, and keep them apart from people with whom they might have had more in common in terms of occupation or class. Tracts like *Namasudra Darpan* make clear, further, that asserting a more respectable identity was vitally dependent on the projection of an alternative 'history'. The subtitle of Roy Pandit's pamphlet promised 'a detailed account of everything related to the Namasudra jati, from its origin to its present situation.' The need for history, paradoxically, was enhanced precisely because identity was far more of a project than a reality with a well-established past.

The Namasudra tracts comprise only a small proportion of the unprecedented flood of both high- and lower-caste writings in Bengali on caste themes, claims, and disputes between *c.* 1900 and the 1920s.[7]

---

[5] *Namasudra Darpan*, p.3. 'Bhadralok', lit. the genteel or polite folk, is the term used generically, in the main, for the three castes mentioned by Roy Pandit, connoting by the late nineteenth century a combination of high-caste status, education, and respectability grounded in aloofness from manual labour. For a related discussion of the term, see also chapter I, fn. 32, above.

[6] As Sekhar Bandopadhyay has pointed out in his recent valuable study, 'Chandal' was probably no more than a generic term used by their social superiors to refer to a wide variety of lower-caste people. Those described as Chandal—and later as Namasudras—in the Census and other colonial accounts fell into no less than twenty-nine endogamous groups, according to H.H. Risley's *Tribes and Castes of Bengal* (1891). Sekhar Bandopadhyay, *Caste, Protest and Identity in Colonial India: The Namasudras of Bengal, 1872–1947* (Richmond, 1997), pp. 19–20, and *passim*.

[7] As I have suggested in an earlier essay, the classified catalogue of printed tracts in Bengali at the India Office Library (now part of the British Library) can provide a rough indicator of this sharp upturn during the first two decades of the twentieth century. Only 24 titles are listed under the 'Castes and Tribes' rubric for the entire period till 1905; the years from 1905 to 1920 include 140, a very large proportion of them written by, or in support of, lower-caste claims. Entries after 1920 are not classified in this manner, but one does get a strong impression that the volume of caste tracts starts diminishing from somewhere around the

'History' entered most of these tracts in ways that were highly diverse, but always crucial for the identities and arguments being projected. An exploration of the specificities of lower-caste handling, appropriations and inventions of history has some intrinsic interest: it can also help to raise a number of important methodological queries.

Basically, I am trying here to interrogate and go beyond a series of polarities that have been common in the current anthropological-cum-historical literature on caste. A brief overview of these questions may be helpful.

As against the 'essentialist' assumptions of many earlier Indologists, anthropologists, and political scientists,[8] there is today a counter-orthodoxy of more or less extreme 'constructivism' that emphasises the 'imagined' nature of caste and other identities, their 'invention' through colonial policies and/or discursive patterns—and here Census classificatory strategies tend to be given pride of place. I intend to argue that while identities like caste are certainly not fixed, given or unchanging, neither can their construction be reduced to colonial discourses alone. Namasudra identity formation was not just a function of Census operations: it also had wider socio-economic and cultural dimensions.

A second polarity has been that between the Dumontian emphasis on structural harmony and consensus through effective and total Brahmanical hegemony,[9] and the binary power/resistance model which, I have argued elsewhere, has been central to the Subaltern Studies approach in all its shifting forms.[10] The first major attempt to extend the latter model to questions of caste, by Partha Chatterjee in

---

mid 1920s. See my 'Identity and Difference: Caste in the Formation of Ideologies of Nationalism and Hindutva', in *Writing Social History* (Delhi, 1997), p. 376.

[8] Indologists with their textual focus had tended to equate caste with unchanging varna, whereas social anthropology, following M.N. Srinivas, visualised jatis capable of moving up or down a fixed, hierarchical ladder. In both types of approaches, however, the entities being studied, varna or jati, were assumed as more or less given or constant.

[9] For a particularly clear instance, see Michael Moffat, *An Untouchable Community in South India: Structure and Consensus* (Princeton, 1979).

[10] I have elaborated this assessment-cum-critique in my *Writing Social History*, chapter 3.

1989, began, significantly, with a critique of Dumont.[11] I share much
of that critique, but find the assumption of a sharp and total disjunction between the domains of high-caste power and subordinate autonomy equally unhelpful. The histories imagined by the Namasudras
developed through selective appropriations and inversions, in the
interstices of dominant Brahmanical-cum-colonial views. To read
them as signs of complete integration or consensus is quite impossible, but neither do they indicate any totally distinct subaltern world.

Such approaches, I feel, are inadequate for understanding—more
precisely, historicising—Brahmanical hegemony. Dumontian structuralism strengthens tendencies towards assuming 'traditional', 'conservative', or 'orthodox' views on caste to have been essentially unchanging. In sharp contrast, the frequent combination more recently of the
twin stresses of subaltern cultural autonomy and colonial discursive
construction can lead towards a virtual elision of high-caste domination within pre-colonial times. Brahmanical controls become either
all-pervasive and conflict-free, or are assumed to have been all-but-
negligible in what becomes a somewhat romanticised vision of a pre-
modern world of flexible, non-authoritarian community life. Paradoxically, extremes meet: indigenous power and oppression tend to
disappear, since even in the second approach these have been reduced
to being epiphenomena of colonial-Western cultural domination
alone. The political implications here can be fairly retrogressive.[12]

[11] Partha Chatterjee, 'Caste and Subaltern Consciousness', in Ranajit Guha,
ed., *Subaltern Studies VI* (Delhi, 1989). Chatterjee's chapter, 'The Nation and
Its Outcastes', in his *The Nation and Its Fragments* (Delhi, 1994), was largely an
elaboration of this article. The same *Subaltern Studies* volume, incidentally, included an essay of mine, also dealing in significant part with caste: it is evident,
I think, at least with hindsight, that I had there already started moving out of
this dichotomous model. 'The Kalki-Avatar of Bikrampur: A Village Scandal in
Early-Twentieth-Century Bengal', *Subaltern Studies VI*, op. cit.

[12] I am thinking particularly of Ronald Inden's *Imagining India* (Oxford,
1990), and the recent work of Nick Dirks. Dirks, to his credit, seems at times
to recognise the political dangers of extreme colonial constructivism in the context of high-caste backlashes against attempts at subordinate-caste affirmations:
see his 'Recasting Tamil Society: The Politics of Caste and Race in Contemporary
South India', in C.J. Fuller, ed., *Caste Today* (Delhi, 1996).

In anthropological and historical research alike, the prevalent tendency has been to research on castes and caste movements more or less singly, or at most upon their interactions at the level of the village or locality selected for fieldwork. This is of course quite understandable in terms of the logic of intensive study of a manageable amount of new empirical material. I have come to feel, however, that at times an alternative, more interactive and intertextual approach might be helpful, juxtaposing high- and lower-caste movements and texts. The present and the following essay form part of a still-unfinished work where I am trying to explore the rise and decline of a 'language' of caste in early-twentieth-century Bengal.[13] Such overall shifts in the relative importance of caste as an issue cannot obviously be explained via studies of the ebb and flow of particular caste movements looked at in isolation from each other. More significantly, perhaps, an emphasis upon interrelationships could have two other advantages. It might help us test more rigorously the opposed stereotypes—of harmonious integration and clear-cut disjunction of levels—about which I have already raised some doubts. And it could reduce the temptation to conceptualise an 'identity'—in this case, caste—in virtual isolation. For, as an important study of the formation of communal ideologies in early-twentieth-century Bengal has pointed out, there is a 'fundamental problem . . . in the obsession with the singularity of collective identities.'[14] The pressures and stimuli of late-colonial

[13] Bengal appears particularly appropriate for such a study of shifts across time. Commonsense today would consider West Bengal to be possibly the one region of India where the articulation of caste in formal politics has so far remained minimal, in total contrast to the notoriety, in this respect, of Bihar. Yet the 1901 Bengal Census Report of G.A. Gait had categorically stated that 'with scarcely an exception . . . claims to higher caste, or to new and more pretentious names, are confined to Bengal proper.' Eleven out of thirteen claims that Gait discussed in the section of his Report entitled 'Disputed Points of Social Precedence' came from Bengal—as against only Babhans and Kurmis from the Bihari-speaking districts of Bengal Presidency. *Bengal Census Report, 1901*, pp. 384, 378–84. This confirms the impression one gets from catalogues of caste tracts—see fn.7 above.

[14] Pradip Kumar Datta, *Carving Blocs: Communal Ideologies in Early Twentieth-century Bengal* (Delhi, 1999), p. 9. Datta goes on to argue that 'A different range of possibilities emerge once communal formations are seen as part of a field

times, after all, constituted conditions of possibility for a more-or-less simultaneous consolidation of not one but a multiplicity of often cross-cutting identities, of anti-colonial 'national', religious or 'communal', regional, ethnic, gender, caste, or class. Identities were therefore not only hardened, they could also simultaneously become more fragile: and herein lay the roots of many of the problems and tensions of twentieth-century South Asia.

My principal focus, however, will remain on Namasudra tracts. This requires some explanation, for they are not all that numerous—less so, in fact, than the available textual productions of several other subordinate-caste formations.[15] My principal reason is that with the Namasudras there is the advantage of an excellent and detailed narrative, indisputably the best so far on the subject of caste in Bengal, reconstructed by Sekhar Bandopadhyay principally on the basis of archival documents.[16] This permits a juxtaposition bringing out the patterns of stresses and omissions in the tracts, for I must emphasise that sometimes they are illuminating precisely through their silences. Important hints about potential fissures emerge, which might help to explain why and how identities may not have continuous and ascendant histories, but can also decline and disintegrate (as seems to have largely happened with the Namasudras after the 1940s).

More generally, I want to use the theme of silences and disjunctures for a brief discussion, in my concluding section, of the potentialities, but also the limits, of the current strong swing away from Marxian class approaches towards a concentration on identity politics alone—a focus that is, moreover, often accompanied by a fairly uncritical

---

in which they have to perforce relate to other collective identities (other than its binary in "Hindu" or "Muslim") such as class, gender or caste affiliations. For what we then behold are the vulnerabilities of that identity, the ways in which its "hardness" has to mediate, compromise, inflect and suppress in order to produce tentative unities that proclaim themselves to be bounded monoliths.' (pp. 9–10)

[15] I am using seven Namasudra tracts, but have seen, for instance, around fifteen Mahishya pamphlets in the collections at the National Library (Calcutta) and the India Office Library (British Library, London): in both cases, of course, a necessarily random sampling.

[16] Sekhar Bandopadhyay, *Caste, Protest and Identity in Colonial India*, op. cit.

valorisation. I am troubled particularly by the tendency to conceptualise identity in a narrowly 'culturalist' mode. My intention, then, is to end with a certain problematisation of my starting-point: identity and history entered through textual study.

II

The flood of caste tracts from around *c.* 1900 onwards seems at first sight to provide strong confirmation of arguments for colonial, and particularly Census, constructions of caste. In 1901, Risley as Census Commissioner ordered for the first (and as it happened, the last) time the classification of jatis according to notions of social precedence prevalent in each locality. This immediately conjured into existence a flood of claims and counter-claims—the famous one-and-a-half mounds of petitions about which O'Malley complained in his Bengal Census Report of 1911.[17] What is less often remembered, however, is that Gait, Risley's successor as all-India Census Commissioner, dropped the whole effort to establish precedence in 1911 as involving too much trouble, and went back to a purely alphabetical classification of jatis.[18] And questions about caste, other than the 'Scheduled' category, have been excluded from all Census operations after 1941, with no visible impact on caste tensions or movements over the major part of the subcontinent.

I have argued elsewhere that there was often a significant input from relatively privileged, high-caste indigenous groups into Census classificatory strategies and other forms of 'colonial knowledge'.[19] More generally, we need to remain aware of the possibilities of the invention of identities and traditions 'from below'.[20] Memorials to

[17] L.S.S. O'Malley, *Report on Bengal, Bihar Orissa and Sikkim, Census 1911*, volume V, part I, p. 440.

[18] E.A. Gait's Notes of 31 May and 14 June 1911, Risley Collection, MSS/Eur.E. 295/11.

[19] See my 'Many Worlds of Indian History', in *Writing Social History*, pp. 22–3.

[20] Gerald Sider takes issue with Hobsbawm and Ranger's very influential edited volume, *The Invention of Tradition* (Cambridge, 1983) for its failure to 'address traditions that are invented "from below" '. I have found Sider's study of the shifting identity claims, internal fissures, and varied productions of history

Census authorities written in English can be a little deceptive in the impression they convey about relative priorities, as Lucy Carroll has pointed out.[21] Such petitions were organised at Census time, and sometimes helped to prod the authorities into accepting caste-names considered more respectable.[22] But caste movements were also engaged in many other kinds of activities, and a striking feature of *Namasudra Darpan*, and indeed the bulk of lower-caste vernacular tracts, is in fact the relative unimportance of the Census within the structure of their arguments. For Roy Pandit, Census statistics were a valuable source of information, but otherwise not central for his project; five of the six other Namasudra texts constituting my sample do not mention the Census at all.[23]

Official accounts like the *Faridpur District Gazetteer* (1925) traced back what the latter described as 'a spirit of sturdy independence . . . shown for some generations past' by Namasudras to certain events

---

of an American Indian community in North Carolina methodologically illuminating and at times almost startlingly appropriate for my present study. Gerald M. Sider, *Lumbee Indian Histories: Race, Ethnicity, and Indian Identity in the Southern United States* (Cambridge, 1993). The quotation comes from p. 291 of this book.

[21] Lucy Carroll, 'Colonial Perceptions of Indian Society and the Emergence of Caste Associations', *Journal of Asian Studies*, February 1978.

[22] Thus, those called 'Chandals' before the 1891 Census were designated as 'Namasudra or Chandal' in 1891, 'Namasudra (Chandal)' in 1901, and 'Namasudras' only from 1911 onwards. *Faridpur District Gazetteer* (Calcutta, 1925), p. 47. It should be noted, however, that officials were generally quite unsympathetic to most such claims, and at times seemed to speak the language of high-caste contempt. Thus E.A. Gait as Bengal Census Commissioner rejected the vast majority of claims in 1901, while his successor L.S.S. O'Malley in 1911 dismissed the petitions of some Namasudras to be considered as Brahmans as 'extraordinary . . . Thus do the pretensions of the low castes grow.' *Census 1901, Volume VI.i* (Bengal), Disputed Points of Social Precedence, pp. 378–84; *Census 1911, Volume V.i* (Bengal), p. 445.

[23] Mahananda Haldar's *Sri Sri Guruchand Charit* (Khulna, 1943), the 600-page biography in verse of the second leader of the Matua sect that played a key role in the Namasudra movement, does give the 1911 Census some space (pp. 238–59)—but only as one incident in a detailed, roughly chronological, and very long account.

in 1872–3 which had little or nothing to do with Census or other direct colonial interventions, and which in fact developed in a world rather far removed even from that of the tract-writers.[24] According to a contemporary police report, Kayasthas and other high castes had refused 'with taunts and reproaches reflecting on the Chundals' an invitation to a funeral feast extended by a rich Chandal of Amgram village in Bakargunj district. In protest Chandals, particularly of the neighbouring Gopalganj and Maksudpur police stations of Faridpur, organised through a meeting of village headmen a massive boycott of all agricultural and other services to high castes (as well as Muslims), threatening to paralyse cultivation, as 'at present fields belonging to Mahomedans and other castes are cultivated by Chundals, who for their trouble take half the produce. . . .' In addition, respectability was sought to be enhanced by stopping Chandal women from going to markets: an important reminder that caste mobility efforts have been associated all too often with the tightening of patriarchal restrictions on women. Chandal village heads complained to the police officer about 'the grievances they suffered from the Hindus, more especially from the Kayesths, whose treatment of them was intolerable.' They also wanted an end to the practice by which Chandal inmates of jails were automatically used as sweepers. That was not at all their caste profession, and, in addition, it went against the government claim 'to treat all castes on terms of equality': in a very interesting hint that elements of a modern discourse of equal rights had already started getting appropriated by a very subordinated and oppressed group.[25] The boycott could not be kept up for long, for Chandal sharecroppers did not have the resources to keep it going. Interestingly, none of the Namasudra tracts that I have seen make the slightest reference to this movement, or for that matter to somewhat similar incidents, with a clearly agrarian-cum-class dimension, in 1907–9. We learn about both only from official records: silences that hint at potential internal fissures, to which I intend to return.

[24] *Faridpur District Gazetteer*, op. cit., p. 47.

[25] Report of W.L. Owen, District Superintendent of Police, to District Magistrate, Faridpur, No. 66, Camp Bhanga, 18 March 1873: Government of Bengal, Judicial Proceedings, March 1873, n. 179.

Sugata Bose has written about a brief 'new frontier of opportunity' for those sections of peasants that could benefit for a time from commercialisation. He refers in particular to Mahishyas, and in central and Eastern Bengal to lower-caste and Muslim agriculturists helped by high jute prices which reigned, with some marked ups and downs, from c. 1907 to the mid-1920s.[26] Significantly, there is a coincidence of dates here with the proliferation of both lower-caste and Muslim vernacular tracts coming out from small towns and villages.[27] For the Namasudras, the more decisive underpinning for efforts at advancement probably came from a transition from fishing and boating to settled agriculture, as marshlands were opened up to cultivation in the course of the nineteenth century.[28] The Gopalganj subdivision of south-west Faridpur, where about a fifth of the total Namasudra population of Bengal came to live, and which became the heart of their cultural and political improvement efforts, had been a 'vast marsh' which by 1921 had a population density of 858 to the square mile. This was a rice-growing area, and jute was unimportant—but Gopalganj was located on an important riverine trade route linking East Bengal jute-exporting areas through Khulna to Calcutta. Orakandi in Gopalganj became the centre of the Matua religious sect, and the metrical biography of Guruchand Thakur has a long account of the trading activities he carried on with great success himself, and urged

[26] A secular decline in agricultural prices set in after c. 1925, to be followed of course by the Depression. Sugata Bose, *Agrarian Bengal: Economy, Social Structure and Politics, 1919–1947* (Cambridge, 1986), pp. 46, 63–4.

[27] For a pioneering account of what he has termed a literature of improvement, particularly of rural Muslim origin, see Pradip Kumar Datta, *Carving Blocs*, chapter 2.

[28] A British account dated 1852 described them as 'fish-sellers, ploughmen, coolies and slaves', but the 1911 Census found 77.94% of Namasudras engaged in agricultural occupations. These were further subdivided into 95.71% tenant farmers, 1.15% rent receivers, and 3.56% field labourers. Cited in Sekhar Bandopadyay, op. cit., pp. 20–1. The possibility of cross-cutting between these categories of course makes all such apparently exact statistics somewhat dubious, but the Namasudras do seem to have become, rather than always been, a predominantly settled peasant caste-group in course of the latter half of the nineteenth century.

on his disciples.[29] But such economic advance tends to be divisive, benefiting only a minority: Sekhar Bandopadhyay provides some data about a growth in the number of Namasudra landless sharecroppers particularly after the onset of the agricultural depression from the late 1920s.[30]

The emergence of lower-caste authors and readers obviously presupposed a certain spread of formal education. A link can be suggested also between the widespread assumption in early-twentieth-century caste tracts about the need for 'historical' arguments, and the new importance given to history in schools of the 'modern' or colonial kind. History of any sort seems to have been absent from the curricula of the traditional *pathshala*, which had concentrated on practical training in language, arithmetic and accountancy, plus bits of religious, moral, and grammatical instruction. The printed Bengali textbooks which the Calcutta School Book Society began bringing out from 1817, in contrast, chose history as a principal subject, and this pattern was only intensified over time, with Vidyasagar, for instance, himself bringing out a vernacular adaptation of a well-known textbook on Indian history.[31]

But it is possible to exaggerate the specific importance of what is usually described as modern, Western, or English education—alternately hailed in historiography as harbinger of renaissance modernity, or denounced as key instrument of cultural subjugation—in creating the conditions of possibility for lower-caste writings and affirmations. What was involved at best, so far as such subordinated groups were concerned, was in any case not English but vernacular schooling, and even there literacy rates remained abysmally low. The Census figures for 1911, for instance, calculated vernacular literacy among Namasudras at 4.9%, and literacy in English to be a negligible 0.22%.[32] Nor

---

[29] *Faridpur District Gazetteer*, pp. 4, 33, 47; *Sri Sri Guruchand Charit*, pp. 61–6, 92–8.

[30] Ibid., pp. 21, 27.

[31] Kazi Shahidulla, *Pathshalas into Schools* (Calcutta, 1987), pp. 15, 23, 29, 33.

[32] The corresponding statistics for the three high castes, normally taken to constitute the Bengali 'bhadralok', in 1911 were: Baidyas 53.2% in Bengali,

need such marginal presence of vernacular literacy have been an entirely new phenomenon, for Adam's famous reports on indigenous education in Bengal (1835, 1838) indicate the presence of a fair number of non-high-caste boys and even teachers in village schools—unlike girls, who appear to have been almost totally absent.[33]

The really new and crucial developments were linked, rather, with the coming of print, and the associated rise of vernacular prose. Through multiplying and cheapening the physical availability of printed texts, these enabled, over time, the emergence of elements of a literary public sphere (to borrow Habermas's term) that was potentially open to groups previously excluded from scribal culture: a growing number of women, a sprinkling of lower-caste men. The other related near-novelty was that open or public argumentation, beyond the boundaries of the traditional high-caste and ulema male literati, now became both possible and necessary over a host of issues—including, notably, caste, particularly from around the turn of the century.

The difference that print culture made can be gauged through a glance back at the kind of evidence historians have had to depend on in efforts at reconstructing the history of caste mobility in pre-print, pre-colonial times. Hitesranjan Sanyal's pioneering study of changes in the status of Sadgops and other upwardly mobile groups in pre-colonial Bengal had proceeded through comparing the caste lists given in two Sanskrit *upapuranas* composed in *c.* thirteenth- and fourteenth-century Bengal with scattered references in later Bengali literary texts. He then correlated these with other available data about

---

20.88% in English, Brahman 39.9% and 10.9%; Kayasthas 30.9% and 9.8%. Cited in Sekhar Bandopadyay, *Caste, Politics and the Raj: Bengal 1872–1937* (Calcutta, 1990), p. 109.

[33] Thus in the 67 vernacular schools in Murshidabad district that Adam surveyed in his 1838 Report, there were 39 Kayastha and 14 Brahman teachers, as against 13 others, including even a solitary Chandal. Of 998 Hindu students, Brahmans numbered 181, Kayasthas 129, and Vaidyas 14. The remaining two-thirds were distributed among no less than 47 castes, including 4 Chandals. William Adam, *Reports on the State of Education in Bengal, 1835 and 1838*, ed. Anathnath Basu (Calcutta, University of Calcutta, 1941), pp. 228, 231.

economic developments and went on to make a highly original analysis of shifts in temple patronage.[34] What Sanyal could not use was
written evidence about the discussions and debates that, one would
guess, must have often accompanied the *vyavasthas* or rulings given
by pandits, or orders issued by kings and chiefs, through which changes in relative status, or rejections of such claims, were sometimes
formalised.[35] Such discussions would have remained at the level of
orality, and, more crucially, be confined to limited numbers of high-
caste literati or courtiers, in a pre-print culture where manuscripts
would inevitably be scanty, easily perishable, and expensive.[36]

    The caste literature of early-twentieth-century Bengal, in contrast,
often gives the impression of an open debate, with a considerable degree of intertextuality across caste lines. Two examples must suffice.
In 1914 a well-known Calcutta-based conservative Brahman journal-
ist, Panchkori Bandopadhyay, blamed Kayastha pretensions to Kshatriya status for the flood of similar claims being put forward by much
more lowly groups 'like Rajbansi, Pod, Jhalomalo, and Kaivartas',
with Namasudras even demanding recognition as Brahmans.[37] The
previous year, an otherwise obscure but equally conservative high-
caste villager from Naldha, Khulna district, had similarly condemned
the spill-over effects of Kayastha claims and ridiculed the argument

[34] Hitesranjan Sanyal, *Social Mobility in Bengal* (Calcutta, 1981), pp. 38–41,
71–4, and *passim*.

[35] Records of such decisions—but not the accompanying discussions—sur-
vive in some abundance in Peshwa-ruled eighteenth-century Maharashtra, as the
late Hiroshi Fukazawa showed in a famous essay: 'The State and the Caste System
(Jati)', in H. Fukazawa, *The Medieval Deccan: Peasants, Social Systems and States,
Sixteenth to Eighteenth Centuries* (Delhi, 1991).

[36] I find Chris Bayly's virtual equation of the pre-print 'Indian ecumene' with
something like a Habermasian public sphere one of the few problematic features
of a very fine study of pre- and early-colonial social communications. C.A. Bayly,
*Empire and Information: Intelligence Gathering and Social Communication in
India, 1780–1870* (Cambridge, 1996), chapter 5. For more nuanced applications
of Habermas, see Tanika Sarkar, *Hindu Wife, Hindu Nation: Community, Religion and Cultural Nationalism* (New Delhi, 2001), chapter 2 and *passim*.

[37] 'Brahman Jati', *Prabahini*, 6 Chaitra 1320/1914, reprinted in Brajendranath
Bandopadhyay and Sajanikanta Das, *Panchkori Bandopadhyayer Rachanabali*,
volume II (Calcutta, 1951), pp. 67–70.

developed by many lower-caste spokesmen that there were no pure Kshatriyas anyway, since an ancient text described all of them having been exterminated by Parashuram. Was Parashuram, an incarnation of Vishnu, then a kind of Sirajuddoulah, he asked rhetorically, in an interesting combination of caste and religious prejudices.[38]

Such intertextuality strengthens my argument about the limitations of the prevalent study of caste movements in isolation from each other. But there is an additional reason why interconnections need careful attention. Lower-caste tracts often acknowledge their indebtedness to individual members of Brahman or other high castes, particularly for guidance concerning Sanskrit texts.[39] Beyond the question of purely personal contacts, there are signs at times of a significant role, that has remained virtually unnoticed so far,[40] of the so-called 'Varna' or 'Patit' Brahmans. These were the ritual experts of 'degraded' status who served castes below the high and the 'Nabasakh' levels.[41] Varna Brahmans could attain respectability only if the caste they served also rose in the social scale. In addition, one encounters fairly often, in contemporary tracts and literary representations alike, the figure of the poor Brahman, ready to preside over rituals, sell

[38] Sirajuddoulah, the last independent Muslim ruler of Bengal prior to the British conquest, generally had a reputation of great cruelty among nineteenth-century Bengali Hindu writers. Guru Umeshchandra Datta Gupta, *Jatimala Sar Sangraha* (Naldha, Fakirhat, Khulna, November 1913). We shall shortly encounter several examples of the multiple uses of the Parashuram legend. For an early instance from Maharashtra, in 1830, see Rosalind O'Hanlon, *Caste, Conflict and Ideology* (Cambridge, 1985), pp. 24–34.

[39] Thus Kaviraj Sashikumar Baroibiswas's *Namasudra-Dwijatattva* claimed to have been revised by a pandit knowing Sanskrit, Srinath Haldar. It also acknowledged help from Madhusudan Sarkar, secretary of a local Kayastha Sabha.

[40] But see Tanika Sarkar, 'A Sudra Father for Our Lord: Balakdashis and the Making of Caste, Sect and Community in Modern Bengal, *Studies in History*, 16.i, n.s., 2000.

[41] Such castes were *ajalchal*: water, or cooked food which would require the use of water, served or prepared by them would pollute the higher caste, but not their touch. Below them were the *antyajas*, whose touch polluted, and who were not served even by Varna Brahmans. For a clear summary of the early-twentieth-century Bengal caste structure, see Hitesranjan Sanyal, *Social Mobility in Bengal*, op. cit., pp. 36–8.

vyavasthas, and generally help in the mobility efforts of lower castes. With at least a smattering of knowledge of sacred texts, both groups could provide valuable assistance in efforts at upward mobility. At the same time, they would be carriers of Brahmanical norms and practices to lower levels, helping to impart to their movements a more strictly sanskritising character.[42] The Varna Brahman presence is most evident in Mahishya tracts[43]—and, not fortuitously, perhaps, this was the most moderate and assimilationist of the major movements in Bengal. But Namasudras also had their 'degraded' Brahmans, some of whom in 1946 organised a petition pleading for official recognition of a higher status.[44]

My analysis of Namasudra texts (section IV) will therefore be preceded by a glance at the ways in which contemporary high-caste writers were looking at histories of caste and caste inequality, in justification, or sometimes as part of reform projects. (Section III) As I have already suggested, the 'traditional' or the 'orthodox' cannot be assumed to be unchanging, and there is a need to bring out some of its early-twentieth-century specificities.

[42] For two instances of orthodox complaints that degenerate or corrupt Brahmans were selling the pass, so to say, see the speech by one of the biggest landlords of Bengal, Brojendrakishore Raychaudhuri, at the inaugural meeting of the Brahman Sabha in Calcutta in March 1911: Bangiya Brahman Sabha, *Brahman Sabhaye Bakrita* (Calcutta, May 1911), and the almost exactly contemporary tract written by an obscure village Brahman: Chintaharan Chattopadhyay, *Brahman* (Faridpur, January 1911). In Satyajit Ray's film *Pather Panchali,* the desperately poor Brahman villager Harihar tries at one stage to raise funds by giving some lower-caste men the sacred thread that is the marker of 'twice-born', high-caste status.

[43] See, for instance, Trailokyanath Haldar, *Mahishya o Mahishyayaji Gouradya Brahman Parichay* (Khari, 24 Parganas, January 1911); Sudarshanchandra Biswas, *Bangiya Mahishya Purohit* (Habashpur, Faridpur, October 1912); and Harishchandra Chakrabarti, *Bhranti-Vijay* (Andul, Howrah, June 1912). The last constitutes exceptionally detailed affirmation of the claims of Mahishya Brahmans, with reference to a large number of specific cases of alleged injustice.

[44] Petition of the Dacca District Namasudra Jajak Brahman Association to the Viceroy, 26 June 1946, Government of India Reforms Office, File No. 115/46-R, cited in Sekhar Bandopadhyay, *Caste, Protest and Identity,* op. cit., p. 252, fn. 37.

III

The textual-cum-mythic justification of varna hierarchy is generally supposed to be grounded in the Purusha Sukta, a possibly late interpolation in the *Rg Veda* where the body of the primal being is sacrificed, and Brahman, Kshatriya, Vaishya and Sudra emerge from its mouth, arms, thighs and feet respectively. Like the more 'philosophical' analogy of the three higher varnas with a hierarchy of moral qualities, *sattva, raja, tama,* this provides no explanation for the multitude of subdivisions or jatis within each varna which constitute for most purposes the more relevant meaning of caste. For that the standard orthodox Brahmanical theory, provided classically in the *Manusmriti,* has been *varnasankara* or miscegenation. The inferior jatis are supposed to have originated from illicit sexual relations violating the ban on intermarriage. Degradation results particularly from *pratiloma,* the woman having intercourse with a man of lower caste: thus for Manu the Chandal is defined as the descendant of a Sudra father and a Brahman mother.[45] Important here is the close interrelationship assumed between right caste and gender hierarchy, for caste depends on purity of lineage, and that demands male control over feminine sexuality. The vision of dystopia conveyed through the motif of Kaliyuga—the last, most degenerate and present era in the endlessly repetitive four-yuga cycle—reiterates this basic assumption by locating the root of evils in the overmighty Sudra and the insubordinate and immoral woman.

The theory of origin through varnasankara is important for medieval Sanskrit texts, such as the thirteenth–fourteenth-century *Brihaddharmapuranam* and the *Brahmavaivartapuranam,* which try to fit the specific intricacies of the Bengal caste structure into this model. A degree of scepticism is probably in order, however, about the reach of these ideas beyond the Brahmanical literati, particularly before the combined impact, in course of the nineteenth century, of Orientalist scholarship, vernacular translations of classical texts, and dissemination through print. Niharranjan Ray was surely right when he pointed out, way back in 1949, that varna was a Brahmanical classificatory

---

[45] Sukumari Bhattacharji, *Literature in the Vedic Age* (Calcutta, 1984), pp. 46–7; Hitesranjan Sanyal, *Social Mobility in Bengal,* op. cit., pp. 13–14.

schema, seeking, not necessarily with much success, to impose order upon a far more variegated and mobile social world.[46] Variations had to be introduced at times to explain anomalies, like the unusually low status of the Subarnabaniks (or goldsmiths) of Bengal despite their pursuit of a profession both respectable and lucrative. The *Ballalcarita*, a medieval text of uncertain provenance and date, attributed this demotion to the arbitrary actions of the Sena king Ballal Sen, thus implicitly admitting that caste order was far from immutable, but quite open to state intervention.[47] One needs to note also another, probably more significant, disjunction, this time between medieval Sanskrit texts and vernacular literary representations of caste. The sixteenth-century *Chandimangala* presented caste distinctions as entirely bound up with distinct occupations, which it enumerated in great detail. The occupational groups were arranged in an order implicitly hierarchical, moving from the Brahmans down to the 'itar' or lowly people (among whom are mentioned the 'Chandals, who sell salt'), but there is no interest at all in explaining this order in terms either of the primal Purusha or miscegenation.[48]

Pre-colonial accounts of caste order thus either present it as a matter of course, or trace it immediately to an origin in a single happening: what is missing in such explanations of hierarchised inequality is any sense of social or historical process. Lower-caste origin myths,

[46] Niharranjan Ray, *Bangalir Itihas: Adiparva* (Calcutta, 1949, 1980), pp. 267–8. Like Georges Duby many years later on the feudal schema of the three orders, this remarkable book argued by implication that classificatory schema are ideological projects formulated by specific groups; they have some connections with social conditions when they are effective, but not any one-to-one correspondence. Georges Duby, *The Three Orders: Feudal Society Imagined* (Paris, 1978; Chicago, 1980), pp. 8–9.

[47] Ray, pp. 269–72. We shall see shortly that the figure of Ballal Sen came in very handy in the late-nineteenth and early-twentieth century in a number of varied projects of caste mobility.

[48] Another striking feature of the account of various groups coming to 'Gujarat', the town newly founded by Kalketu—where this caste list is located—is that the description begins with Muslims, who are sub-divided similarly into occupational groups. 'Kavikankan' Mukundaram Chakrabarti, *Chandi*, c. 1570s–1590s (first printed in Bat-tala, Calcutta, 1820; Basumati, Calcutta, n.d.), pp. 68–72.

transmitted orally and recorded by colonial or post-colonial investigators, do not appear all that different in narrative form, though the accompanying values might be not justificatory but a shifting combination of acceptance-cum-resentment. The emphasis there, once again, is on an original pollution through a single mistake, or sometimes a trick, played on the ancestors of the community.[49]

The major change that came about in the colonial era was through the emergence and development of the Aryan myth, so central to Orientalism, from the time of William Jones onwards. Based on a dubious leap from linguistic to racial affinity, this in diverse forms has become so much the dominant common sense that it is often difficult to be aware of its insidious presence even in liberal discourses about cultural 'integration', 'unity in diversity', or 'civilisational values'. In inverted ways, it has been quite central also even for most oppositional, anti-Brahmanical theories of caste.[50] 'History', of some kinds, has clearly entered the scene now, but its critical potential tends to get recuperated by essentialisms of race or ethnicity.

Jogendranath Bhattacharya's *Hindu Castes and Sects* (1896) can

[49] I find it difficult to accept Gyan Prakash's assessment, in a case study of the Bhuinyas of Bihar, that the pollution clichés in their origin myths indicate an insertion of the 'historical' and 'cultural' into the 'natural': 'one is not born, but rather becomes, a Bhuinya.' Prakash equates high-caste theories of origin entirely with the Purusha myth. But the notion of debased origin through human error or violation is very much present also in the Brahmanical theory of varnasankara. Gyan Prakash, 'Becoming a Bhuinya: Oral Traditions nad Contested Domination in Eastern India', in Douglas Haynes and Gyan Prakash, eds, *Contesting Power: Resistance and Everyday Social Relations in South Asia* (Delhi 1991), pp. 147, 158. For a similar critique, see Sekhar Bandopadhyay, *Caste, Protest and Identity*, op. cit., p. 45.

[50] Obvious examples would include Dravidian or Tamil counter-myths; Phule on Marathas as the original peasant-warriors of Maharashtra; assumed to be a region conquered unjustly by Aryan-Brahman invaders from the North; and the plethora of 'Ad'-movements among subordinated caste groups in early-twentieth-century India. The striking exception is Ambedkar: see his *The Untouchables: Who Were They and Why They Became Untouchables?* (Delhi, 1948), where he tries to explain the Hindu/Untouchable divide not by racial or even occupational difference, but in terms of a combination of uneven transitions from nomadic pastoral life to settled agriculture, and the subordination of groups that had remained loyal longer to Buddhism.

provide a convenient benchmark to gauge the extent of changes brought about through colonial developments in high-caste justifications of caste. The apologetic dimension is muted but never absent in this detailed study written by a Nadia pandit-cum-lawyer just around the time discussions in Bengal of caste were beginning, rather abruptly, to become a flood.[51] Bhattacharya has little patience with the varnasankara theory of the origin of 'mixed' castes, for this assumes an unlikely knowledge of 'irregular marriage and illicit sexual intercourse'. He also recognises that the occupational bases of caste distinctions have become very porous. But caste remains valuable for him as providing 'bonds of union between races and clans . . . the legislation of the Rishis was calculated not only to bring about union between the isolated clans that lived in primitive India, but to render it possible to assimilate within each group the foreign hordes that were expected to pour into the country from time to time.'[52] A wide range of Bengal intellectuals, including for a time Rabindranath, would elaborate justifications of caste in terms of such a model of differentiated yet harmonious unity during the next, Swadeshi decade.[53]

It would be simplistic, however, to reduce the shifts in the conceptualisations of caste to an unilinear flow of acculturation or derivation from dominant Orientalist-colonial discourses. Three qualifications are needed, in terms of variations in colonial constructs, their highly selective Indian appropriations, and evidence of considerable interpenetration. What emerged over time was a discourse as much, if not more, Brahmanical as colonial.

Trautmann's study[54] has highlighted the many variations within the Aryan myth, shifts and tensions which make highly problematic the homogenised assumptions about 'Orientalism' made so influential by Said and sought to be applied to India by Inden and many

[51] Thus Bhattacharya reduces the question of caste antipathy to an occasional 'little hitch', and has nothing but contempt for 'low-caste parvenus' who aspire to higher status. Jogendranath Bhattacharya, *Hindu Castes and Sects* (Calcutta, 1896; rpt. 1968), pp. 3–4.

[52] Ibid., pp. 4, 10, 11.

[53] For some details, see below, as well as my *Many Worlds of Indian History*, in *Writing Social History*, pp. 26–30.

[54] Thomas R. Trautmann, *Aryans and British India* (California, 1997).

others. I am concerned much more in this essay, however, with Census reports, obviously the most relevant kind of official discourse for questions of caste. These too reveal a remarkable fluidity of classificatory schema. Thus information regarding caste was placed by Beverley in the first Bengal Census Report (1872) in a chapter entitled 'Nationalities, Races and Tribes of the People'. Sixty years later, the 1931 Report was still admitting that returns under the 'Caste, Tribe and Race' schedule remained 'most unsatisfactory and troublesome', and noted that the indigenous Bengali term, *jat*, and its derivatives, could be applicable to communities of race, tribe, caste, and nationality alike.[55] The choice of caste as the key building-block of Indian society was a gradual process, in which the decisive moves were made by H.H. Risley in the course of compiling his ethnographic glossary of Bengal tribes and castes published in 1891. The central assumption, as Risley acknowledged, came from Sir Alfred Lyall's *Asiatic Studies*: 'the gradual Brahmanising of the aboriginal non-Aryan or casteless tribes'.[56] This implied an evolutionary sequence from tribe to caste, in a civilising process presided over by the men of Aryan race led by their Brahmans. Historical in appearance, Risley's framework in fact was deeply shot through with assumptions both essentialist and racist. Thus he admitted—in fact, emphasised—that often customs and ceremonies had been borrowed by lower castes 'in the most liberal fashion from the higher castes'.[57] E.A. Gait, who was in charge of the Bengal Census in 1901, went so far as to confess that 'the more ignorant classes have very little idea as to what caste means . . .'[58] Yet Risley remained determined to ground caste difference in race. At one point he explicitly stated the political advantages of this move, and proceeded to locate that difference in anthropometry, the measurement of heads and noses to establish physical race distinctions between high and low castes. The alternative view of Nesfield, who had

[55] *Bengal Census Report, 1872*, volume v, chapter v; *Census 1931*, volume v.i, Bengal and Sikkim Report, p. 421.

[56] H.H. Risley, *Tribes and Castes of Bengal/Ethnographic Glossary* (Calcutta, 1891; rept. 1981), p. xv.

[57] Ibid., p. xix.

[58] *Bengal Census Report (1901)*, volume vi.i, p. 347.

argued that caste was essentially related to occupation, and that the Aryan/non-Aryan divide was no longer very significant, was therefore rejected.[59] It did not entirely disappear, though, and occasionally surfaced in some later Census reports as well as in Indian discussions around caste.[60]

Ten years before the publication of Risley's ethnographic glossary, the Protestant missionary M.A. Sherring, in a similarly entitled volume, made a violent attack on caste, attempting a 'natural history' where responsibility for its many evils was fixed on Brahman selfishness and conspiratorial, divide-and-rule designs.[61] There has been a strong tendency, particularly in recent years, to represent such views to have been dominant within colonial attitudes, since they seem to fit so well with Christian missionary and Utilitarian–rationalist–'Enlightenment' assumptions alike. But Risley, almost certainly, was far more typical at least of late-colonial officialdom when he took up with great consistency a diametrically opposite stance, thus once again demonstrating that colonial discourse was never a monolith. His 1891 volume went very far indeed in its display of sympathy for Brahmanical values, to the extent of virtually supporting infant marriage in 'oriental' conditions—for that ensured parental control over marriage and purity of caste lineage, which was of course an essential

[59] Risley referred in 1891 explicitly to the 'political value [that] may attach to the demonstration that a given population is or is not composed of homogeneous ethnic elements . . .' Ibid., p. 20. Ten years later, as Census Commissioner of India, he argued that 'race sentiment' supplied 'the motive principle of caste', animating its sense of hierarchy. Anthropometry for Risley had become a dogma, with caste hierarchy corresponding to the gradation from the 'finest' to the 'coarsest' nose: 'The status of the members of a particular group varies in inverse ratio to the mean relative width of their noses.' *Census of India 1901*, volume I.i (H.H. Risley's Report), pp. 489, 498.

[60] Thus E.A. Gait in his report on Bengal in 1901 tried to combine a somewhat toned-down version of Risley's race theory with elements from Nesfield's stress on the occupational basis of caste. Artisanal castes, he suggested, may have had their roots in 'guilds' that 'gradually hardened into endogamous groups.' *Bengal Census Report* (1901), volume VI.i, pp. 359, 361.

[61] Rev. M.A. Sherring, *Hindu Tribes and Castes*, volume III (London, 1881; Delhi, 1974), pp. 220–35, and *passim*.

part of his race theory of caste.[62] Risley advocated greater respect for what he called 'the standard Indian theory of caste', and was sure that his views would meet with approval 'from the leaders of the Hindu community in all parts of Bengal, among whom both the orthodox and the advanced lay considerable stress upon the purity of their Aryan descent . . .'[63]

Such divergences created conditions for widely different, even mutually opposed, Indian appropriations, with for instance a strong element of a Brahman conspiracy theory entering the assumptions of radical lower-caste thinkers like Jyotirao Phule, with some inputs probably from early missionary influences.[64] And Risley's confidence was certainly not misplaced. In 1896, Jogendranath Bhattacharya began his book with a violent attack on Sherring and considerable approval for Risley.[65] But interaction rather than appropriation might be the more relevant term at times, so far as relations between sections of the high-caste literati and colonial officials were concerned. Data for the 1891 survey had been collected with the help of 190 local correspondents. Being literate, most of them would have been necessarily high caste.[66] In 1901 Risley ordered the classification of castes in each locality in census reports 'by social precedence as recognised by native public opinion at the present day.' His subordinate, Bengal Superintendent of Census E.A.Gait, added an important, practical gloss. Since 'it often happens that a Hindu knows or cares but little of any caste other than his own . . . the decision must rest with enlightened

---

[62] Risley (1891), pp. xcii–xciii. What made this sympathy particularly significant was that 1891 was the year of the passing, amidst enormous controversy, of the Age of Consent Act.

[63] Ibid., pp. xxv, xx.

[64] Rosalind O'Hanlon, *Caste, Conflict and Ideology: Mahatma Jyotirao Phule and Low-Caste Protest in Nineteenth-Century Western India* (Cambridge, 1985), chapters 3, 6.

[65] *Hindu Castes and Sects*, op. cit., pp. 1–2, 9, and *passim*.

[66] The correspondents—among them men of the stature of Bankimchandra Chattopadhyay and Aswinikumar Dutta—were asked 'to go for their information to the persons most likely to be well informed on questions of custom, such as priests, marriage brokers, genealogists, headmen of caste panchayets, and the like.' Except for the last category, all the others would have been high caste. Risley (1891), p. xiii; Sekhar Bandopadhyay, *Caste, Politics and the Raj*, op. cit., p. 33.

public opinion, and not with public opinion generally'—once again, high-caste literati opinion would evidently enjoy a very high premium.[67] The two-way flow continued: the sevenfold structure that Gait worked out for Bengal caste on the basis of this data has remained the basis for all later academic analysis.[68] It is not to be found with such clarity in Jogendranath Bhattacharya's account of 1896.

The question of caste hierarchy remained somewhat marginal in high-caste debates and activities till around the 1890s, no doubt largely because, unlike in Phule's Maharashtra, it was not yet perceived as under serious threat. The major divisive issues in bhadralok life till then concerned religious beliefs and rituals (particularly image worship, under severe attack from Christians and Brahmos), and the condition of women. I have argued elsewhere that though references to caste hierarchy did sometimes enter the dominant conservative discourse of *adhikari-bheda*, this was usually as means towards the defence of beliefs in many gods, image worship, and patriarchal values.[69] Major social reform initiatives were related primarily to themes of gender injustice within the reformers' own middle-class, high-caste milieu. The Brahmos did occasionally attack caste, but their concrete initiatives in this regard tended to remain tokenistic, confined in practice to themselves giving up the Brahmanical sacred thread and promoting intercaste marriage within their own, overwhelmingly educated high-caste, community. Even the theoretical critiques—as for instance some stray comments by Rammohan Roy—focussed upon the barriers caste distinctions set for patriotic unity, rather than social injustice.[70]

[67] *Census Report (India)*, 1901, volume I.i, p. 538; *Census Report (Bengal)*, 1901, p. 354.

[68] Compare, for instance, Hitesranjan Sanyal, *Social Mobility in Bengal*, op. cit., pp. 36–8 with *Bengal Census Report (1901)*, pp. 367–73.

[69] *Adhikari-bheda* (literally, differential rights, claims and powers) conveyed the notion of the propriety of each caste and sect having its own rituals and beliefs in an unified but hierarchically differentiated structure within which each accepted its appropriate place. It thus neatly combined catholicity with conservative maintenance of norms appropriate to a group's location within the overall hierarchy. For more details, see my 'Identity and Difference', op. cit., pp. 368–74.

[70] Thus Rammohan in 1821 had criticised *jatibheda* (caste distinction) as 'the

The first book-length Brahmo attack on caste, Sibnath Shastri's *Jatibheda*, came out only in 1884. This did include an impressive historical account of multiplicity of jatis as a degeneration compared to early Vedic times,[71] produced by the subordination of non-Aryans and, interestingly, the restricted transmission of high culture along hereditary lines because of the absence of print. There was also a passionately indignant chapter, making effective use of the diatribes against Sudras in the *Manusmriti*, while the valorisation already well developed in much bhadralok writing of ancient Hindu glory, as contrasted with decline under 'Muslim tyranny', was implicitly subverted: for Sibnath associated the Buddha, Muslim rule, and of course the colonial period, with progress in the conditions of the Sudras. The *Manusmriti* passages cited by Sibnath, along with many of his historical arguments and assumptions, were to be frequently used in many later tracts written by or on behalf of lower castes. But even for Sibnath, the primary evil of jatibheda concerned 'divisiveness and lack of fraternal feeling'. In addition, he felt that it hindered high-caste improvement through its insistence upon eugenically harmful marriage restrictions. Caste also encouraged contempt for manual labour and intellectual narrowness among high castes (by banning sea voyages, for instance). Significantly, *Jatibheda* revealed no awareness at all about the Faridpur Namasudra movement of the previous decade.[72] Judging from the official press excerpts, Bengali newspapers of 1873 had also been totally silent about that early act of lower-caste agrarian affirmation.[73]

Things changed dramatically from around the turn of the century with the development of lower-caste agitations, stimulated, significantly though not solely, by colonial policies like Census efforts to

---

root of all disunion', and in a letter dated 18 January 1828 argued that caste 'had entirely deprived (Indians) of patriotic feeling.' Ibid., p. 365.

[71] The contrast between Vedic (or Upanishadic) times, and later degeneration, a standard assumption of much Orientalist scholarship, had already been given a central place in the arguments of reformers like Rammohan when preaching monotheism and attacking customs like sati.

[72] Sibnath Shastri, *Jatibheda* (Calcutta, 1884), ed. Dilip Biswas (Calcutta, 1963), pp. 33–6, 40–9, and *passim*.

[73] I was unable to find a single reference to these happenings in the weekly *Report of Native Papers (Bengal)* for January–June 1873.

determine social precedence (1901), or Gait's abortive Circular in July 1910. The latter suggested an exclusion from the 'Hindu' category of those not allowed entry into temples and Brahman services, or considered polluting by touch or proximity. Two kinds of high-caste responses need to be distinguished here.

The first was a more aggressive assertion of hierarchy or adhikari-bheda, and specifically of the need for Brahman hegemony, set in a cultural-nationalist context in which caste was presented as a way of maintaining order and stability that was superior to Western statism, individual rights, and class conflict. I have elsewhere given instances of such attitudes from the writings of a Bengali adherent of Positivism engaged in developing a highly conservative and Brahmanical reading of Comte, and from the pages of a journal very influential in Swadeshi days, Satish Mukherjee's *Dawn*. Thus, already by 1900, the Positivist Jogendrachandra Ghosh was fearful of a 'dangerous upheaval from the lower depths of Hindu society'. In August 1903 *Dawn* argued that 'in all ages and by virtue of a law of nature, there shall be inequalities and distinctions between man and man.'[74] Less sophisticated versions of similar values were expressed at the Brahman Sabha meeting held in Calcutta in March 1911 with the specific objective of refuting Kayastha claims to twice-born status, and in a spate of high-caste tracts written by obscure Brahmans from small towns or villages. In the latter, not unexpectedly, the old kinds of textual arguments based on the *Purusha-sukta* and Manu's theory of varnasankara still often retained a prominent place.[75]

The second, apparently opposite, trend tried to develop an alternative self-image of upper-caste leadership, formulated in terms of paternalist philanthropy and sanskritising reform-from-the-top that would 'uplift' or 'purify' lower castes and so build 'Hindu' and/or

---

[74] Jogendrachandra Ghosh, *Brahmanism and the Sudra, or The Indian Labour Problem* (Calcutta, *c.* 1900), pp. 11–13; Satish Mukherjee, 'The Question of Caste', *Dawn*, August 1903. For more details, see my *Writing Social History*, pp. 27–33, 378–9.

[75] *Brahman Sabhaye Baktrita*, op. cit. Examples of tracts devoted to outlining and justifying right (i.e. Brahmanical) order, sometimes collectively termed *jati-mala* literature, include the already cited *Brahman* of Chintaharan Chattopadhyay, and Pandit Asutosh Mukhopadhyay's *Jati-Vigyan* (Durgapur, Post Office Joynagar, 24 Parganas, May 1915).

'national' unity. P.K. Datta has established the centrality here of U.N. Mukherji and his extremely influential series of articles in the *Bengalee* entitled *Hindus: A Dying Race* (1–22 June 1909).[76] The articles began with some Census data and projections from 1891 onwards that seemed to indicate a relative decline in the proportion of Hindus to Muslims in Bengal, attributed this to the wretched conditions of lower castes as contrasted to the supposedly more virile, energetic and prosperous Muslim peasants, and urged paternalistic upliftment at Brahmanical initiative as the means to Hindu survival, unity, and rejuvenation. Social reform was thus given a new, caste focus, but simultaneously sought to be appropriated to a vision of ineluctable biological rivalry between Hindu and Muslim: a theme that, in changing forms, has remained central to Hindu chauvinist tendencies until today. Links are evident here with Census discourse and other colonial efforts at stimulating a divisive numbers game in the context of the beginnings of representative institutions.[77] But there was also an important class dimension, for Mukherji's articles coincided exactly with an essay in the *Modern Review* entitled 'What can be done for the Namasudras' by Binod Lal Ghosh, pleader from Madaripur, Faridpur district, suggesting a series of concrete ameliorative measures. These had become urgent, Ghosh argued, because some Namasudras 'egged on by their half-educated brethren' had started a 'misguided and suicidal agitation', cutting off connections with high castes and even ceasing to cultivate 'the lands of the higher class Hindu landlords as *burga* [sharecropping] tenants.'[78]

[76] Pradip Kumar Datta, ' "Dying Hindus": Production of Hindu Communal Commonsense in Early-Twentieth-Century Bengal', *Economic and Political Weekly*, 19 June 1993, and *Carving Blocs*, op. cit., chapter 1.

[77] The demand for a separate electorate raised by the just founded Muslim League was granted with suspicious ease by the Morley–Minto Reforms of 1909, and there were also some gestures in the way of appointments and educational facilities extended to Namasudras and other lower castes in the new province of East Bengal and Assam that had been set up in 1905 by partitioning Bengal. In July 1910 the Gait Circular threatened to reduce sharply the number of officially recorded 'Hindus' by siphoning off large numbers of lower castes—to which U.N. Mukherji responded with another pamphlet, *Hinduism and the Coming Census* (Calcutta, March 1911).

[78] *Modern Review* (June 1909). For a more detailed study of these agrarian-cum-class aspects, see chapter 3 below.

Binod Lal Ghosh's specific suggestions were confined to the starting of night schools, free dispensaries, and co-operative banks for Namasudras, along with a very limited change in modes of social intercourse extending to them the same status that the bhadralok granted to 'those non-Namasudras from whose hands the high-caste Hindu does not drink water'. In a curious mismatch between diagnosis and remedy, nothing further was said about agrarian relations. More generally, caste reform geared primarily to projects of Hindu unity was repeatedly undercut by persistent high-caste assumptions. What they did stimulate at times, however, were more determined efforts at caste uplift and self-organisation. Here a crucial link role was played by a Brahman reformer undeservedly forgotten today, Digindranarayan Bhattacharya of Serajgunj, Pabna district, who had been hailed in his lifetime by a lower-caste activist (Manindranath Mandal, a Pod) as comparable to the Buddha, Chaitanya—and Muhammad.[79] Across three decades, Digindranarayan wrote copiously against caste, spoke frequently at lower-caste gatherings, and composed histories for them. His *Jatibheda* (1912) interestingly combined arguments drawn from Mukherji's *Dying Race* with Sibnath Shastri's more radical tract of 1884, and also launched a direct attack on adhikari-bheda couched in terms of what is recognisably a discourse of rights.[80] In his most radical phase, around the mid-1920s, Digindranarayan tried to bring together caste and gender reform. He passionately denounced the horrors of austere widowhood in terms reminiscent of Vidyasagar, and at the same time expressed his reservations about narrow, purely Sanskritising movements both for being divisive and for imposing tighter restrictions on women in imitation of Brahmanical norms.[81] The anti-Muslim note remained muted in Digindranarayan, despite his being for some time an office bearer of

[79] Manindranath Mandal, *Bange Digindranarayan* (Calcutta, 1927).

[80] God, he argued, has given 'the same powers to all human beings, just as he has made the same sun for Brahman and Chandal.' *Jatibheda*, pp. 4–5. The title of this pamphlet itself could have been an implicit tribute to Sibnath Shastri's tract with the same name.

[81] Digindranarayan Bhattacharya, *Bidhabar Nirjala Ekadashi* (Calcutta, 1926)—which targeted the custom of making widows go without water on *ekadashi* day, twice every month; ibid., *Chaturvarna Bibhaga* (Serajgunj, 1917; Calcutta, 1925), and *Nipirita Sudrer Nidrabhanga* (Calcutta, 1926).

the Hindu Mahasabha, and despite occasional mention in his writings of Mukherji's *Dying Race* motif of Hindu demographic decline. Unlike Mukherji, again, Digindranarayan encouraged Manindranath Mandal in his efforts to organise a joint front of lower-caste groups, the Bangiya Jana Sangh floated in 1923.[82]

But it is time to turn to the writings and initiatives of the lower castes themselves, approached through a selection of Namasudra texts.

IV

My sample consists of three kinds of writings. I look first at four tracts affirming Namasudra identity and developing claims to high status on the basis primarily of 'historical' arguments: these come closest to my theme as formulated in its title.[83] There is also an autobiographical text, written by a man claiming to be an untouchable (*patit*) activist of Namasudra origin,[84] and finally two long hagiographies in verse of Harichand and Guruchand 'Thakur' (Biswas), leaders of the Matua religious sect which provided a core organisational and ideological focus for the Namasudra movement in the Faridpur–Khulna region.[85] It may be noted that while stylistically these lower-caste texts are not noticeably more colloquial or rustic than the average high-caste tract, they do tend to use much more verse.[86] The very high

[82] In the introduction to his pamphlet entitled *Bangiya Jana Sangh/Bengal People's Association* (Khejuri, Midnapur, 1923), pp. i–ii, Manindranath recalled how U.N. Mukherji had discouraged, and Digindranarayan enthusiastically welcomed, his initial efforts to start such an organisation around 1919. He also acknowledged the help received from some Mali, Namasudra, Rajbansi, Jhalla-Malla, and Pod leaders while eventually organising the inaugural conference of his association in Calcutta on 5 February 1922.

[83] Rashbihari Roy Pandit, *Namasudra Darpan* (1909), op. cit.; Kabiraj Sashi-kumar Baroibiswas, *Namasudra-Dwijatattva* (Barisal, April 1911), p. 104; Balaram Sarkar, *Namasudra-Jnanabhandar* (Boltoli School, Olpur, Faridpur, May 1911), p. 94; and Jadunath Majumdar, *Namasudrachar-Chandrika* (Jessore, June 1913).

[84] Haridas Palit, *Bangiya Patit Jatir Karmi* (Calcutta, 1915).

[85] Tarakchandra Sarkar, *Sri Sri Harileelamrita* (Olpur, Faridpur, 1916; 2nd edn, Rampal, Khulna, 1924); Mahananda Haldar, *Sri Sri Guruchand-Charit* (Kalibari, Khulna, 1943).

[86] Rajbansi tracts also often slip into verse: see for instance Narendranath

proportion of illiterates or neo-literates among groups like the Namasudras or the Rajbansis probably demanded a greater reliance on oral
communication of texts and their retention through memory, which
is of course always easier in verse.

Namasudrachar-Chandrika (June 1913), the briefest of these tracts,
proceeds through a simple contrast of the description of Chandals
given in the *Manusamhita* and other Sanskrit texts as executioners by
profession obliged to reside away from all other people, and the evidently very different life of the Namasudras. The latter, the author
argues, are actually descendants of a Brahman sage, Namas, son of
Kashyap, who had legitimately married a Sudra woman. This inverted the ascription by Manu of origin through an illicit, degrading
pratilom relationship of a Brahman woman with a Sudra, while the
Kashyap–Namas story is sought to be grounded in a passage in a
Tantric text. Rashbihari Roy Pandit's 1909 tract, *Namasudra Darpan*,
had already presented this origin myth in much greater detail. His
account was based on a surprisingly knowledgeable appropriation of
select Brahmanical texts—to which Roy Pandit added the rudiments
of a historical narrative. Kashyap's descendants settled in an isolated
part of south-central Bengal, started losing their Brahmanical ways
because of their life in proximity with Chandals (giving up, for instance, the sacred thread as an inconvenience while hunting), and then
got degraded through the machinations of Ballal Sen. The Namasudras,
further, could not benefit from Muslim rule, unlike the educated
Brahmans, Kayasthas, and Vaidyas, for they had become peasants
who neglected education. Muslim rulers, too, had no interest in starting schools in villages—in sharp contrast to the British—and the
pamphlet ends with a loyalist effusion replete with gratitude also for
Christian missionaries.

Namasudra-Dwijatattva (April 1911) uses similar textual arguments to claim that Namasudras are 'pure Aryan Brahmans' unjustly
deprived of that status by Ballal Sen, and ends with a call to take on
the sacred thread once more. (None of the Bengal lower-caste tracts

---

Adhikari, *Rajbansiya Kshatriya-Samaj* (Rangpur, 1910, 1911), and Maniram
Kavyabhushan, *Rajbansi-Kshatriya-Dipak* (Village Kishamat-Paharbhanga, Post
Office Pharabari, Dinajpur, August 1911).

that I have seen, it may be mentioned here in parenthesis, claimed a non-Aryan heritage, unlike counterparts in other parts of the country like Tamil Nadu and Maharashtra: in that sense a complete break seems never to have been sought with sanskritisation.) But it also has occasional passages indicative of more radical, even rationalistic, moods. Textual exegesis, it suggests, has to be combined with reason, and so the theory of varnasankara, with its assumption of perfect knowledge of past illicit sexuality, is plainly ridiculous. The *Purushasukta* argument is also given an interesting twist: it states, after all, that even Sudras came from the body of the same Brahman. The initial division was in terms of occupation and function alone and did not imply hereditary inferiority. The subsequent degeneration was attributed in part to a kind of Brahman conspiracy at the time Buddhism was being suppressed, producing a system more cruel 'than anything in any other part of the world.' For—and here the author suddenly turns to verse—'The babus keep foreign dogs, eat and sleep with them/That doesn't take away the caste of a Hindu /But caste goes if he touches a Namasudra . . .'[87]

For Balaram Sarkar, the author of *Namasudra-Jnanabhandar* (May 1911), however, the question of Brahman origin is less important than education, with which is immediately associated a call for economic improvement through prudence, hard work, frugality, keeping away from idle amusements—a veritably puritanical programme, in fact. It is probably not a coincidence that this tract seems to have been written by a schoolteacher, and came out from Olpur village in Faridpur, the place of publication five years later of the metrical biography of Harichand Biswas, the founder of the Matua sect. The Matuas came in course of time to advocate a similar combination of learning with petty entrepreneurship. The Australian Baptist missionary Mead helped them to set up a high school at Orakandi, the home of the Biswas family, and their motto neatly combined a simple, non-ritualistic religious faith with economic enterprise: '*Haté kām mukhé nām*', doing worldly work while chanting the holy name.[88]

---

[87] *Namasudra-Dwijatattva*, pp. 33–4, 36.

[88] Sekhar Bandopadhyay, *Caste, Protest and Identity*, p. 42, and *passim*; Bandopadhyay, 'Popular Religion and Social Mobility in Colonial Bengal: The Matua Sect and the Namasudras', in Rajat Ray, ed., *Mind, Body and Society: Life and Mentality in Colonial Bengal* (Calcutta, etc., 1995).

The pamphlet, unusually for a lower-caste tract, also contained a social reform strand. It condemned child marriage and advocated the remarriage of widows and education for women, all largely on the grounds of producing healthy, well-trained children for the community.[89]

All four tracts have 'Namasudra' in their titles, and, despite evident differences in emphasis and argument, they share a common assumption—or project—of caste identity. The term, in contrast, is not particularly common in the other three writings in my sample. In them, identity repeatedly gets diffused in often contradictory directions. There is the communion of a dissident sect in the first Matua text; a solidarity of the poor and underprivileged against their superiors, occasionally in all three but most of all in parts of *Patit Jatir Karmi*; satisfaction and pride flowing from achieved entry (for the author and some associates, though clearly not for the bulk of his intended audience) into the ranks of the respectable, paradoxically quite obvious in other passages of that same autobiography; and traces of a passage from initial heterodoxy to growing conformity with high-Hindu practices and politics, which become evident if the two verse hagiographies are compared with each other.

Haridas Palit—a pseudonym, we are told[90]—introduces himself at the beginning of his *Bangiya Patit Jatir Karmi* (1915) as 'a Hindu, by jati a Namasudra': and that is virtually the only reference to his specific caste identity in the book.[91] Palit is interested not, like the tract writers, in inventing a Namasudra history as a way of affirming higher status for a specific caste, but in a personal narrative of successful upward mobility which he tries to extend to those around him, and projects as a model for the poor and socially despised. He had started life in a Burdwan (West Bengal) village working, like his mother and sister, as a servant in the house of an upper-caste master. Conditions had been bad, with frequent insults, beatings, and a

---

[89] Balaram Sarkar, pp. 78–81.

[90] The author assures us that his is a true story, only he has changed the specific names of people and places. Parts of the book read too much like a model improvement tale to be entirely believable. But the facticity of Palit's story is less relevant than the insights it can provide about one kind of lower-caste perception, imagination—and limits.

[91] *Bangiya Patit Jatir Karmi*, p. 1.

general treatment of his community as untouchables. Life there had been much worse, it appears, than in the Faridpur–Bakargunj region which constituted the heart of the Namasudra movement, for in West Bengal they were a small minority—bonded servants and sharecroppers—rather than a big chunk of the Hindu landholding peasantry.[92] There are passages, however, where the author derives some pride and confidence from his recollections of an early life of manual labour. For through making lower castes do all the work, the bhadralok have become parasites, hopelessly dependent really on them. There is, he hints, a potential for a kind of inversion here, through the skills and capabilities developed through subordination.

From such abject beginnings, the author tells us with much pride, he has risen to become a successful lawyer, landlord, District Board Chairman.[93] This success he attributes above all to the guidance of an uncle, who gave Haridas's family shelter when famine drove them out of their village to Hooghly district with its many jute mills. The uncle had worked as a jute millhand, saved up much of his wages instead of wasting them, like most fellow-workers, on drink and occasional luxuries, and gradually bought some land, with which he combined some small-trading activities—and Haridas became his assistant. To this theme of improvement through petty commodity production is quickly added education. Education of a specific kind, however, the book repeatedly emphasises, quite different from the upper-caste bhadralok habit of using degrees just to get clerical jobs in offices, for that would be only another kind of *gholami*.[94] Lower castes taking to education must not cut themselves off from, or begin to despise, productive manual work—which is identified primarily

[92] Palit recalls how his master always had a wash after giving him a thrashing. Ibid., pp. 12–13. For a comparison of conditions with those in the Namasudra heartland of South-Central Bengal, where they were not systematically treated as completely untouchable, see Sekhar Bandopadhyay, *Caste, Protest and Identity*, pp. 15–16.

[93] Ibid., pp. 7, 56.

[94] Palit here appropriates an auto-critical theme about the dasatya of chakri—bondage of clerical office-work—which had been much in vogue in some bhadralok circles from the late nineteenth century. See for instance my 'Kaliyuga, Chakri and Bhakti: Ramakrishna and His Times', in *Writing Social History*, chapter 8, and chapter 1 above.

with peasant agriculture, as contrasted to the dependence of wage-labour in factories. Thanks to his uncle, Haridas got himself a good education, in course of which he made friends with a number of upper-caste classmates. The benevolent landlord-father of one of them became his second patron. The book ends, in a mixture perhaps of a bit of reality and much utopian imagination, with Haridas and his friends setting up a chain of night schools for labouring groups in the Burdwan countryside, along with co-operative stores and other improvement projects—and the combination of education and entrepreneurship allegedly creates a general collective atmosphere of improvement, the benefits of which are shared in by a wide variety of lower-caste groups, even some Santal tribals and Christians. The more selfish of the bhadralok are upset, however, for they see small business and trade passing into the hands of lower castes and Muslims, and find it difficult to get servants: for them, it is the Kali-yuga, the inversion of right order.

The combination of economic improvement with education which is Palit's panacea has affinities with parts of the Matua creed, but otherwise *Patit Jatir Karmi*, like the four other tracts examined so far, is an entirely secular text that makes no reference to that religious sect. Conversely, the verse biography of the Matua founder Harichand (1811–78), composed by the village poet Tarakchandra Sarkar and published, we are told, only after much delay due to lack of funds in 1916,[95] has little to say about specifically Namasudra caste aspirations. It emphasises, rather, a devotional communion of song (*kirtan*), ecstatic dance, and miraculous healing across caste, gender, even occasionally Hindu–Muslim divides, in the spirit of much medieval bhakti. The text tries to follow the format of the epics and medieval *mangalkavyas*, with many repetitions and numerous digressions into subsidiary tales, mostly dealing with the miraculous achievements of Harichand and some of his disciples. Taking up what is quite a standard Vaishnava theme—that Kali-yuga despite its evils was also blessed, for in it the humble could attain salvation easily through devotion

---

[95] A preface, by Ramanikanta Biswas, describes how the money for its publication had to be raised by 'begging'. The book came out two years after the death of its author, who had been an intimate disciple of Harichand himself. Tarakchandra Sarkar, *Sri Sri Harileelamrita*, op. cit., p. i.

alone—*Harileelamrita* goes on to add an interesting gloss further privileging the underprivileged. Vishnu is incarnating himself lower and lower down the social scale: from Ram the Kshatriya through Krishna reared in a 'Gop' (Vaishya) family down to today's avatar, the Namasudra Harichand. Strikingly, the Buddha is described as predicting Harichand's advent, while there is also a reference to 'the Yavana [Muslim] weaver Kuber [Kabir], a great devotee of Ram.'[96] More concrete hints about power relations are not entirely absent. Thus Harichand's family had had to leave their home village of Safala due to a quarrel in which his brothers beat up a wicked official of the local Brahman zamindar. This was not quite a landlord–peasant clash, however, for the fight had been about that *gomastha* official reneging on a loan he had taken from Harichand's elder brother. An entrepreneurial streak is therefore present from the beginning, with Hari Thakur miraculously producing double crops on his land, starting an oil shop, turning to trade and teaching disciples to do the same.[97] But repeatedly the references to an improvement ethic get swamped by tales of miraculous healing (in return for which Harichand gets gifts of rice and money), while to the occasionally mentioned formula of '*haté kām mukhé nām*' is often attached the tag '*bhakti-ee prabal*' (devotion is mighty) which seems to have been dropped later on. What is totally absent are references to education, jobs, missionary contacts, Census status—the staple of much Namasudra politics from *c.* 1900 onwards—and this though the text was published in 1916.

With Mahananda Haldar's 600-page biography in verse of Harichand's son, Guruchand Thakur (1847–1937), we are clearly in a different world, indicating transformations within the Matua sect and the Namasudra movement alike. The author had been a lawyer at Bagerhat (Khulna), and the book's copyright-holder was Guruchand's grandson P.R.Thakur, who had a British barrister's degree and was successively member of the Bengal legislature and the Constituent Assembly of independent India. Publication costs had been met by a Matua Mahasangh, and a long prose preface laid much emphasis

[96] Ibid., pp. 15–16.
[97] Ibid., pp. 49–51.

on Namasudra identity and history.[98] Sect and caste movement alike have acquired far more crystallised forms now, but simultaneously they have become, in significant part, instruments in the very successful upward mobility of a family and its entourage.

Stylistically the traditional format is still sought to be retained, with much repetition—almost cyclicity—and there is at times a self-conscious archaism, as when the Baptist missionary Mead is called *rajpurohit* (royal priest), or in descriptions of meetings of Guruchand with high British officials that read like accounts of princely darbars in epics. But the basic order is chronological, with precise dates given for important events in Namasudra history. For some of these, in fact, like the first Namasudra assembly around 1880 in Dattadanga (Khulna), and the contacts of Guruchand with Mead concerning the setting up of a high English school at Orakandi in 1908 and subsequent Census petitions, the text is the principal and at times the only source.

Miracle tales and accounts of ecstatic devotion are rare in this text, in sharp contrast to the biography of Harichand. His son, we are told, was firmly opposed to piety detached from work. The basic stress on householder devotion, *grihastha sanyas*, as opposed to otherworldly renunciation, is a common bhakti theme, but to this has been added an insistence on improvement almost reminiscent of the Puritan ethic. Predictably, this finds principal expression in the twin fields of economic enterprise and education. In both, as with Haridas Palit, 'modernity' displays somewhat paradoxical consequences. It has clarified awareness of exploitative relations of caste and class,[99] and

[98] The history that it presents is the now-familiar tale of descent from a Brahman-Shudra marriage, and debasement due to Buddhist loyalties and the machinations of Ballal Sen. But the story is at once made more concrete and focused on Harichand's lineage. This is traced back to a Maithili Brahman who had migrated to Jessore, been impressed by the courageous, unjustly degraded Namasudras, and married his son to a Namasudra girl.

[99] Thus, to cite one instance among many, this is how Guruchand supposedly convinced his followers to stay away from bhadralok nationalists during the Swadeshi movement of 1905: 'If a rich man and a poor man walk along the same path/The rich always makes the poor carry his luggage/And introduces him to others as his servant/. . . How oppressive the zamindars are/Have they [bhadralok nationalists] ever tried to stop such things?/Don't touch, don't touch, say the Brahmans and Kayasths/Has anyone tried to broaden their hearts?' Ibid., p. 174.

simultaneously instrumentalised that awareness into a project of upward mobility of a small part of the community—for individualistic improvement, in conditions of extremely meagre resources, tends always to be highly divisive. Thus there is a whole section on the entrepreneurial activities of Guruchand from the late 1860s onwards, through entering very successfully the riverine trade of the Orakandi region in rice, jute, and mustard seeds, as well as by giving loans to poorer peasants. He urged his followers to adopt similar ways, and we are assured that Guruchand's loans did not really amount to the usual kind of oppressive moneylending: and yet land accumulated in his hands, for he generously cancelled the debts of those who surrendered their lands to him![100]

Both class awareness and its manipulation are clearest in the section on Guruchand's educational efforts. The rationale suggested for Namasudra education is interestingly different from what we know about the motivations animating the efforts of bhadralok men or women. Not jobs, or non-utilitarian broadening of mental horizons, but mitigation of class tyranny is foregrounded in this section, for the landlord and moneylender constantly trick the illiterate peasant in everyday matters of rent or debt-payment receipts. The Kayasthas opposed the proposal of a benevolent bhadralok to start a high school in a Namasudra village, for they were afraid their sharecroppers and servants would no longer work for them if they became educated. That, they are reported as arguing, would disrupt the age-old principles of adhikari-bheda, as enshrined notably in the *Ramayana*. The biography explains that it was such bhadralok hostility that made Guruchand accept the help of Mead's Baptist Mission, and it is also very careful to emphasise that the motives were entirely pragmatic—to get financial help for the school and also obtain access to British officials: there was never any desire to become Christians. And yet the detailed exposure of class oppression culminates in a section, grandiloquently entitled *Namasudra Jagaran, 1907* (Namasudra awakening), where all that happens is that through Mead's intercession some relatives of Guruchand, and a few others, manage to get minor administrative posts.[101] *Guruchand-Charit*, a hagiography unusually detailed

[100] See p. 100, and *passim*.
[101] Ibid., pp. 100–10, 140–66.

and precise about numerous events far removed from the conventionally 'religious', remains totally silent about the Namasudra sharecropper withdrawal of services around 1907–9 in the Gournadi region of
Bakargunj (quite close to the Matua heartland of Gopalganj) that had
alarmed Binod Lal Ghosh.[102] Like the earlier movement of 1872–3,
this found no mention in any other Namasudra tract either, so far
as I know. And towards the end of *Guruchand-Charit*, Guruchand
is quoted as stating with engaging frankness that it was sufficient if
some Namasudras get jobs: the rest should presumably remain content with their life as toilers.[103]

It is in such—ultimately, class—terms that it seems most plausible
to contextualise the increasing strength of what Sekhar Bandopadhyay
has termed 'accommodative' tendencies among the Namasudras, and
indeed very many other caste movements. The pattern involved also
the growing acceptance of high-Hindu divinities and rituals, a sharper
stress on the seclusion and subordination of women, and the entry
of an apologetic undertone into accounts of continued Namasudra
self-distancing from bhadralok-led anti-colonial nationalism. Thus
the closing sections of *Guruchand-Charit* include a description of the
entry of first Durga and later Kali worship among the Matuas. A concluding summary of Matua teachings insists on keeping women
secluded and wives always obeying and worshipping their husbands.[104]
It has to be added that there had been strong indications of patriarchal
values right from the beginning of the Namasudra upthrust. The
seclusion of women was an important element in the social boycott
of high castes even in 1873, and Guruchand had insisted on it at the
Dattadanga conference in 1880.[105]

But assumptions of a seamless transition from 'alienation to integration' will not really do, for implicit in some passages of this text,
as well as in its silences, are numerous indications of tensions.[106] Several times Guruchand is depicted violently abusing his followers, as for

[102] For some details of the Gournadi developments, see chapter 3 below.

[103] Ibid.. p. 530.

[104] Ibid., pp. 518, 567–74.

[105] See above, p. 73, and *Guruchand-Charit*, p. 131.

[106] 'From alienation to integration' is the title of Sekhar Bandopadhyay's two
concluding chapters in *Caste, Protest and Identity*, dealing with leaders and
peasants successively. To be fair to Bandopadhyay, the data and analysis in his

instance when many of them got swayed initially by Swadeshi propaganda in 1905. There is also a hint about the leader getting rather
distanced from even close followers, and some resentment on that
score.[107] Even the insistence on patriarchal values may not be as simple or automatic as it might seem. Child marriage was discouraged,
and even widow remarriage actively debated, in 1907 and again at the
1923 conference, which actually split partly on the latter issue. *Guruchand-Charit* remains a little coy about details in these matters, and
offers no explanation as to why and how widow-remarriage had
become such a vital issue: yet another revealing silence. Repeated discussions surely indicate both tension spots and possibilities of argumentation that would have been absent earlier.[108]

The Namasudra texts that I have seen were all written by men, as
were the overwhelming majority of available tracts brought out by or
on behalf of other subordinate-caste movements. But the point
regarding shifts and tensions is amply confirmed and extended by
Mahishya-Mahila, a bi-monthly journal edited by a woman (Krishnabhabini Biswas) for women of the upwardly mobile Mahishya
community. The first number, dated July 1911, appears firmly con-
formist, with Mahishya women asked to remain (or become) housebound, and contribute to the cause of their menfolk through prayers
alone. There was a need to educate girls in childhood, but solely in
order to produce good wives and mothers, and a poem by Giribala
Dei urged Mahishya women to be worthy of their lofty Aryan birth
by always obeying the commands of husbands, parents-in-law, and
all elders. An article by the same Giribala in a later issue of the journal
in early 1914, however, appears significantly different. Two Calcutta

---

book actually often contradict the impression which a hasty reader might get
from these titles, whether in approval or criticism.

[107] Ibid., pp. 236–7.

[108] Ibid., pp. 253, 442. Even the convergences with conservative high-caste
positions could sometimes flow from rather different and largely internal pressures, as emphasised recently in a fine study of Rajbansi participation in the anti-
Muslim abduction agitation of the mid-1920s: Pradip Kumar Datta, 'Abductions and the Constellation of a Hindu Communal Bloc in Bengal of the 1920s',
Studies in History, xiv.i, January–June 1998; and Datta, *Carving Blocs*, chapter 4.

girls had just burnt themselves to death, realising that their parents did not have the dowry money to get them husbands, and many had hailed this immolation as worthy of comparison with the *jauhar-vrata* by wives of medieval Rajput warriors. Giribala lashed out at the crassness of such 'greedy, devilish men', and pertinently reminded readers that neither Sabitri nor Sakuntala had thought of committing suicide. Articles and poems redolent of patriarchy remained abundant in the later numbers of *Mahishya Mahila*, but alternative voices kept surfacing: as when in early 1915 a piece entitled *Streer Patra* (A Wife's Letter) detailed the sorrows of an oppressed and neglected wife whose husband had married a second time.[109]

Maybe the point I have been trying to make about textual fissures and silences can be sharpened by a coincidence of dates: 1943, the date of publication of *Guruchand-Charit*, was also the year of the Bengal Famine. This virtually shattered the Namasudra small-peasant economy in districts like Faridpur and Bakargunj, which along with some adjoining areas had constituted the heart of their caste movement. Yet Namasudra assembly members remained supporters of the Muslim League ministry, and Mukunda Behari Mullick, one of the most prominent of their political leaders from *c.* 1912 onwards, played down the devastating effects of this awesome human tragedy. He even supported the very unpopular and disastrous government decision to hand over sole procurement of foodgrains to the notoriously profiteering Ispahani business house.[110]

V

Let me end by touching on a wider theme. It seems to me that the data and argument I have been presenting can help to problematise

[109] Krishnabhabini Biswas, ed., *Mahishya-Mahila*, published by Damodar Biswas, Post Office Kumari, Nadia, volume I (Calcutta, 1318/1911); volume III, 5–6 (Magh-Falgun 1320/1914); volume IV, 5–6 (Magh–Falgun 1321/1915). The *Streer Patra* piece is particularly interesting, as the title is identical with that of a famous short story of Rabindranath written in the voice of an oppressed and ultimately rebellious housewife, which had been published just six months earlier: *Sabuj-Patra*, Sravan 1321/1914—a very striking instance of inter-textuality across caste–class divides. See chapter V below.

[110] Sekhar Bandopadhyay, *Caste, Protest and Identity*, op. cit., pp. 200–1.

a little the current worldwide swing away from class analysis towards valorisations of identity politics. The first is often assumed today to be always incorrigibly economistic and reductionist: the second gets formulated overwhelmingly in terms of cultural 'authenticity'. A politics of 'recognition' of subordinated identities gets pitted against what are thought to be the dangerously homogenising implications of modern-Western post-Enlightenment rationality and universalist equal rights, as embodied in liberalism and Marxism alike.

There is no doubt at all that earlier approaches had numerous blind spots: most obviously, for Left-inclined Indian politics and historiography, the virtual silence till quite recently, on caste. I need go no further in search of a telling example than an instance from my own earlier research. Working on caste in early-twentieth-century Bengal, I have had to go back to the literature of vernacular tracts that had constituted one major kind of material for my first research project, on the Swadeshi era. I feel astounded today that I had virtually ignored caste tracts and movements. And yet I often wonder whether, today, other kinds of silences are not becoming quite as disabling.

I have argued elsewhere that the assumption of a total disjunction between the 'domains' of power and autonomy or resistance fits in well with culturalist conceptions of pure or authentic identity.[111] Much in the later trajectory of Subaltern Studies becomes explicable in the light of that affinity. There is also a strong tendency to collapse the cultural into the religious in the search for the authentic autonomy of the non-West or non-modern. For Partha Chatterjee, therefore, the interesting but extremely marginal story of the Balarami oppositional religious sect becomes the empirical core of the study of 'the nation and its outcastes'.[112]

Neither of these two assumptions, of dichotomous power/autonomy and the centrality of alternative forms of religious life in subaltern-caste protest, fits the early-twentieth-century Bengal material. Subordinate castes were quite often oppositional, but hardly ever autonomous in the sense of being free from high-caste religious, social and historical assumptions. The pattern, we have seen, was neither total integration nor the building up of a distinct domain, but marked

111 See chapter VI below.
112 Partha Chatterjee, *The Nation and Its Fragments*, chapter 9.

by complicated, shifting and selective appropriations. As for religion, the Namasudras appear almost unique among Bengal lower-caste formations in developing their movement around a dissident religious sect. But even in their case, I have suggested, one has to be wary about exaggerating the centrality of the Matuas. The overlap between heterodox religious sect and Namasudra caste affirmation was real but far from exact. The five Namasudra tracts in my sample that are not hagiographies do not mention the Matuas, while the biography of the Matua founder says very little about caste identity.

Over time, the Matuas lost much of their anti-orthodox edge, and sections of Namasudra and many other lower-caste movements could on occasion develop links with chauvinistic high-caste-led formations like the Hindu Mahasabha. Sekhar Bandopadhyay's study reveals shifting patterns of relationships, including several major riots, between Namasudras and Muslims. There are hints, in many cases perhaps unrecoverable in any detail, of moments when gender tensions sought expression, as we saw in some issues of *Mahishya Mahila*. And Bandopadhyay has amassed considerable evidence that Namasudra peasant and sharecropper mobilisation was far from developing only around caste identity. Periodic agrarian struggles—consistently ignored by Namasudra tracts and caste organisations, as we have seen—included the movements of 1872–3 and 1907–9, as well as the combination in 1928–9 of Namasudra and Muslim sharecroppers demanding two-thirds share of the crop. This *tebhaga* demand was generalised into a powerful movement under Communist and Kisan Sabha leadership in 1946–7, primarily among the Rajbansis of North Bengal, where the long-established caste organisation found itself completely sidelined by this explicitly class-grounded upsurge, but also in some Namasudra-dominated areas in Faridpur, Bakargunj, Khulna, Jessore and Dacca.[113]

Clearly, studies of caste identities in isolation will not do. We need to avoid essentialisms not only of class, but also of caste. Class struggle and identity politics both have to be conceptualised not as given or inevitable constants, but as no more than constructed, contingent projects playing on specific kinds of pressures and tensions in varying ways and magnitudes. But I have some problems with eclectic

[113] Sekhar Bandopadhyay, *Caste, Protest and Identity*, pp. 145, 235–6.

approaches which merely emphasise oscillations in relative importance, and which in effect look upon class as just another kind of identity, remaining satisfied with a model of fleeting solidarities all more
or less on the same level of importance. As projects, one needs also
some evaluation in terms of potential implications. Here, the original
Marxian project had visualised the proletariat as a very distinct kind
of social group, as the potentially 'universal' class, the identity of
which has to be simultaneously affirmed and ultimately transcended
through a politics of hegemony. Lower-caste politics in sharp contrast
has been quite remarkably fragmented, as Digindranarayan angrily
emphasised in a mid-1920s pamphlet: Namasudras look down upon
the Chandals, Mahishyas distinguish themselves from the Kaibartas,
the Rajbansis say they are utterly distinct from the Koch, and so it
went on, he complains.[114] Of course, similar things happen in class
movements, too, and Marx's faith in the potentialities of the working
class would appear highly utopian to very many today. The point,
rather, is that the contemporary theoretical emphasis on identity and
authenticity, and above all the widespread rejection of any and every
potentially universalist values and projects, tend to erect a major problem into an ideal.

---

[114] Digindranarayan Bhattacharya, *Chaturvarna-Vibha* (Serajgunj/Calcutta,
1925), pp. 68–77.

CHAPTER III

Intimations of Hindutva
Ideologies, Caste, and Class in
Post-Swadeshi Bengal*

J AWAHARLAL NEHRU recalled in his autobiography that, on his return from England in 1912, he found 'India . . . politically, very
dull.'[1] Historians had till recently generally agreed with this, and
considered the years between the decline of the Swadeshi movement
and the First World War interesting only in terms of a continuing
saga of revolutionary terrorism. Things start looking rather different
once we recognise that there can be many histories and not just one,
and move away a little from the assumption that everything about
late-colonial India (or, in the context of this essay, Bengal) can be
neatly encapsulated within a single narrative of colonialism vs. anti-
colonial nationalism.

The trough between the two waves of major anti-colonial struggle,
Swadeshi and Non-Cooperation–Khilafat, is now coming to be recognised as crucial for the development of high-caste ideologies and
activities that were in some ways constitutive of the Hindutva of the
mid-1920s and later. The Swadeshi—and particularly the immediate
post-Swadeshi—years in Bengal were marked by numerous lower-
caste affirmations, notably among Namasudras, Mahishyas and Rajbansis. Caste had been relatively marginal in nineteenth-century

---

*Revised version of a paper presented at the Calicut Session of the Indian
History Congress, December 1999.

[1] Jawaharlal Nehru, *An Autobiography* (Bodley Head, London, 1936), p. 27.

social-reformist endeavours in Bengal in which the 'women's question' had been pre-eminent, and one gets an impression of a decline in importance again from around the mid-1920s. In between, however, it enjoyed a discursive and political centrality. It might be interesting to explore why.

I have a twofold agenda in this essay. First, I intend to highlight the interconnections between high- and lower-caste developments, and the emergence, in part from out of that interaction, of discourses of aggressive Hindu unity. Such themes are usually considered separately, with caste in particular being studied through movements of individual jatis—except where they are unhelpfully collapsed into frameworks that assume a Dumontian structural unity, harmony, and fundamental changelessness. Contemporary newspapers, journals, and pamphlets provide considerable material on such interconnections. Second, I seek to explore some possible, so far largely unnoticed connections between the new centrality of caste and religious identity-formation, and certain specificities of agrarian tensions in the 1900s. Connections, but also important discordances: for my argument is that important relationships do often exist between class relations and forms of identity politics, but the links are seldom of a neat or reductive kind.

II

Pradip Datta has emphasised the importance of U.N. Mukherji's serialised essay in the *Bengalee* in June 1909,[2] entitled 'A Dying Race'. Striking a theme that has had many resonances in Hindu communal ideology down to present times, this sought to instil a demographic panic through selective use of some Census data and projections which seemed to suggest that Muslims were breeding much faster in Bengal than Hindus. Hindu weakness and disunion, he suggested, was rooted 'in our treatment of our co-religionists'. What today would be called a 'sanskritising' uplift of lower castes at bhadralok initiative was necessary to build anti-Muslim Hindu unity in a situation

---

[2] Datta, *Carving Blocs* (Delhi, 1999), chapter 1; as well as Datta, 'Dying Hindus: Production of Hindu Communal Commonsense in Early Twentieth Century Bengal', *Economic and Political Weekly*, 19 June 1993.

where, at the end of each year, 'they [Muslims] count their gains, we calculate our losses.'[3] The series was very widely welcomed in both Bengal bhadralok and other upper-caste circles.[4]

Bhadralok reformism concerning caste, however, remained severely limited. 'A Dying Race' was very dismissive of contemporary lower-caste self-improvement efforts, and a decade later its author tried to dissuade the Pod activist, Manindranath Mandal, from floating a Bangiya Jana Sangh as an autonomous united platform for subordinate jatis.[5] Mukherji's own concrete efforts at caste upliftment seem to have been confined to attempts at persuading barbers and washermen to extend their services to lower jatis like Malis—without disturbing, it should be noted, the pollution taboos imposed by the bhadralok themselves.[6] And even this very restricted kind of reform was not liked by many bhadralok spokesmen. I have shown elsewhere[7] that if papers like the *Bengalee* or the Brahmo-edited *Modern Review* supported Mukherji, the very influential cultural-nationalist *Dawn* took a rather different line, much more openly affirming Brahmanical hierarchy and apparently not much moved by the demographic scare.[8]

Anticipations of what today would be called Hindutva moods and

[3] *Bengalee*, 1–22 June 1909, in 19 parts, generally carried on the editorial page. The quote is from 22 June 1909.

[4] A letter of support came immediately from Lala Lajpat Rai, and the response was particularly enthusiastic in Panjab and Delhi, with several suggesting the Arya Shuddhi method as model for lower-caste upliftment. *Bengalee*, 22 June, 10 July, 11 July 1909.

[5] Manindranath Mandal, *Bangiya Jana Sangha* (Khejuri, Midnapur, 1925), Introduction; see also my previous chapter, pp. 65–6.

[6] *Bengalee*, 8 June 1909; Manindranath Mandal, *Bangiya Jana Sangha*, op. cit., p. i; U.N. Mukherji, *The Malis of East Bengal* (Calcutta, April 1911). A Barisal District Conference in August 1908 passed a similar resolution recommending the extension of barber-washermen services to the Namasudras. Fortnightly Report, Eastern Bengal and Assam, second half of August 1908, Government of India Home Political A, October 1908, n.104.

[7] Sumit Sarkar, *Writing Social History* (Delhi, 1997), chapter 9.

[8] Well before Mukherji's articles, the *Modern Review* ('Decrease of Hindus', April 1907) and the *Bengalee* (Editorial entitled 'Decrease of Hindu Population', 1 March 1908) had used Census data to express alarm about Hindu decline, and had suggested the need for limited reforms to improve the status and conditions of lower castes so that they did not break away from the Hindu fold. The *Dawn*,

formulations—along with internal variations and tensions that have remained characteristic of that ideological formation—became very striking indeed for a time around November–December 1910. The context was the abortive move by Census Commissioner Gait to exclude castes not served by Brahmans, kept out from temples, or suffering from similar disabilities, from the 'Hindu' category. High-caste protests focused upon the question of defining the Hindu and sought to combine, in varying proportions, an argument of basic unity and catholicity embracing multiple variations, with retention of hierarchical inequality. Thus the *Daily Hitavadi* of 5 November 1910 declared that 'whoever calls himself a Hindu is a Hindu': differences of belief were irrelevant, but of course 'Hindu social customs remained obligatory—which surely meant caste above everything else. And, once again anticipating the basic thrust of Savarkar's key thesis in *Hindutva: Who is a Hindu?* (1923), priority was sought to be given repeatedly to the question of authentic origin. Differences were a secondary matter given origin within Bharatvarsha, and, being unimportant, could be retained, even reiterated. The same newspaper cited (19 December 1910) a *vyavastha* given by some Nabadwip pandits defining as Hindus 'all those people who have inhabited Bharatvarsha before the time of the crossing of the Indus by the Musalmans', and, 'at the present time, all Indians who are not Christians and Musalmans.' It immediately went on to defend the exclusion of lower castes from temples and Brahman services, and pollution taboos in general. Internal variations remained considerable. If the reformist *Sanjivani* (on 1 December) denounced untouchability as 'a disgrace' to Hinduism, the extreme-conservative *Nayak* (17 November) initially went so far as to welcome the Gait Circular as a barrier against caste mobility. 'No true Hindu likes the idea of his society being filled with un-Hindus following *mleccha* habits.' It backtracked quickly (22 November), having learnt, it said, that Gait's move was related to

---

in significant contrast, repeatedly came out with open and aggressive justifications of caste hierarchy as much superior to what it described as the Western 'doctrine of rights', and in January 1911 deplored the obsession with population statistics as a surrender to alien 'secular' and 'utilitarian' values. 'Social Movements Round a Centre', *Dawn*, August 1897; 'The Question of Caste: Some Sort of an Analysis', ibid., August 1903; 'Who are Hindus and Who are Not', ibid., January 1911.

Muslim League pressure to reduce the number of Hindus in Census enumeration.[9] Hindu unity thus remained the ultimate common denominator, emphasised by the *Sanjivani* as much as by orthodox papers.

The unusual prominence of caste issues during these years had evidently much to do with political conjunctures. The declining Hindu scare had been launched by Census Commissioner O'Donnell way back in 1891.[10] This evoked widespread interest and alarm only from around 1907 onwards, in the declining phase of the Swadeshi movement. The attempt to build a united mass struggle had clearly foundered, with Hindu–Muslim riots breaking out at Iswargunj in May 1906 and Comilla and Jamalpur in March–April 1907, and with Muslim and lower-caste Hindu peasants either indifferent or hostile to bhadralok calls for boycott and swadeshi. Swadeshi, for the first time, brought home to bhadralok nationalists the need for mass mobilisation, and hence the political importance of Muslims and lower castes, but the methods often used for that purpose (such as social boycott of recalcitrants, and the closure of village markets by gentry order) frequently proved counter-productive.[11] And the numbers game constructed around identities of religion and caste, made possible by Census enumeration, had suddenly become more vital for politicians and educated middle-class people, with the simultaneous onset of a measure of representative government and separate electorates.

All this is well known and indisputable, as are the standard explanations in terms of British divide-and-rule, or what seems its updated version—the discursive patterns imposed by colonial knowledge. Assumptions of automaticity of response need to be avoided, however, and for all levels. Thus bhadralok ideology and politics in the early-twentieth century had started getting conditioned also by

[9] The extracts and references in this paragraph are all from the relevant Report on Native Papers (Bengal) series, November–December 1910.

[10] He had even made the startling prediction that if the present differentiated growth-rates continued for Bengal Muslims and Hindus, the latter would cease to exist in 700 years. *Census 1891, volume iii (Bengal)*, chapter 9, p. 146.

[11] For details, see my *Swadeshi Movement in Bengal, 1903–8* (New Delhi, 1973), chapters VI–VIII, and *passim*. I am amazed, however, today by my near-total blindness then to the question of caste.

lower-caste pressures, which were not mere reflexes of Census stimuli, as has been assumed at times. The opportunity for upward mobility provided—briefly—by Risley's effort in the 1901 Census to classify jatis according to regional notions of social precedence was no doubt important.[12] But Sekhar Bandopadhyay's pioneering work has revealed that the Namasudra upthrust in South-Central Bengal began in the 1870s, quite independently of Census or other official stimuli, through a brief agrarian protest on a question of honour, followed by the more sustained Matua dissident religious movement.[13] Again, Census status was seldom the sole or even primary theme in the lower-caste vernacular tracts that started coming out in considerable numbers from *c.* 1900 onwards. It is not even mentioned in five out of the seven Namasudra tracts, six of them published between 1909 and 1916, that I have examined in detail in the preceding chapter. More important contexts were arguably provided by a degree of economic advancement, some educational opportunities, and, above all, the democratising potential of the spread of vernacular print-culture.[14] Whatever their other differences, post-Swadeshi high-caste discussions around social hierarchy tended to have in common a sense of alarm about lower-caste assertions. Thus a letter supportive of U.N. Mukherji in *Bengalee* urged the need 'to meet the rising tide of the new aspirations of that large and fast-growing class of educated men who derive their origin from the humbler castes.'[15]

III

But can caste conflict in post-Swadeshi Bengal be reduced entirely to a question of conflicts between educated 'elites' and 'counter-elites'?

[12] It is seldom remembered, however, that this experiment lasted only for a decade. Gait as Commissioner of the very next Census, that of 1911, went back to a purely alphabetical listing of castes. *Writing Social History,* pp. 376–7; also see chapter 2, above.

[13] Sekhar Bandopadhyay, *Caste, Protest and Identity in Colonial India: The Namasudras of Bengal, 1872–1947* (London, 1997), chapter 2. See also chapter 2 above.

[14] See above, chapter 2. For an earlier brief discussion of these themes, see my *Writing Social History,* chapter 9.

[15] It went on to refer directly to the 'mass of literature that is springing for the exaltation of castes'. *Bengalee,* 10 July 1909.

The subordinate jatis consisted predominantly of peasants, share-croppers, artisans, or other rural labouring groups, and literacy rates among most of them remained abysmally low in the vernacular and almost non-existent in English.[16] In the wake of Swadeshi decline, a few perceptive and self-critical bhadralok commentators, most notably Rabindranath Tagore, in a number of his post-1907 essays as well as in the novels *Gora* (1907–9) and *Ghare-Baire* (1915–16), drew pointed attention to the vast gap between the overwhelmingly upper-caste Hindu gentlefolk and the Muslim or lower-caste rural masses.[17] The concordance between class and religious-cum-caste differentiation in large parts of Bengal has in fact become something like a truism. The problem is, however, that this most often gets treated as a historical constant, and so is not entirely satisfactory as an explanation for the evident sharpening of agrarian, caste and communal conflict in particular times and places, as in the Swadeshi and post-Swadeshi years.

Here a juxtapositioning of two works of recent research, written without any knowledge of each other—Sekhar Bandopadhyay's detailed study of the Namasudras, and the outstanding yet so far sadly little-known analysis of changing agrarian relations in East Bengal, *c.* 1870–1910, by Nariaki Nakazato[18]—can prove quite illuminating. Through a rigorous statistical analysis of Dacca Division Registration Department and Court of Wards records, Nakazato raises serious doubts about the widespread current assumption of a relatively undifferentiated peasant community in early-twentieth century southeast Bengal (as distinct from sharper internal divisions towards the north and the west).[19] Differentiation meant, not so much any proliferation of 'depeasantised' landless labourers, but a major drive on the

---

[16] Thus in 1911 Namasudra literacy was estimated at 4.9% in Bengali and 0.22% in English—up considerably, however, from the corresponding 1901 figures of 3.3% and 0.04%. The extent of educational differentiation along caste lines becomes clear from the figures in 1911 for Kayasthas: 34.7% in vernacular and 9.80% in English. Calculated from Census data by Sekhar Bandopadhyay, *Caste, Politics and the Raj: Bengal 1872–1937* (Calcutta, 1990), p. 109.

[17] *Swadeshi Movement in Bengal*, pp. 79–86, 90–1, and *passim*.

[18] Nariaki Nakazato, *Agrarian System in Eastern Bengal, c. 1870–1910* (Calcutta, 1994), is not included among the references in Sekhar Bandopadhyay (1997).

[19] This model of ecologically differentiated regional distinctions—a contrast, notably, between the 'moribund' and the jute-growing 'active' delta—was

part of the gentry to shift from cash·rents to produce rent-paying *barga* (sharecropping) tenures—in the context particularly of rising grain prices in the early twentieth century. An addtional incentive was provided by the fact that sharecropping was not subject to the legal restrictions on rent enhancement imposed by the 1885 Tenancy Act, nor would occupancy rights accrue to land leased out in that manner. Many of the predominantly bhadralok zamindars and tenure-holders, moreover, had begun to combine rent extraction with trade in grain. What was rapidly developing, as one exceptionally perceptive official (J.C. Jack) noted in 1912, was a produce rent 'of modern growth . . . where raiyats holding at cash rent have been converted by moneylenders or petty landlords into bargadars.' He saw in this the development of 'competition rent', unrestrained by custom or law, extracted mainly from bargadars—unlike the cash rents from occupancy raiyats that had been regulated to a considerable extent by the Tenancy Acts of 1859 and 1885.[20] It may be noted that zamindars, tenure-holders, *mahajans*, and sections of richer peasants could all participate in this barga drive. What was happening, then, was not so much a change in the balance of power in the countryside from zamindar to upstart jotedar—as often portrayed in Bengali literature which has at times been marked by a degree of sympathy for the more 'traditional' kind of landlordism—as a shift in the form of exploitation from which diverse groups could benefit.

The one legal possibility of resistance to this gentry drive for produce rent came from Section 40 of the 1885 Act, which gave occupancy raiyats being pushed into sharecropper status an option of applying

---

suggested by Partha Chatterjee ('Agrarian Structure in Pre-Partition Bengal', in Asok Sen, *et al.*, *Perspectives in Social Sciences 2*, Calcutta, 1982, and *Bengal 1920–1947: The Land Question*, Calcutta, 1984), and elaborated by Sugata Bose (*Agrarian Bengal: Economy, Social Structure and Politics, 1919–1947*, Cambridge, 1986). With Chatterjee, it served as a basis for the 'Subalternist' conception of a fairly homogeneous peasant 'community-consciousness' manifested through Muslim, or at times lower-caste, identity: see for instance his 'Agrarian Relations and Communalism in Bengal, 1926–35', in Ranajit Guha, ed., *Subaltern Studies I* (Delhi, 1982).

[20] J.C. Jack, 'Commutation of Rents', in Government of East Bengal and Assam, Revenue Department, Revenue Branch, September 1912, Progs. 81–2, cited in Nakazato, pp. 90–1.

for commutation into cash rates. This had become very attractive for peasants, particularly because of the early-twentieth-century rise in grain prices, which created an enormous gap between the actual burden of rents extracted in produce and in money. The burden was greatest in areas where barga was taking the form of *dhankarari*, rent as a fixed amount of paddy, rather than a third or (much more often) half-share of the actual produce in a particular year. Thus Jack, then Settlement Officer of Bakarganj and Faridpur, noted in January 1909 that dhankarari rent, if translated into money terms at current prices, would amount to at least Rs 12 per acre in North Bakarganj, as contrasted to the prevailing cash rates in the same area of Rs 3 or 4.[21]

Matters came to a head around 1907–9 in the Gaurnadi police station area of North Bakarganj. A region with a particularly heavy bhadralok concentration and a major bastion of the Swadeshi movement,[22] it was also the one pocket in Bakarganj where dhankarari had become common. A big proportion of the peasants and sharecroppers here were Namasudras, members of a social group among whom efforts at self-improvement and assertions of higher status already had a long history, going back to the early 1870s.[23] The catalyst came from

---

[21] J.C. Jack to Dacca Divisional Commissioner R. Nathan, 13/20 January 1909, in J.C. Jack, *Bakarganj Settlement Report, 1900–1908* (Calcutta, 1915), Appendix G: correspondence concerning the commutation of rents, p. xlvi.

[22] For some details, see my *Swadeshi Movement in Bengal*, pp. 381–90, and *passim*. Batajore, the home village and estate of Aswinikumar Datta, head of the Swadesh Bandhab Samiti and one of the most prominent and respected of the Swadeshi leaders, fell within Gaurnadi thana. J.C. Jack in January 1909 described Gaurnadi, with an area of 130 square miles and population of 162,000, 23,000 of them bhadralok, as 'a Mecca to high-caste Hindus.' He also mentioned 'the Dutts of Batajore' as among the many zamindars and tenure-holders who had been shifting in a big way to *dhankarari*, combining it with 'a large trade in rice.' Jack to Nathan, 13/20 January 1909, op. cit.

[23] Gaurnadi was not far from Gopalganj subdivision in south-west Faridpur, within which lay Orakandi, headquarters of the Matua sect, as well as of an Australian Baptist Mission. The Matua leaders of the Namasudra movement seem to have used the missionaries as a resource for starting a high school and for developing contacts with white officials, but very few became converts. The Namasudra concentration, usually on marshy land which they had opened up for cultivation, extended from Gaurnadi and Swarupkhati in Bakarganj, through Gopalganj in Faridpur, to Magura and Narail subdivisions of Jessore and Sadar

the settlement operations, which started in the Gaurnadi region in
1903–4. These were headed by two successive officials, Beatson-Bell
and Jack, who happened to be rather sympathetic towards cultivators
and felt that information about the legal provision that allowed commutation during settlement operations should reach those being
coerced into dhankarari. Applications poured in for commutations,
with the lead apparently taken by some Christian peasant converts.
Namasudras, according to one (unsympathetic) official report, at
times formed combinations that allegedly spread rumours that the
government was on their side, and used social boycott on those community members who were hesitant about applying. Jack, who saw
in dhankarari parallels with the metayer system which Arthur Young
had found so oppressive in pre-Revolutionary France, went so far as
to appoint a special officer who, between June and August 1908,
looked into 1164 applications and granted commutations in all but
30. But zamindars and tenure-holders hit back through false cases of
rent arrears, pleaders and local courts backed the gentry (being indeed
overwhelmingly drawn from, or dominated by, rentier groups), and
in August 1908 the Bakarganj settlement policy was abruptly reversed
by Jack's superior, Savage. The latter halted the commutation proceedings, responding to a petition presented to him at Barisal 'by a
body of pleaders and Brahmin priests' who claimed that gentlefolk,
more particularly purohits and high-caste widows, were suffering
acutely as the commuted cash rents were insufficient for purchase of
rice at the prevailing high prices. The struggle continued for some
time more, with scattered reports of Namasudras withdrawing barga
and other services to the bhadralok gentry both in Bakarganj and a
few pockets in neighbouring districts. But the brief moment of some
official sympathy had passed as quickly as it had come.[24] Contrary

---

and Bagerhat in Khulna. Sekhar Bandopadhyay, *Caste, Protest and Identity*, chapter I; see also the District Gazetteers for these four districts, where lived more than
half of the Namasudra population of Bengal. A kind of 'inside' view is provided
by a long hagiography in verse of the second Matua leader: Mahananda Haldar,
Sri Sri Guruchand-Charit (Kalibari, Khulna, 1943), discussed in chapter 2 above.

[24] Jack learnt his lesson and did not try to go in for commutations in his next
assignment (as Settlement Officer of Faridpur) despite considerable similarities
in conditions. In his famous *Economic Life of a Bengal District* (London, 1916)

to what could have been expected, even at this peak moment of anti-British agitation among the bhadralok, class affinity apparently proved stronger than race—especially when peasants seemed on the point of developing an organised agitation of their own.[25]

The combination of lower-caste assertion and agrarian protest certainly troubled the bhadralok, and there is at least one striking coincidence of dates which suggests a fairly direct link of such pressures with attempts to shore up Hindu unity in combination with limited reform from above. In June 1909, precisely the month when U.N. Mukherji's 'A Dying Race' was being serialised in the *Bengalee*, the *Modern Review* carried an article by a Madaripur (Faridpur) pleader, Binod Lal Ghosh, entitled 'What Can be Done for the Namasudras'. This regretted that Namasudra peasants in parts of Bakarganj and Faridpur, allegedly incited by 'their half-educated brethren' and Christian missionaries, had started a 'misguided' and 'suicidal' agitation, withdrawing services—particularly of barga—from the gentry. The remedy lay in convincing the Namasudras that they were 'a part and parcel of the Hindu society'. A series of bhadralok-initiated ameliorative reforms were then suggested (schools, free dispensaries, a slight relaxation in pollution taboos, etc.)—but nothing that remotely touched questions of barga or basic land relations.[26] It is also

---

analysing Faridpur data, he presented a rather rosy view of a fundamentally undifferentiated and prosperous peasant community. He left for posterity, however, the texts of his correspondence about Bakarganj commutations, in a fascinating Appendix G of the Settlement Report of that district. My account is based on the material in this Appendix, particularly the Note of H. Savage, First Member of Board of Revenue, Eastern Bengal and Assam, 20 August 1908, and the letter of J.C. Jack to R. Nathan, Commissioner of Dacca Division, No. 937, 13/20 January 1909. *Bakarganj Settlement Report*, Appendix G.

[25] Sekhar Bandopadhyay (1997), pp. 76–80, gives a summary of the Gaurnadi developments based on the *Bakarganj Settlement Report*, but does not draw out the more general implications in terms of changes in agrarian structure. Nor does he draw attention to the interesting differences within the colonial bureaucracy. Nakazato, chapter VII, and *passim*, provides an excellent and original analysis of the significance of the shift towards 'new barga'. The format of his work, however, does not allow any detailed study of caste.

[26] A number of broadly similar articles came out around this time in some other journals, in particular the *Nabyabharat*, edited by a man with Faridpur

interesting that August 1908, when a Barisal District Conference passed a resolution expressing a limited degree of sympathy for Namasudras,[27] was also the precise moment when pleaders and purohits presented a successful petition to Savage in that same town to halt commutations. And meanwhile the local nationalist weekly, *Barisal Hitaishi*, was carrying on a bitter campaign against the Gaurnadi effort to curb the growth of produce rent.[28] Bhadralok intransigence regarding the drive towards what Nakazato has termed 'barga landlordism' only deepened with the years. In 1909, a key Calcutta High Court judgement ruled that arrangements with bargadars did not 'by itself create relationships of landlord and tenant'.[29] Every effort to give some legal rights to sharecroppers during the run-up to the 1928 Tenancy Amendment was blocked by landed groups fully backed by Swarajists, and that legislation finally abrogated Section 40, which had enabled commutation.

Such limits were perhaps natural enough among the bhadralok: more surprising are the silences in lower-caste tracts and journals. We may take *Guruchand Charit* as an example. Signs of class anger are not infrequent in this Namasudra view from within. Thus we are told that Guruchand accepted missionary help in starting a high school at Orakandi after local Kayasthas had opposed its foundation, allegedly on the grounds that sharecroppers and servants would no longer work for them if they became educated. Literacy, further, was vital for peasants, for otherwise high-caste landlords were constantly tricking them in matters of rent receipts and indebtedness.[30] But the key

---

connections, Debiprasanna Raychaudhuri—which had focused fairly often on Namasudra problems already from the 1890s. See Madhusudan Sarkar, 'Sparsha-dosh pratha uthiye dao', *Nabyabharat*, Asar 1314/1907; Pyarisankar Dasgupta, 'Namasudra', ibid., Agrahayan 1315/1908; and Kaliprasanna Chakrabarti, 'Banglar Bartaman Hindusamaj', ibid., Caitra 1316/1910.

[27] Fortnightly Report for second half of August 1908, in Government of India Home Political A, October 1908, n.104.

[28] *Barisal Hitaishi*, 3 August, 17 August, 7 September 1908—translated excerpts in the Report on Native Papers (Eastern Bengal and Assam) of the relevant weeks.

[29] Nakazato, p. 82.

[30] The text describes Kayasthas to be arguing that education of Namasudras would disrupt the age-old principles of adhikari-bheda (hierarchical order), as

moments of agrarian struggle by sections of the Namasudras of the Faridpur–Bakarganj region, in 1872–3 and 1907–9, are completely ignored in this very long metrical hagiography which, unlike most representatives of that genre, focusses very largely on quite mundane developments. And if this reticence is significant, even more striking is the way *Nihar* (Contai), weekly journal of the Mahishyas of Midnapur, developed in summer 1909 a sustained critique of settlement operations in parts of that district, entirely from the point of view of relatively privileged rural strata.[31]

What can explain such discordances? Clearly, a part of the explanation lies in major variations in conditions of life, both across regions and within subordinated castes. Thus a District Gazetteer described the Mahishyas of Midnapur as representing 'all interests in land ranging from the proprietor to the cultivator.'[32] Namasudras on the whole tended to be located at humbler socio-economic levels, but even among them there were great local variations and many signs of growing differentiation. The dhankarari issue, for instance, so vital in Gaurnadi, did not have much relevance for Gopalganj, and a whole section in the biography of Guruchand hailed the success of his entrepreneurial efforts as trader-cum-moneylender. Evidently it is this upwardly mobile strata which would have access to print, thus producing a particular kind of alignment in available sources of lower-caste origin.

But of course it does not follow that the appeal of a language of caste was confined only, or always, to emergent counter-elites. Which among a great range of potential solidarities—of caste, class, religious community, region, nation, gender—becomes pre-eminent among a particular group clearly varies with circumstances and times. A crucial

---

enshrined notably in the Ramayana. *Guruchand Charit,* pp. 100–10, 140–66. For more details about this text, see my 'Identities and Histories', and chapter 2 above.

[31] A series of articles in *Nihar* between 20 April and 20 July 1909 attacked the giving of *parchas* (title-deeds) to bargadars (i.e. treating them as tenants rather than labourers), attempts to implement Section 40, and efforts to extend occupancy rights to *korfa* raiyats (sub-tenants). *Nihar,* 20 and 27 April, 11, 18, and 25 May, 19 June, and 13 and 20 July 1909—Report on Native Papers (Bengal), relevant numbers.

[32] L.S.S. O'Malley, ed., *Midnapur District Gazetteer* (Calcutta, 1911), p. 58.

element here, I would like to suggest, is provided by what might be called the horizon of expectations at particular moments. Signs of a rift between British authorities and nationalist-inclined landlords during the Swadeshi years probably stimulated peasant hopes, particularly where—as in Gaurnadi—settlement operations were being conducted by somewhat sympathetic British officials. This helped to produce combinations along class lines—which were less evident, however, as Jack noted, in neighbouring Faridpur tracts, where too the dhankarari drive was under way, for officials, after being pulled up in Bakarganj, did not inform peasants there about the Section 40 option.[33] At the other end of the Namasudra country, in the Narail and Magura subdivisions of Jessore, a demand for what would later become famous as tebhaga (sharecroppers claiming two-thirds of the harvest) was raised jointly by some Muslims and Namasudras in 1909. Bargadar agitations revived in the 1920s in several districts, in the context of much discussion about an impending change in tenancy laws, and then in 1946–7 came the greatest *bhagchasi* upsurge of all, the Communist and Kisan Sabha-inspired Tebhaga upsurge.[34] It had some strongholds in Namasudra-dominated areas, and its major base among the Rajbansis of North Bengal—the third big lower-caste group in the province which for several decades had followed with apparent loyalty the privileged leaders of a moderate, sanskritising type of caste movement. But there have also been long years when the horizon of expectation of radical change in agrarian relations shrank, and when for most it probably seemed more sensible to adhere to other kinds of identity. This could be religious solidarity, in the context of upper-caste overtures of limited sanskritisation from the top, or, to come to an obvious contemporary instance, the pinning of all hopes on reservations. Such moves would directly benefit only a minority, but others might hope to gain a little through kinship ties and clientage connections—or at the least enjoy a bit of vicarious pride at the success of a few of their caste brethren.

What is needed, then, are studies of class, caste, religious, or other identities in their shifting interrelations, and not in isolated or essentialised ways. To go back to the theme with which I had begun: the

[33] J.C. Jack, ed., *Faridpur Settlement Report* (Calcutta, 1916), *passim*.

[34] For a summary account of the anticipations of tebhaga, see Tanika Sarkar, *Bengal 1928–1934: The Politics of Protest* (Delhi, 1987), pp. 40–1.

intimations of Hindutva among sections of the bhadralok in the immediate post-Swadeshi years appear related, fairly clearly, to a felt sense of threat from lower-caste/class groups—a pattern with many later manifestations, one hardly needs to add.

CHAPTER IV

Two Muslim Tracts for Peasants
Bengal 1909–1910

I HAVE SUGGESTED in an earlier chapter that the high degree of concordance between class and religious-cum-caste differentiation in
large parts of pre-1947 Bengal—most landlords bhadralok Hindu,
most peasants Muslim or lower caste—has been conducive for somewhat deterministic, 'structural' interpretations of communal and
caste tensions. Thus the emergence of a distinct and powerful Muslim
political identity in the wake of the anti-Partition movement of the
bhadralok, once explained in Indian nationalist historiography in
terms of British and/or Muslim elite machinations, came to be widely—and, up to a point, helpfully—read in terms of 'distorted' class
struggle, or as the expression of a more-or-less homogeneous, already-
existent, Muslim peasant 'community-consciousness'.[1] A necessary
search for mediations, however, began in 1981 with Rafiuddin Ahmad's pathbreaking work. Ahmad opened up a forgotten world of
cheap vernacular printed tracts spreading notions of a reformed Islam
in villages and small towns from the late nineteenth century onwards.
Together with practices of public religious debates and gatherings
(*bahas*, and *waz mahfil*), such manuals of religious instruction (*nasihat
nama*) were shown to have contributed to the formation of a much

---

[1] My *Swadeshi Movement in Bengal 1903–8* (New Delhi, 1973), chapter VIII,
and Partha Chatterjee, 'Agrarian Relations and Communalism in Bengal, 1926–
35' (in Ranajit Guha, ed., *Subaltern Studies I* (Delhi, 1982), can be taken as
instances of such interpretative strategies.

more widespread, grass roots-level sense of distinct and unified Muslim community identity than seems to have been evident earlier.[2]

What remained unexplained, however, is why significant sections of Bengali Muslim peasants responded with such eagerness to the proselytisation campaign of reformist mullahs in the countryside: the 'class' and 'religious' interpretations still remained somewhat detached from each other. Here a very significant contribution has been made by P.K. Datta through his focus on the emergence, in the early twentieth century, of a relatively new 'peasant improvement' theme in many of the vernacular tracts directed to village audiences. These combined the inculcation of a puritanical ethic of diligence, hard work, avoidance of extravagance, and 'individual profit', with insistence on 'collective betterment' through strengthening the solidarity of the Islamic community. Datta brings out the mutually productive interrelations between such an ethos and the aspirations and fears of an upwardly mobile stratum of peasants, mostly Muslim in East Bengal, trying to pull themselves up by their bootstraps during what proved to be an all-too-brief, relatively favourable, conjuncture of soaring jute prices.[3] At the same time, he emphasises the fluidity and open-endedness of the processes of multiple identity formation. For while improvement ideology was obviously very open to appropriation along anti-Hindu, communal lines, there remained alternative possibilities for other kinds of solidarity—of Bengali language and culture, and, notably, of class. These could, and occasionally did, undercut projects of Muslim communal mobilisation, as indicated for instance by some pamphlets of the 1920s preaching united class war through peasant associations against zamindars.[4]

My purpose here is a modest one—of adding something like a footnote to such ongoing work, through presenting material from an

[2] Rafiuddin Ahmad, *The Bengal Muslims, 1871–1906: A Quest for Identity* (Delhi, 1981), chapters II, III, and *passim*.

[3] Pradip Kumar Datta, *Carving Blocs: Communal Ideology in Early Twentieth-century Bengal* (Delhi, 1999), p. 73, and chapter 2, *passim*.

[4] Notably Khondakar Mohammad Badiazzaman, *Banger Zamindar* (Mijangunje, Ullapara, Pabna, 1332/1925), and Mohammad Moazuddin Hamidi, *Krishaker Unnati o Dukho Durdashar Pratikar* (P.O. Kolaroa, Khulna, 1929). Datta, op. cit., pp. 79–80.

exceptionally interesting pamphlet I came across in the British (previously India Office) Library collection of vernacular tracts. This is Muhammad Mohsin Ulla's *Bureer Soota* (Calcutta, 1909/1910),[5] roughly translatable as 'The old woman's thread'—an interesting title, to be explicated shortly. To the best of my knowledge, this tract has not figured so far in any historical account. I want to juxtapose it against another, near-contemporaneous pamphlet which is better known: a long poem entitled *Krishak Bandhu*, by 'Garib Sayer'(Calcutta, 1910: reprinted, 1921).[6] The two are close to each other from the points of view of date and, up to a point, provenance—the enormous differences nevertheless in content and overall thrust are therefore all the more worthy of analysis.

II

I will be brief about *Krishak Bandhu*, since a fair amount has been written about it already. The 112-page poem has a well-thought-out, near-seamless structure, and represents an almost copybook instance of class issues being simultaneously evoked, and effectively subordinated, to developed communal discourse. It begins with around 20 pages on the woes of the peasant, on whose back-breaking labour society rests, but who is oppressed by all: zamindar, mahajan, police, shopkeeper, even the village headman. The exploiters then start getting merged into the figure of the 'babu' or bhadralok Hindu, who is also the Congressman—while the peasant gets collapsed into the Muslim, and is urged to cultivate solidarity with his co-religionists. A number of possible rough edges are deftly removed through sheer silence: that a fair number of zamindars were Muslims, for instance, including the very big landlord, Nawab Salimulla of Dacca, who just then was in the forefront of Muslim political opposition to the Swadeshi movement. As Datta notes, a passing reference to lower-caste

---

[5] The text consists of two parts, bound together in the British Library copy. Part I came out initially in March 1909, while the version I have seen is its second edition, dated 14 September 1910. It is bound together with part II, 1st edition, 26 November 1909.

[6] I discussed this extensively in my *Swadeshi Movement*, op. cit., pp. 462–4, and it has been explored again in Datta, *Carving Blocs*, pp. 70, 79.

Hindus—'Namasudra, Pod, Kaibarta' being also ill treated by high-caste bhadralok gentry is not allowed to develop into any theme of possible class solidarity of all peasants irrespective of religious difference.[7] For the central message of the poem is improvement, indissolubly combined with Islamic reform-cum-unity. The Muslim peasant is urged to open up new lands for cultivation (through migration to thinly populated Sylhet, Cachar, Assam, the Sunderbans, the Tarai region), diversify crops, get educated with the primary aim of learning up-to-date farming techniques, turn to trade, and, simultaneously, acquire the proper Islamic values.[8] Religious solidarity, it is implied, will prevent the enterprising upwardly mobile Muslim peasant getting alienated from the rest of the community and becoming an oppressor himself. Correct Islamic values are spelt out to include the avoidance of unnecessary expenditure on weddings and litigation, regular readings of the Koran and payment of *zakat* to the mullah, and a sharp rejection of syncretistic cults of the *baul* kind.[9] All this is combined with repeated attacks on the Congress, moderate as much as extremist, as an essentially Hindu conspiracy seeking a swaraj that Hindus will surely dominate, and calls to rally round the recently formed Muslim League.

'Garib Sayer' is obviously a pseudonym, and the entire text is marked by a certain anonymity—one that signifies here not plebeian origin, as it might be tempting to presume,[10] but its precise opposite: for the poem, on careful reading, reveals several signs of being part of an organised, 'elite' kind of project, seeking to proceed enirely from top downwards. The peasant is an 'Other', who is sought to be 'embraced' at the end of each six-line stanza, by the 'Friend of the Peasant' (Krishak Bandhu), Garib Sayer—who, despite his claim to be poor ('garib'), is evidently not a peasant himself.[11] The text seeks to display

---

[7] *Krishak Bandhu*, p. 19; Datta, p. 79.

[8] *Krishak Bandhu*, pp. 58–68, 74–6.

[9] Ibid., pp. 26, 39, 46, and *passim*.

[10] For anonymity as a weapon of the weak, see E.P. Thompson, 'The Crime of Anonymity', in Hay, Linebaugh, Rule, Thompson and Winslow, *Albion's Fatal Tree* (London, 1977).

[11] The refrain, repeated with minor variations throughout the poem, is 'Esho bhai drirabhabe kori alingan' ('Come, brother. let me hold you fast in embrace').

its knowledge of local rural conditions—by enumerating possible migration zones and districts suitable for particular new crops, for instance—but is also subject to sudden slippages into near-absurdity. The advice to plead with the government to construct canals on the Punjab model, for instance, seems excessively unreal for peasants living for the most part on the deltaic flood plains of East Bengal.[12]

The one indication that *Krishak Bandhu* provides about its precise provenance confirms what I have been trying to tease out of the text. It was published from 40, Kareya Gorosthan Lane, Calcutta, and a passing reference in *Bureer Soota* tells us that this was the office of a well-known Muslim monthly, *Islam Pracharak*, edited by Muhammad Reazuddin Ahmad.[13] Reazuddin, prominent in Calcutta Muslim journalism since the 1890s, had connections with *Mihir-o-Sudhakar*, the newspaper which was the most aggressive advocate of Muslim identity politics in Calcutta in the Swadeshi and post-Swadeshi years. He also had links with Munshi Meherulla, the anti-Christian polemicist of rural origin who helped to displace *bahas*, which had emphasised debate, with monologic *waz* sermons as the predominant form of rural Muslim congregational assembly. Reazuddin subsequently became important in the entourage of Pir Abu Bakr of Furfura, identified by Datta as the organisational lynchpin in the production of increasingly communalised cheap vernacular tracts in the 1920s.[14] The easy and painless subordination of class to aggressive community identity in *Krishak Bandhu* need therefore cause no surprise.

III

Unlike *Krishak Bandhu*, *Bureer Soota* is very explicit about its author as well as about the people who had helped in its publication. In this it is similar to many lower-caste tracts of the early twentieth century—like Rashbihari Roy Pandit's *Namasudra Darpan* (1909), for instance.[15] Mohammad Mohsin Ulla describes himself as resident of

[12] *Krishak Bandhu*, p. 31.

[13] *Bureer Soota*, part II, p. 44.

[14] Anisuzzaman, *Muslim Banglar Samayik Patra, 1831–1930* (Dacca: Bangla Akademi, 1376/1969); Rafiuddin Ahmad, op. cit., pp. 97–9; Datta, op. cit., chapter II.

[15] See above, chapter II, pp. 38–9. Otherwise entirely obscure villagers would

'mouza Alaipur, thana Natore, post-office Natore, district Rajshahi'. The text is in formal terms quite different from Garib Sayer's single, long and well-structured poem. *Bureer Soota* comprises a number of separate brief essays, a few poems, plus texts of some resolutions and reports of proceedings of two rather different organisations that seem to have had key roles in subsidising and circulating the pamphlet. Mohsin Ulla perhaps should be better described as its compiler rather than author, and the connections that the text displays reveal a corresponding variety.

Part I of *Bureer Soota* (1909; 14 September 1910), the text informs us, was distributed free at a meeting of the 'Naogaon Mohammadan Association': perhaps publication costs might have been met in part by the latter. The back page of this part describes the aims of this subdivisional organisation as 'spreading education among Muslims, starting schools and maintaining them, providing necessary assistance to needy schoolboys, etc.' . Nothing is said about any specific peasant grievance or demand, and two Muslim lawyers of Naogaon town are indicated to be the organisers. Acknowledgements are made also to Sheikh Abdur Rahim, 'ex-editor, weekly *Mihir-o-Sudhakar*', as well as to Munshi Sheikh Muhammad Zamiruddin. The latter was closely associated with Munshi Meherulla's anti-Christian and proselytising campaigns.[16] So far we seem to be on ground not dissimilar to that from which *Krishak Bandhu* had emerged.

But this impression quickly gets modified as one starts reading the text, for even Part I consists overwhelmingly of accounts of peasant grievances and exploitation, with little or no reference to any Muslim identity or demands on its behalf. And Part II (dated 26 November 1909) seems to have had a different kind of organisational linkage. It was distributed free at a 'Natore Krishak Sammilani'. A brief note sketches the history of this organisation. It was founded on 27 February 1908, with Munshi Wahed Uddin Ahmad (of 'Mallikhati, Natore, Rajshahi') as its Secretary, and it had held three subsequent

---

naturally like to see their names in print, while lack of resources might make getting access to publication something like a collective endeavour. Those who had helped in various ways, particularly if little-known themselves, would likewise expect public acknowledgement.

[16] Rafiuddin Ahmad, p. 99 and *passim*.

meetings down to November 1909. Memorials had been drafted for presentations to East Bengal and Assam Lieutenant-Governor Hare (17 December 1908), and, via the Rajshahi District Magistrate, to the Viceroy (7 August 1909). Four schools had been set up, the government had been approached to help start a quaintly named 'The First Bureer Soota Bank'—presumably to provide co-operative credit facilities—and the note ended with the claim that the organisation was now spreading from Natore subdivision into neighbouring districts. It even optimistically envisaged the emergence over time, from this nucleus, of a 'Bharatiya Krishak Sabha'. The memorials and account given in Part II of the Krishak Sammilani make no mention whatsoever of any specific demand raised on behalf of Muslims. Its objectives are summed up on the end page of Part II as 'peasant education, protection of their land rights, and improvement of agriculture.'[17]

An implicit contrast seems to emerge between Naogaon and Natore, adjacent subdivisions of the district of Rajshahi, in Central Bengal. Two official accounts not too distant time-wise from *Bureer Soota*—O'Malley's *Rajshahi District Gazetteer* (1916) and W.H.Nelson's *Rajshahi Settlement Report, 1912–22* (1923), do indicate important differences between these subdivisions, and it is tempting to correlate some of them with the 'Mohammadan Association'/'Krishak Sammilani' distinction. Naogaon, lying to the north and west of the district, was healthier, more prosperous, with a density per square mile of 889 in 1921, the highest in Rajshahi. Natore, in the south and east, famous at one time in Bengal history, had become a decaying region, much afflicted by malaria, with a big tract of swampy land from which rivers had moved away (the Chalan Bil). Density had gone down here by 23% since 1872, and was now 514. Jute covered 18% of the land in Naogaon, only 9% in Natore. We would expect to find more upwardly mobile peasants in the first, mainly Muslim (who comprised 77% of the Rajshahi population), and possibly more open to an improvement-ethic-based Muslim identity politics.[18] Both Gazetteer and Settlement Report, however, emphasised a high degree of Hindu–Muslim 'amity' as characteristic of Rajshahi. Hindus made offerings to dargahs, Muslims sacrificed goats to Kali

[17] *Bureer Soota*, part II, pp. 23, 44–54, and end page.
[18] *Rajshahi District Gazetteer*, pp. 49–54; *Rajshahi Settlement Report*, p. 23.

and recited the Padma-Puran when their children fell ill.[19] Rajshahi was also a district marked by much landlord oppression, where zamindars had used their considerable quasi-judicial powers to hike up rents to rates higher than in East Bengal. One zamindar, for instance, had been making 'regular collections for the education of his son as a barrister in England.'[20] But there were also several examples of effective peasant resistance, including a powerful and long-sustained combination in a part of Naogaon during the 1880s—while in 1907 the Naib of a particularly oppressive small zamindar had actually been tied down by tenants and set on fire.[21] Conditions were favourable, then, for non-sectarian peasant organisation—particularly perhaps in Natore by the early 1900s where agrarian decline may have lent an additional edge to unrest. And Natore was also the subdivision where settlement work began in July 1910: a time often conducive for peasant protest, as we saw in an earlier chapter pertaining to Bakargunj Namasudras.

One must not overemphasise, though, the extent of distinction between 'Muslim' and 'krishak' organisation, for clearly *Bureer Soota* to some extent straddled both. Part I, distributed at the Naogaon Muhammadan Association, included Krishak Sammilani Secretary Wahed Uddin in its acknowledgements list. The account of the Natore Krishak Sammilani in Part II made particular mention of *Mihir-o-Sudhakar* and *Islam Pracharak* as giving regular coverage to its activities. Most worthy of note, the bulk of the large number of essays in the pamphlet dealing with specific peasant grievances are actually reprints from *Mihir-o-Sudhakar*, carefully acknowledged and dated.

'Association', 'Sammilani'—it will be noticed: the Muslim organisation has an English name, the peasant its Bengali equivalent. Do we have, then, what amounts to a planned division of labour by the same

---

[19] *Rajshahi Settlement Report*, p. 24 ; *Rajshahi District Gazetteer*, p. 66.

[20] *Rajshahi District Gazetteer*, pp. 95–7. Incidentally, the Gazetteer makes a special point of mentioning one striking exception to this general picture of gross landlord oppression. This is Rabindranath Tagore's estate at Patisar, marked by efficient, yet benevolent, management, with considerable remissions for poor harvests, construction of schools and dispensaries, the starting of an agricultural bank, and tight control over subordinate staff. Ibid., p. 127.

[21] *Rajshahi Settlement Report*, p. 32.

group of Muslim activists, probably the one associated with *Mihir-o-Sudhakar*, deliberately using two kinds of idioms to attract audiences that differed in linguistic attainment and class? I think that, too, would be an oversimplification. The *Mihir-o-Sudhakar* extracts do occasionally mention the banning of cow slaughter as one instance of zamindari oppression, but otherwise there is very little stress on specifically Muslim peasant grievances. In this the pamphlet may have been showing considerable selectivity, if the excerpts from that weekly in the official *Reports on Native Papers* are any guide.[22] Careful reading also reveals certain rifts or faultlines—and in one striking instance, towards the end of Part II, a clear contradiction, between an article reproduced from *Mihir-o-Sudhakar*, and another, not published there, which seems to be engaged in its systematic (though undeclared) refutation.

It is time to take a closer look now at the content of *Bureer Soota*. The title, first. Part I explains it as related to a folk tale, presumably one current in the Rajshahi region. What we see as spots on the moon are the faces of an old, very poor peasant, and his wife, who spins yarn on her charkha to help make ends meet. They are poor because both Rahu—an official of the distant 'Maharaja' of the heavens—and sundry 'gods' keep robbing them . Poverty leads to quarrell, and the old man often tears up the yarn spun by his wife in anger and beats her up. The old woman carefully stores up the torn threads so that she can complain if, someday, the Maharaja visits the moon. A rather moving tale, replete with peasant suffering and exploitation, which also has a kind of political implication. Immediate superiors are always oppressive, while, like the 'little father' of Russian peasants in

[22] Unfortunately that not necessarily reliable official series seems to be the only way one can find out about the contents of *Mihir-o-Sudhakar* today. The Reports indicate a far more systematic and aggressive anti-Hindu polemic than the *Bureer Soota* essays suggest. To take two specific instances: the *Mihir-o-Sudhakar* of 20 March 1908 reported a campaign by Zamiruddin for boycott of Hindu sweetmeat shops in Dinajpur, a district adjoining Rajshahi. That of 19 March 1909 condemned the prosecution of Munshi Reazuddin Ahmad (described as the 'conductor' of *Mihir-o-Sudhakar*) for bringing out two allegedly obscene anti-Hindu tracts. Such activities and travails of two men who figured in the *Bureer Soota* acknowledgements were ignored by the pamphlet. *Report on Native Newspapers (Bengal)*, weeks ending 28 March 1908, 27 March 1909.

Tsarist times, the distant king is benevolent, and, hopefully, might some day intervene.[23]

The imagery becomes more explicit—indeed, strikingly historical—in the poem with which Part I actually begins:

> The ears that had heard the cry of the *sati*, of the sacrificed child, of those oppressed by indigo-planters / Why does it not pay heed to the peasant's tears / And so the old woman's torn threads are flying in the skies . . . O King, look once at how your peasants have to live . . . Your laws are praised as being as pure as the Bible, the lamb and the tiger are said to drink from the same pool thanks to your even-handed justice . . . And so the old woman's torn threads are flying in the skies . . .[24]

A predictable appeal to the distant superior, of course, but one that is praised not just for intervening against white indigo planters but— much more unusual for the early twentieth century—for social reform legislation banning widow immolation and infanticide.[25] There are traces also of an implicit gendered note—the one most oppressed is the peasant wife, and it is her stored-up complaints that are flying up to the heavens for redress—though this is not a theme developed in the rest of the pamphlet.[26] And while the tone is certainly loyalist, this is a loyalism rather different from that displayed in Garib Sayer's poem. The closing sections of *Krishak Bandhu* had bluntly declared that sedition was 'sinful', and seemed very confident of a virtual alliance between rulers and Muslims. Such confidence is conspicuously lacking in *Bureer Soota*: succour from the distant 'Maharaja' clearly remains uncertain, there are inconsistencies between British professions and practices so far as peasants are concerned, there is need for at least a determined presentation of grievances.

Such presentation is the burden of the bulk of the essays in *Bureer Soota*, mostly reprints, as we have seen, from *Mihir-o- Sudhakar*.

---

[23] *Bureer Soota*, part I, p. 47.

[24] Ibid., p. 6.

[25] Late-nineteenth or early-twentieth-century nationalist writings were much more likely to hail the 'heroism' of the sati, or even admire the 'beauty' of self-immolation.

[26] There is one brief poem entitled 'Krishak Mata' (the peasant mother), describing her woes, in highly generalised terms, however, and ending with a conventional call to the sons to rescue her. Ibid., part I, pp. 41–3.

Unlike *Krishak Bandhu*, once again, where the description had remained fairly general, these are full of concrete, local detail, and often seem extremely realistic and convincing. Take the 'Appeal of Gunu Pramanik', for instance. Its author describes himself as coming from 'Shidhni, station Baraigram, subdivision Natore, district Rajshahi', and at the end of a two-part article states that he has been ruined, his lands have been taken away by the zamindar through a false court case and the terrorising of witnesses. Government officials at local levels, Pramanik argues, are really often heavily dependent on zamindars. Such a perception, born out of direct experience of injustice, makes Pramanik move, for a moment at least, to a very nearly anti-colonial position a world apart from Garib Sayer:

> In this magic land of Bengal your laws have no efficacy . . . you are meek before the strong, a terror for the weak. . . . We have seen your laws, your courts, your clever tricks, and have understood that you come from a land of traders, you have come for trade and profit—you do not consider it your job to look after your subjects.[27]

A second, slightly later, series of extracts from *Mihir-o-Sudhakar*, again replete with local detail, described the decline of fisheries due to the drying-up of water resources, notably in the Chalan Bil area of Rajshahi. The Decennial Settlement of Cornwallis (made permanent in 1793), it argued, had arbitrarily deprived the 'prajas' of their traditional right to dig ponds, and so the British were in part responsible for this degradation of natural resources. The Arms Act was also criticised for depriving peasants of weapons with which to drive out wild animals from their fields—with the result that wild boar was destroying crops in parts of East Bengal and Assam. The concluding part of this series listed a series of specific demands: rent-reduction, the extension of praja rights to land, an end to the constant landlord encroachment on traditional customs (*deshachar*), government efforts

[27] Ibid., pp. 7–19; reprinted from *Mihir-o-Sudhakar* (27 Agrahayan, 11 Paus, 10 Magh 1314/November 1907–January 1908). But for a brief reference to peasants being persecuted by landlords for cow slaughter, it would have been impossible to guess, by name or by the contents of his articles, that Gunu Pramanik was probably a Muslim. The *Rajshahi Settlement Report* had noted (p. 24) that the lack of sharp Hindu–Muslim distinction in that district was indicated by the fact that 'names of Muhammadans are not always distinctively Muhammadan.'

to introduce improved farming methods, the provision of free legal aid for poor tenants, and restrictions on excessive interests.[28] Another extract from *Mihir-o-Sudhakar*, dated June 1908, urged the government to implement its talk of free primary education, and, welcoming the settlement operations that had started in parts of East Bengal, called on all friends of peasants to supply necessary technical advice to them about existing claims, precedents, and rent regulations.[29] Similar demands were raised by two memorials to the Lieutenant-Governor and the Viceroy, in December 1908 and August 1909. The issues specified in December 1908, for instance, included eviction from 'legitimate' holdings, arbitrary landlord fees for permission to sell plots, and high rates of interest. Tenants should be given back the right to dig ponds, and, more generally, the constant zamindari infringements of '*deshachar*' (local custom) must stop.[30]

The demands raised clearly have a certain tilt towards, if not necessarily the rich, at least the relatively better-off, landholding peasants. It would have been surprising if this had not been so. References to settlement operations being helpful for peasants, if properly utilised, remained significantly silent about possible benefits for bargadars. There was no mention of Section 40 of the 1885 Act permitting commutation of barga to money rent, the dissemination of information about which by J.C. Jack had stimulated a brief share-cropper upsurge in the Gaurnadi region of Bakargunj, precisely around 1908.[31] Yet some 8% of Natore lands were under barga around the time of *Bureer Soota*, and the proportion was increasing as it was so much more profitable for landlords.[32]

Bureer Soota, one might say, may be indicative of the kind of local developments—almost entirely unexplored so far—which must have constituted the preconditions for the Kamariar Chak peasant rally in Jamalpur subdivision of Mymensingh in 1914, which Abul Mansur Ahmad has hailed as the first step in the formation of the Praja

[28] Ibid., part I, pp. 27–40 (*Mihir-o-Sudhakar*, 15 Baisakh, n.d., 19 Bhadra 1315/April–August 1908).

[29] Ibid., part II, pp. 10–19.

[30] Ibid., p. 23.

[31] For details, see chapters II and III above.

[32] *Rajshahi District Gazetteer*, pp. 94–5.

movement. The demands raised by that meeting were, once again, 'rents, cesses, restrictions on felling trees and digging ponds, barriers to the free sale or transfer of peasant holdings, etc.': nothing about sharecropping.[33]

Yet, in two key respects, *Bureer Soota* does stand apart from the usual run of Muslim peasant improvement tracts that Datta has explored. The improvement theme is not absent, but far less prominent here: the central thrust is clearly towards the detailing of grievances, of the nitty-gritty of landlord exploitation as well as of reducing its burdens. More significantly, the link with Islamic reform-cum-solidarity, so ubiquitous in other tracts, is here largely ignored—and over one, specifically political, issue, came to be directly challenged.[34]

From around the summer of 1908 onwards, and obviously in the context of the impending 'Morley–Minto' Council reforms, some of the *Mihir-o-Sudhakar* extracts given in the pamphlet began urging the need for some peasant representation. In August 1908 the *Mihir-o-Sudhakar* suggested such representation in local boards, juries, and government committees.[35] The Krishak Sammilani memorial to the Lieutenant-Governor (17 December 1908) somewhat hesitantly proposed 'representation on behalf of peasants' in the Provincial Legislative Council as something that 'might be considered.'[36] By the following year the demand was less vague and bolder: but simultaneously an important, if largely implicit, divergence had become noticeable.

The *Mihir-o-Sudhakar* excerpt dated 11 Bhadra 1316/August 1909, entitled, significantly, 'Muslims and Peasants in Legislative Reform', simultaneously hinted at a potential difference between

---

[33] Abul Mansur Ahmad, *Amar Dekha Rajnitir Panchash Bachhar* (3rd edition, Nawroze Kitabistan, Dacca, 1975), p. 23.

[34] There is also a poem (not, perhaps significantly, a *Mihir-o-Sudhakar* reprint) which can be read to suggest a strongly this-worldly, secular meaning: 'Who says that this world is nothing / Where can dharma be pursued except here? / How can religious rites be performed without resources attained on this earth? / . . . The Merciful One awards heaven to those who do their work properly on earth / This world comes before paradise / This earth cannot but be the gateway to heaven . . .'. 'Duniya', *Bureer Soota*, II, pp. 27–8.

[35] *Mihir-o-Sudhakar*, 19 Bhadra 1315, reprinted in *Bureer Soota*, I, pp. 33–40.

[36] Ibid., part II, p. 24.

'Muslim' and 'Krishak' interests, and sought to eliminate that possibility. It justified an extension to peasants of the kind of occupational representation already given in the Council to zamindars,
business interests, and Muslims, on the grounds that this would really
enhance the proportion of Muslims. This seems to have been the real
reason why this highly communal paper—or at least some of its contributors—had become advocates of such an apparently radical proposal. However, the article went on to admit there was a difficulty:
many Muslims were hostile to the suggestion. They forget that 'fif-
teen-and-a-half of sixteen Muslims in Bengal are peasants', hence
Muslim and peasant interests are interdependent. The article regretted that many Muslims, themselves born of peasant families, try to
abjure their lowly origins once they get educated. Muslims should,
rather, elect as their representatives (under the separate electorate just
granted to them) men not connected with landlord interests, but with
peasant sympathies. By implication, it might be noted, the article
admitted that a Muslim community was not something given, but
remained in need of continual formation, and that the 'Muslim' it
was referring to when outlining political perspectives, actually meant
a much narrower 'elite' group which tended to get alienated from
peasants even when they sprang from such plebeian roots.[37]

The *Mihir-o-Sudhakar* article, then, may be not unfairly characterised as an exercise in appropriation. In *Bureer Soota*, it is followed
immediately by another essay, this time *not* a reprint from *Mihir-o-
Sudhakar*, which was almost certainly intended as a tactful but firm
refutation. 'Muslim' has disappeared from the title of this second
article (which has no author's name, nor date), which is called *Krishaker Samaj o Sabha* ('Peasant Society and Association'). Its theme is
not any specific demand like Council representation for peasants, but
the need for peasant organisation—which, it emphasises, must rise
above religious distinctions by situating itself on the ground of immediate material needs (the phrase used is '*peter dohai*', needs of the
belly):

In today's circumstances, the defence of common interests requires the
coming together of people of different religious beliefs . . . the easiest way
to achieve this is to unite on the basis of the needs of the belly. These have

[37] *Sashan-Sanskare Musalman o Krishak*, in *Bureer Soota*, part II, pp. 29–34.

become so urgent now that it seems likely that all peasants would respond to such an appeal . . .[38]

The essay then moves on to expound, in simple and effective language, the norms and logic of democratic functioning of such 'krishak sabhas'. These would need to thrash out issues of common concern among peasants. As it is unlikely that there would be unanimity on all or even most matters, everyone must agree that decisions would have to be taken by a majority vote. No consideration of superior learning or prestige would be allowed to stand in the way. Thus we can see emerging a quest for a village assembly very different from bahas debates among religious experts, or the monologic sermons of waz.

Finally, this utterly remarkable essay returns to the theme of overcoming sectarian barriers: 'We, as Muslims, will drive out all Hindus from the country and become supreme, or we Hindus will drive out all Muslims—such silly ambitions must be abandoned. Forgetting all narrow interests and village factional rivalries [*daladali*], it is the duty of all to join the Krishak Sabha.' Differences are bound to remain, the unknown author is practical enough to admit, between religions, texts (shastras), castes (jatis), and particular material interests; but it would be futile to bring such divisive issues into Krishak Sabha meetings. Still on a practical note, the essay states that the accounts of the Sabha must always be open to inspection by all members (*sarbasadharan*) and that, in villages with acute daladali, separate sabhas could be set up first, which could then try to evolve a kind of confederation from below. A suggestion is made also that such federative organisation from below might eventually lead to unity between peasants and other sections of the people, ultimately producing a 'Bharat samaj'. Instead of proposals for some peasant representation in existing official structures (and the *Mihir-o-Sudhakar* never made clear whether such representation should be by nomination, or election; and, if the latter, on how wide a franchise), here we seem to be seeing elements of an alternative, far more radical political vision.[39]

[38] *Bureer Soota*, part II, pp. 36–7.

[39] Though it should be added that the article, at one place, does suggest—maybe again on practical grounds—that village *pradhans* (heads) should take the initiative in the starting of Krishak Sabhas in each village. Ibid., p. 41.

I have left till the end what had seemed to me, on first looking at the pamphlet, to be its most remarkable sentence, and one that I cannot explain. Part I of *Bureer Soota* begins with brief passages translated from Aristotle and Adam Smith: most unexpected, of course, in a pamphlet being compiled in an obscure Natore village. Perhaps one of the more learned urban patrons or associates of Mohsen Ullah had picked these up from some college texts; and the passages are nothing remarkable, being merely statements about the value of agricultural work. Part II repeats these quotes, but adds one more. Inexplicably, across centuries and continents, comes an echo of the English Peasant Revolt of 1381, inspired by Wat Tyler and the rebel priest John Ball:

> *Soota kate Haba, Adam chashe hal,*
> *Se dine ke bhadra chhilo, hayere kapal.*

> (When Adam delved and Eve span,
>   Who was then the gentleman?)[40]

---

[40] But I have recently come across another reference to the labour of Adam and Eve as argument for human equality in Muhammad Yaqub 'Ali, *Jater Barai* (Simulia Village, Kareswari, Dacca, 1333/1926). Couched in entirely Islamic terms, it rejected arrogance of birth or wealth as contrary to the Prophet's teachings. Its author was secretary of the Anjuman, Ahl-i-Hadis, a sect which, in the Bengal of the 1920s, was headed by Akrem Khan, who combined fundamentalist adherence to the letter of the Quran and hadis with devotion to Hindu–Muslim unity and Swarajist politics. He had tried to start a peasant agitation in 1925, but had been pulled up by Swarajist landlords. The pamphlet contained a quote from *al Eslam*, a monthly edited by Akrem Khan. *Jater Barai*, published at a peak moment of communal strife, did not directly advocate Hindu–Muslim unity, but the absence of any anti-Hindu message and frank admission of sharp intra-Muslim tensions along class lines remains significant. Datta, pp. 94–6; Kenneth McPherson, *The Muslim Microcosm: Calcutta, 1918 to 1935* (Weisbaden, 1974), p. 86; Muhammad Jahangir, *Muhammad Akrem Khan 1868–1968* (Jibasi Granthmala, Dacca 1987), vol. 1.

CHAPTER V

Nationalism and 'Stri-Swadhinata'
The Contexts and Meanings of Rabindranath's *Ghare-Baire*[1]

'In Europe a band of modern women feel ashamed even of being women. They are embarrassed about giving birth and serving their husband and children. . . . Sweeping floors, bringing in water, grinding spices, serving food to relatives and guests and eating only afterwards—in Europe all this is considered oppressive and shameful, but for us it indicates the high status of the *grihalakshmi* [bounteous goddess of the home], their sanctity, the respect that is shown towards them . . . the more women look upon even husbands without any striking qualities as divine, the more they are invested with purity and true beauty . . . Europe claims that all human beings have the right to have or become everything. But in reality everyone doesn't have the same right, and it is best to accept this profound truth from the very beginning'—Rabindranath, *Nababarsha* (The New Year), read at Santiniketan on the occasion of the Bengali New Year, Baisakh 1309/April 1902).[2]

---

[1] This is a modified and extended version of an essay entitled 'Ghare-Baire and Its Times', being published in Pradip Kumar Datta, ed., *A Companion to Rabindranath Tagore's 'Ghare-Baire'* (Delhi, 2002). I have been greatly helped by the comments and criticisms of Pradip Kumar Datta and Tanika Sarkar.

[2] *Rabindra Rachanabali*, Centenary Edition, hereafter *RR* (Calcutta, 1961), volume XII, p. 1264. My translation.

'My wife—does that amount to an argument, much less the truth? Can one imprison a whole personality within that name?'— Rabindranath, *Home and the World* (English translation of *Ghare-Baire*, 1322/1915–16, by Surendranath Tagore, London, 1919; rpt. Delhi, 1999, p. 64).

I BEGIN WITH two excerpts from Rabindranath, both expressing views about the norms of proper womanhood, between which a chasm seems to yawn. The first is from an essay written on the eve of some years of intense involvement in nationalist politics, during the Swadeshi movement set off by the partition of Bengal of 1905. The second comes from an interior monologue of the character in *Ghare-Baire* who is clearly nearest to the views of the author himself, at a time when Rabindranath had become very critical of chauvinistic forms of nationalism. Primarily through a reading of *Ghare-Baire*, I intend to explore the contexts and implications of this transition.

A well-established historical commonsense counterposes nineteenth-century middle-class social reform centred around issues concerning women,[3] with twentieth-century anti-colonial nationalism subordinating such issues to the struggle for freedom.[4] Partha Chatterjee's widely accepted thesis about the 'nationalist resolution of the women's question' is in fact a refinement-cum-modification of this commonsense. His argument begins with the assumption of 'a rather sudden disappearance' of women's issues 'from the agendas of public debate from towards the close of the nineteenth century', and goes on to explain this apparent occlusion by 'nationalism's success in situating the 'women's question' in an inner domain of sovereignty, far removed from the arena of political contest with the colonial state.' While major changes took place in the lives of middle-class women during the decades of nationalist struggle, a predominant ideology of *ghar* and *bahir*, the 'home' and the 'world' produced a fundamental

[3] Women's education, widow immolation, widow marriage, polygamy, age of consent, child-marriage, seclusion of women—the bundle of reformist issues sometimes termed in the 1860s and 1870s 'stri-swadhinata'—the emancipation, or more precisely the 'freeing' of women.

[4] The earlier, naively nationalistic assumption of a straightforward connection between the struggle for freedom and improvements in the conditions of women finds few takers today.

contrast between early-twentieth-century Indian and Western women's movements. In India, Chatterjee tells us, the transformations took place entirely inside homes, outside the arena of political agitation, and legal reforms about 'marriage rules, property rights, suffrage' became legitimate only after independence.[5]

There can be little doubt that the home/world disjunction was frequently in evidence, and probably the Swadeshi-cum-Extremist era in Bengal marked a high point in its importance. A passage from *Gora*, the novel Rabindranath wrote during 1907–9 and published in book form in 1910, provides a particularly clear expression of that ideology. Gora is rebuking his friend Benoy, who is showing signs of interest in a Brahmo girl, Sucharita:

> Men and women are two distinct parts of society, as day and night are of time. When society is in good health, the woman is not publicly visible . . . she comforts us in the privacy of our times of rest, contributes to our well-being. . . . If we drag women into the public arena, the health and peace of society gets disrupted, a madness enters social life . . .

Gora's espousal of this separate spheres model, through much of the novel, is related to an equally aggressive defence of caste hierarchy and Hindu orthodoxy—all of which he tries to justify on patriotic grounds, by arguments of authenticity and cultural nationalism. He has been through a spell of iconoclasm in early youth, admiring Keshab Sen and critical of traditional values, but has then reacted violently to 'an English missionary abusing Hindu shastras and rituals in some newspaper . . . While he had himself often criticised such things, the contempt of a foreigner for Hindu society stung him to the quick.'[6] Perhaps Rabindranath was recalling a not dissimilar shift in Bankimchandra following an attack on Hinduism in the pages of *The Statesman* in 1882 by a missionary named Hastie.

[5] Partha Chatterjee, *The Nation and Its Fragments* (Delhi, 1993), pp. 116–17, 120, 133. See also the first exposition of this argument in Chatterjee, 'The Nationalist Resolution of the Women's Question', in Kumkum Sangari and Sudesh Vaid, eds, *Recasting Women* (Delhi, 1989).

[6] *Gora* was serialised in *Prabasi*, 1314–16/1907–9, and published in 1910. My quotes in this and the preceding paragraph come from pp. 78–9 and p. 22 of *RR*, volume IX and have been translated by me.

Yet the model does have problems and inadequacies. To begin with, the terms 'nationalist' and 'resolution' in Chatterjee's formulation stand in need of some unpacking. 'Nationalist' is often used nowadays in ways diffuse enough to refer to virtually every member of the colonised literati, irrespective of their specific stances regarding colonialism. But the conservative-patriarchal appeal of a home/world kind of disjunction was not necessarily associated with overall anti-colonial critique. To invert an influential formulation of Lata Mani concerning sati, maybe nationalism could sometimes become a 'site' for the refurbishing of patriarchal values. This seems to have been the case, notably, with the Calcutta newspaper *Bangabasi*, in the forefront of the agitation against the Age of Consent Bill in 1891, and, for that specific moment, violently cultural-nationalist,[7] but otherwise consistently loyal and very critical of all forms of anti-colonial politics even during the Swadeshi years. Conversely, a fair number among those involved in diverse forms of indisputably nationalist activities were quite supportive of broadly 'modernising' change in matters concerning greater freedom or equality for women. The 'resolution' of the women's question through displacement into the 'home' was, therefore, never stable, unchanging, final. A striking instance is provided by the ultimately successful agitation for the enfranchisement of women (limited and property-based, of course, as was the case also for men, right down to independence) in the early 1920s. The agitation was started in Bengal in the wake of the Montagu–Chelmsford extension of the franchise by women's groups like the Bangiya Nari Samaj. No doubt these represented no more than an élite of educated women, but the agitation was indisputably public and political, and not waged within any domestic sphere. Rejected in September 1921 by a Legislative Council dominated by Loyalists and Moderates due to the Non-Cooperation–Khilafat boycott of elections, it was passed in August 1925, after the Swarajist return to the Council, precisely because of the support extended by the more

---

[7] Tanika Sarkar, 'Rhetoric Against Age of Consent: Resisting Colonial Reason and the Death of a Child-Wife', *Economic and Political Weekly*, 4 September 1993; reprinted in her *Hindu Wife, Hindu Nation* (Delhi, 2001). Mrinalini Sinha, *Colonial Masculinity* (Manchester, 1995), chapter 4.

anti-colonial nationalist male politicians.[8] Virtually every section within the nationalist political spectrum also backed the Sarda Act of 1929 raising the minimum age of marriage: the stereotype breaks down again.

Other essays in this volume suggest that the decline of the Swadeshi movement by *c.* 1908 and the subsequent lull in mass anti-colonial nationalist politics till Non-Cooperation–Khilafat may have afforded spaces for alternative initiatives and mobilisations around caste, religious community, perhaps also class.[9] Perhaps an opening-up took place with regard to women's issues too. That, I suggest, could be an appropriate context for a re-reading of *Ghare-Baire*, along with some contemporaneous short stories and essays of Tagore.

II

Ghare-Baire has never been a comfortable text for many of its readers. Even its author's enhanced stature as winner of the Nobel Prize in 1913 did not prevent sharp contemporary criticism. There is even a report that the book was withdrawn for a time from the Calcutta University library.[10] One would expect many to have been shocked by the novel's depiction of Sandip, the unscrupulous Swadeshi-Extremist politician, seeking to seduce Bimala, wife of his old friend Nikhilesh, at whose house he was staying. Sandip's politics of aggressive Hindu-nationalist demagogy, combined with the coercion through landlord pressure of Muslim and lower-caste peasants unwilling to boycott British goods, are shown to lead to communal violence. A charge of unfair criticism of patriots engaged in heroic anti-colonial struggle probably still lingers, with many readers feeling even now that Rabindranath in *Ghare-Baire* betrayed a certain softness towards colonial cultural-political domination. It is interesting, though, that contemporary criticism of the novel seems to have related primarily to the portrayal of Bimala, her adulterous passion for Sandip being thought intolerable for a Hindu wife, and a gross violation of the Sita

---

[8] See the detailed study by Barbara Southard, *The Women's Movement and Colonial Politics in Bengal: The Quest for Political Rights, Education and Social Reform Legislation, 1921–1936* (Delhi, 1995), chapter 3.

[9] See chapters 3 and 4 above.

[10] Asok Kumar Sarkar, *Sabuj Patra o Bangla Sahitya* (Calcutta, 1994), p. 58.

model. This is the charge that Rabindranath tried to respond to, in two brief rejoinders in 1915 and 1920.[11]

Criticisms on the ground of insufficient patriotism imply an assumption, still far too widespread in different forms, that the entire field of early-twentieth-century Bengal (and Indian) history was, or should have been, occupied by the single colonial/anti-colonial binary. Everything else has to be accepted as of secondary importance, and nationalism valorised without qualification provided it appears sufficiently anti-colonial, in politics and/or in its indigenous cultural authenticity. I find this quite unacceptable, but have some problems also with the alternative reading put forward by Ashis Nandy in an influential study of Tagore. This in effect inverts the value judgements implicit in such charges by hailing the author of *Ghare-Baire* for being, precisely, a great critic of conventional forms of nationalism. I would go with Nandy part of the way. The novel, along with numerous other writings of Tagore around that time, does represent a valid and still highly relevant critique of the many dangers of aggressive, chauvinistic forms of nationalism, whether of the West or the non-West. What I find difficult to accept is the attempt to assimilate Rabindranath—despite the well-known debates with Gandhi—into Nandy's own favoured kind of anti-modernism, and thus to locate him as ultimately 'a critic . . . by implication, of modernity'. For Nandy, Tagore, like Gandhi, was among the 'dissenter among dissenters' who sought the alternative to nationalism not in any 'homogenised universalism' still grounded in some version of the 'Enlightenment concept of freedom', but in 'a distinctive civilisational concept of universalism embedded in the tolerance encoded in various traditional ways of life in a highly diverse, plural society.'[12] I feel

---

[11] The appendix to *RR*, VIII, pp. 525–6, 527 contains these rejoinders of Tagore, first printed as 'Teeka-Tippani', *Sabuj Patra*, Agrahayan, 1322/1915; and 'Sahitya Bichar', *Prabasi*, Chaitra, 1326/1920. His replies pointed to the cultural-nationalist subtext of these criticisms, the attempts to confine literary debate to the degree of conformity or otherwise of a character to the supposed norms of the 'true Hindu woman' ('Teeka-Tippani'). Rabindranath's tone was sharper in 1920: so many would like to 'make of national literature a literature of frogs in the well.'

[12] Ashis Nandy, *The Illegitimacy of Nationalism: Rabindranath Tagore and the Politics of Self* (Delhi, 1994), pp. 2, x–xi.

that this does less than justice to a very significant change in Rabindranath's trajectory in his post-Swadeshi phase, embodied notably in *Ghare-Baire*. Above all, it fails to adequately comprehend the new elements in the handling of gender relationships and images, in the novel as well as in certain near-contemporaneous short stories of Tagore.

Ghare-Baire has to be located within a crucial era of transitions, for Rabindranath, and in his times. Its fuller understanding demands some exploration of a fairly dense web of texts and events. Constituted primarily by other writings of Rabindranath around that time, this has to extend to other kinds of documentation about Swadeshi and immediate post-Swadeshi years, both official and non-official. A glance at some contemporary debates and narratives around questions of gender would be particularly vital, for this is a novel where political debate is intricately interwoven around the triangular relationships of Nikhlesh-Bimala-Sandip.

Like his hero Nikhilesh, Rabindranath had tried without success to promote swadeshi habits and enterprises long before they became popular. He had also been one of the earliest and sharpest critiques of the 'mendicancy' for which the Moderate Congress had become notorious, merely begging for concessions from the rulers, without avail. Where the novelist differed from his hero was in initial enthusiasm, around 1905–7, for the new agitational methods of the boycott of foreign goods and schools, and the other kinds of passive resistance adopted by Bengal's middle-class nationalists as a reaction to the partition imposed on their province by Curzon in 1905. A movement predominantly of upper-caste Hindu bhadralok who tended to have rentier interests in land cultivated, in the main, by lower-caste Hindus and Muslims, Swadeshi often sought mass contact through a highly emotional Hindu revivalism, particularly as it turned militant or Extremist.[13] A parting of the ways between Tagore and the Swadeshi movement came, however, with the shock of Hindu–Muslim riots

---

[13] Rabindranath had in fact suggested some of the new agitational methods, like appropriating the Hindu rite of Rakhi-bandhan on Partition Day, 16 October 1905. He also composed a series of stirring patriotic songs, often replete with Hindu imagery, at times merging Mother Bengal with the mother-goddess Durga in a manner not far removed from Bankimchandra's 'Bande Mataram'.

in some villages of East Bengal in the early months of 1907. The evident ebbing of hopes in a mass movement led some Extremists towards methods of individual terror, accompanied often by an intensification of aggressively Hindu revivalist moods. For Tagore, in sharp contrast, the riots demanded deep introspection and auto-critique, expressed first through a series of essays around 1907–8, some passages of which would be almost echoed in the reflections of Nikhilesh eight years later.[14] The internal debate through which Rabindranath was passing found vivid embodiment in the pages of *Gora* (1907–9), and traces of it are discernible, in more oblique ways, also in the novel that just preceded *Ghare-Baire: Chaturanga*, serialised likewise in *Sabuj Patra* in 1914, and published in the following year. Then came the onslaught on nationalism through lectures in Japan and the USA during 1916–17, published in book form as *Nationalism* (1917). And there was another, related, but much less noticed evolution. Revivalist nationalism was often associated with certain conceptions of ideal Hindu womanhood that, once again, Rabindranath had briefly shared, but then came to very sharply repudiate. *Gora* is marked by the signs of this second debate, possibly as one not yet decisively resolved. Then, between 1914 and 1917, came a spate of short stories, published, like *Chaturanga* and *Ghare-Baire*, in *Sabuj Patra*, itself an experimental, in some ways quite iconoclastic monthly which Rabindranath had helped Pramatha Chaudhuri to start in 1914.[15] There were ten such *Sabuj Patra* stories, among them the remarkable, proto-feministic 'Streer Patra' (The Wife's Letter, Sravana 1321/July–August 1914). The title of the monthly itself implied an evocation of youth and novelty,[16] while 'Streer Patra' and *Ghare-Baire* share the distinction of being the first works of Rabindranath written in the *calit* (colloquial) Bengali prose. As contrasted to the prevalent, more

[14] For a more detailed account of the shifting patterns of the Swadeshi movement and of Tagore's responses, see my *Swadeshi Movement in Bengal 1903–1908* (New Delhi, 1973).

[15] For some discussion of the significance of *Sabuj Patra*, and the hostility it evoked, see Asok Kumar Sarkar, *Sabuj Patra o Bangla Sahitya* (Calcutta, 1994), and Arunkumar Mukhopadhyay, *Birbal o Bangla Sahitya* (Calcutta, 1960, 1968).

[16] *Sabuj Patra* translates as 'Green Leaves'.

formal and Sanskritised, *sadhu bhasha*, this must have been intended as a democratising move.

I propose to tackle my theme at two levels. A novel—even one as specifically contextualised as *Ghare-Baire*—has of course no obligation to be an accurate representation of its times, and the question of the 'fairness' or otherwise of Tagore's account of Extremism is not a very vital one. Yet it is difficult to avoid it altogether, and I begin therefore with briefly juxtaposing *Ghare-Baire* with other documentation from the Swadeshi years, highlighting—as I had done many years ago, in my research on that era—its considerable relevance for an understanding of the limits of that movement in terms of mass involvement. In terms of the novel's manifest content, and looking upon it more or less as one kind of 'source' among others, I turn to the deeper aspects of Rabindranath's critique of Extremist nationalism, its fetishising of the Nation, and to the subordination of morality to its worship. (Here a brief discussion of Nandy's analysis will be necessary.) I plan to move then to a more textual approach, focussed upon the handling of themes of domesticity and gender, using as the lynchpin of my move to this second level what I consider to be a key passage about halfway through the novel. Here Tagore makes Sandip link up the many facets of what is a male dream of power, a hard, aggressive conception of masculinity that relates, in a totally exploitative and instrumentalist manner, to other men, women, and Nature alike. This of course is Sandip in the privacy of his interior monologue. On the surface, in his conversations with Bimala, he is, in apparent contrast, placing her on a pedestal, an object of eroticised, patriotic, near-religious worship who somehow embodies the Motherland. One has to consider, then, why the two had come to appear near-identical for Rabindranath, the woman on a pedestal as one form of male power. This is certainly not how he had seen things always, for, as I have already suggested, he too had been attracted by the ideology of a home/world divide where the woman would be honoured precisely through being kept within a segregated space of domesticity and motherhood. The *Sabuj Patra* stories, along with *Ghare-Baire*, I would like to argue, represent a decisive break, and their novelty demands emphasis—and explication. Here I suggest, as a tentative part-explanation, the possible impact of a *cause celebre* of January 1914, the Snehalata case.

Ghare-Baire, however, provides an additional, and to my mind quite crucial, complication. It presents a sincerely reformist husband hoist with his own petard. Nikhilesh had encouraged his wife to come out into the 'world', but then Bimala chooses a trajectory that, for him, his creator, and the intended readership alike, is utterly disastrous. We need to ask why Rabindranath deliberately chose to complicate matters in this way. I suggest that the internal conflicts that ensue in Nikhilesh constitute the real heart of the novel, for through them Rabindranath is trying to work out an alternative conception of masculinity. Diametrically opposed to that embodied in Sandip, this seeks to move, through self-examination and auto-critique, towards a non-instrumentalised recognition of the autonomy of the Other. Nikhilesh responds to the crisis through a reaffirmation of his reformist values, but also begins to recognise the limits of a reformism which had paid little heed to the subjectivity of women, the need, above all, for women to develop their own autonomy, *atmasakti.* *Ghare-Baire,* then, can be read in terms of a conflict between alternative notions of masculinity—meaning by that term, of course, not just ways of relating to women but the cluster of values thought to be most appropriate for true manhood. It is in terms of this problematic that I will turn to Bimala, and pose a problem concerning the extent of Rabindranath's readiness and ability to accept the autonomous subjectivity of the woman.

Tagore had certainly tried to foreground such subjectivity in the *Sabuj Patra* stories as well as through the interior monologues of Bimala. In 'Streer Patra', remarkably, he had even attempted to write in the persona of a rebellious wife, linking up in a way, it has been suggested, with the rich tradition of women's autobiographies in Bengali from the 1860s onwards.[17] The contexts of *Ghare-Baire* therefore need to be enriched through exploration of the contemporary voices of women themselves. Extant gender-sensitised research on women's writings in the Swadeshi-post-Swadeshi years—not just autobiographies, but novels, stories, plays, poems, monthly magazines edited by women—unfortunately seems much scantier than for the nineteenth century. I can only end with a few scattered instances,

[17] Tanika Sarkar, 'Mrinal: Anya Itihaser Svakhshar', in her *Adhunikatar Du-Ek Dik: Dharma, Sahitya o Rajniti* (Calcutta, 2001).

taken from different social realms: indicators, perhaps, of the wealth and reach of discourses still largely unexplored.

III

There is a marked affinity between *Ghare-Baire* and a number of essays written by Tagore around 1907–8, so far as specific social critique is concerned. The one entitled 'Sadupay' (The Right Way), published in *Prabasi* in Sravana 1315 (July–August 1908), provides a particularly clear instance. It begins with a reference to the hostility of large numbers of Muslim and subordinate-caste Namasudra[18] peasants to boycott in the East Bengal countryside. Some of them were now sticking to foreign salt and cloth even when their Swadeshi substitutes were cheaper, and Rabindranath found this understandable. 'We have demanded closeness and brotherhood from them without ever having tried to be close to them earlier . . . We imagine that the Mother has become real for the whole country through songs and emotional ecstasy alone.' The problem of the alienation of the bhadralok from Muslims, lower castes, and the peasant masses in general was being compounded, he felt, by the easy recourse to force when support was not forthcoming. Herein lay a crucial limitation, with implications going far beyond defective strategies of mobilisation alone. 'Our misfortune is that we want freedom, but we do not believe in freedom in our hearts . . . Threats of consigning forefathers to hell, social ostracism through withdrawing the services of washermen and barbers, burning homesteads, beating up recalcitrants on village paths . . . all these are ways of making slave mentalities permanent within us.'[19] The Swadeshi experience made Tagore more deeply aware of the divisive and oppressive nature of caste and community barriers, the coercion associated with their maintenance. It led him, in this essay to perceive a basic incompleteness in the Swadeshi

---

[18] Numerous in parts of south and south-east Bengal, Namasudras constituted, along with Mahishyas in the south-west and Rajbansis in the north, the three major subordinate-caste formations in the province. The particular prominence of Namasudras in Tagore and other bhadralok writings of that time was probably due to a certain militancy around caste status, as well as on agrarian issues. For more detail, see chapters II and III above.

[19] *RR*, x, pp. 527–8. My translation.

concept of freedom. It is this notion of freedom, of individual human rights affirmed, if need be against community discipline, that lay at the heart of Rabindranath's more general critique of nationalism— and it would also provide the basis for a widening of his horizons concerning gender in the post-Swadeshi era.

Ghare-Baire enters these problems through the sub-plot of Ponchu. Near-landless, surviving through bartering cheap imported cloth and trinkets for grain from women of Namasudra households in a segregated area amidst swamps, Ponchu has to mortgage the little land he has due to his wife's illness, and then has his Brahmin-dominated panchayat impose a monetary *prayaschitta* (ritual penance) on him when she dies.[20] This is very reminiscent indeed of some key passages in *Gora*. The hero of that novel, whose burning patriotism had made him seek communion with the motherland through a rigorous upholding of Hindu-traditionalist rituals and values and wanderings among the peasants, comes to discover in the depths of the countryside that the ties of the community (*samajer bandhan)* 'provide no help in times of need, no comfort in troubles, they only enforce disciplinary commands that add to the problems . . . No longer could Gora delude himself with the roseate hues of his own imagination.'[21]

Ponchu's woes are then compounded by the additional burden of Swadeshi. He becomes a target of bullying by Sandip's student cadres (back home for the vacation from Calcutta) for the crime of petty trading in foreign goods which is necessary for this sheer survival. While Nikhilesh, as benevolent and paternalist zamindar, refuses to force boycott on his tenants, the notoriously oppressive neighbouring landlord Harish Kundu earns a great reputation as Swadeshi hero by having Ponchu beaten up and planning to evict him from his tiny

[20] *Ghare-Baire, RR,* IX, pp. 466–7; *Home and the World,* pp. 88, 99.

[21] *Gora, RR,* IX, pp. 318–19. While Gora's ultimate transformation comes about through the fortuitous revelation of his Irish birth, the novel makes it clear that experiences like these had already deeply unsettled his revivalist-nationalist faith. He greets the news, therefore, with exhilaration. The gates of all the temples of India have closed in his face, he declares, and it is this that has made him truly Indian ('Bharatiya') for the first time, worthy of bowing to the 'Lord whose temples are ever open to all . . . who is the Lord of Hindus, Muslims, Christians and Brahmos alike, who is the divinity, not of the Hindus alone, but of all Indians.' Ibid., pp. 349–50. My translation.

homestead. Meanwhile the incessant and aggressive Hindu imagery deployed by Sandip's band culminates in plans for organising a massive Durga Puja, for which Harish Kundu levies additional cesses on his largely Muslim tenantry. This leads to a Muslim backlash, encouraged by mullahs from Dacca. The novel ends amidst the fires of communal violence.

Rabindranath was distorting, or imagining, little of all this. Government records speak of Hindu shrines constructed by landlords through an 'Ishwar-britti' cess. These became preferred targets of Muslim iconoclasm in the riots of May 1907 in Mymensingh district.[22] Officials in the winter of 1907–8 started enquiries into the alleged oppression of tenants by big zamindars suspected of Swadeshi involvement, notably on the estate of Gauripur in the same district, held by the leading Swadeshi supporter Brojendrakishore Raychaudhuri.[23] Nationalist newspapers were indignant that the government was encouraging in this manner the 'withholdings of payment of rent' by peasants. They may well have been right in suspecting a strong element of selectivity in the choice of zamindars investigated, the working of a divide-and-rule strategy. But even a mild criticism of oppressive absentee landlords made at that time by a nationalist newspaper, *Daily Hitavadi*, did not fail to add that swaraj required the strengthening of 'social ties', and 'zamindars are heads of society.' As for the methods of social boycott, so roundly condemned by Rabindranath in *Ghare-Baire*, this is what the same paper had to say on 23 February 1908: 'It would be easy to convert illiterate and half-educated villagers to Swadeshism, subjecting them to social control and threatening them with social boycott. . . . The dread of being deprived of the services of the priest, the barber and the washerman will act powerfully to keep the refractory spirits under control.'[24]

[22] 'It is particularly worthy of note that both at Bakshigunj and at Dewangunj the rioting began by an attack upon the idol which had been erected by the hated Iswarbritti.' Note by R. Nathan, July 1907, in Government of India Home Political Progs A, December 1907, n.58.

[23] Government of India Home Political A, February 1908, n.102–3: Conduct of zamindars of Gauripur in connection with the political agitation in Mymensingh district.

[24] *Daily Hitavadi*, 11 Februry, 24 February, 23 February 1908, in *Report on Native Papers* (Bengal) for the weeks ending 15 February and 29 February 1908; *Swadeshi Movement in Bengal, passim*.

The social critique developed in Tagore's 1907–8 essays and *Ghare-Baire* had its limits, however. It did not go beyond the nexus of a dangerous kind of nationalism—unscrupulous politicians as typified by Sandip, their deluded student followers, and oppressive landlords and their agents. The alternative—ineffective, as the novel ends in unrelieved tragedy—is presumably paternalist zamindari, embodied in Nikhilesh (in large part Rabindranath himself), riding out alone and unarmed into the sunset to fight communal violence. A sense of failure and isolation pervades the novel. And here there may have been reasons deeper than those the author himself perceived. At the time of writing *Ghare-Baire*, it seems likely that he would have had little quarrel with the *Daily Hitavadi* characterisation of zamindars as natural 'heads of society'—provided the landlord was someone like Nikhilesh/Tagore.[25] But recent research—notably of Nariaki Nakazato on agrarian history and Sekhar Bandopadhyay on Namasudras—indicates that it was not just a question of particular oppressive landlords, or even the long-term, structural, landlord/peasant class divide, overdetermined often by Hindu/Muslim, upper caste/lower-caste distinctions. An earlier chapter has tried to explore a more specific conjuncture: the coincidence in time between the Swadeshi movement and a sharpening of tensions in the countryside. Gentry efforts to shift towards produce-rent forms of surplus appropriation in the context of rising prices produced acute conflict between rentier bhadralok, and Muslim and Namasudra peasants and sharecroppers—notably in the Gaurnadi region of Bakargunj where, interestingly, lay the estates of one of the most idealistic Swadeshi leaders, Aswini Kumar Datta, who had a long record of sustained philanthropic work in the countryside.[26]

The more profound dimension of the *Ghare-Baire* critique of Swadeshi–Extremist nationalism is really its rejection of any fetishisation of the Nation, and of efforts to subordinate morality to its worship. Towards the beginning of the novel Bimala (who, unlike Nikhilesh and Sandip, is throughout recollecting its events in retrospect, making for a rather unusual narrative structure) recalls that her husband had anticipated much of Swadeshi, but 'had never been able

[25] The Soviet visit of 1930, however, seems to have made Tagore more self-critical even about benevolent zamindari.

[26] For details, see above, chapter III, pp. 87–91.

to accept the mantra of Bande Mataram as the ultimate value. He used to say that he was willing to serve the country, but reserved his worship for the Being who is above the land. If we make the country the object of worship, we will be leading it to disaster.'[27] Bankim's hymn, with its indissoluble mingling of devotion to the Motherland with worship of Durga and Kali, had a well-known alienating impact on Muslims when it was made central to Swadeshi nationalism. But Rabindranath's critique goes much beyond the question of failed patriotic mobilisation and Hindu–Muslim unity alone. The disaster, the novel makes clear, resides in a ruthless instrumentalisation of everything else to the presumed cause of the Nation. Of critical importance here is what Rabindranath puts in the voice of Sandip. 'Sandip's story' begins with the following assertion:

> The impotent man says: 'That which has come to my share is mine.' And the weak man assents. But the lesson of the whole world is: 'That is really mine which I can snatch away.'. . . . The world into which we are born is the world of reality. When a man goes away from the market of real things with empty hands and empty stomach, merely filling his bag with big-sounding words, I wonder why he ever came into this hard world at all . . . What I desire, I desire positively, superlatively.[28]

What Rabindranath is repudiating here is much more than a specific, Extremist form of Indian nationalism. Reduced to that alone, Sandip might appear to be something of a caricature in his utter villainy.[29] The unremittingly dark portrayal of Sandip is redeemed only once, in *Ghare-Baire*, pp. 460–3, where Sandip confesses to a certain sense of guilt—which of course he considers to be a weakness—about the way he is deceiving his old friend Nikhilesh. The target is something much more general, what might be called a creed

---

[27] *Ghare-Baire, RR*, VIII, p. 419. My translation. Here, as in several other instances, the English version inexplicably omits an important passage.

[28] *Home and the World*, pp. 45–6.

[29] The unremittingly dark portrayal of Sandip is redeemed only once, in *Ghare-Baire*, pp. 460–3, where Sandip confesses to a certain sense of guilt—which of course he considers to be a weakness—about the way he is deceiving his old friend Nikhilesh. Perhaps some awareness of this problem, which does weaken the novel, led Rabindranth to introduce, as a foil to Sandip, the transparently sincere and dedicated young revolutionary Amulya.

of political 'realism', made harsher through the assumption of universal and inevitable competitiveness—the moods, we might say, of Social Darwinism. Here Rabindranath seems to be grasping, in embryo as it were, certain possibilities that have become frighteningly manifest in today's India, more so perhaps than in the times of the novel. Resonances with contemporary aggressive, chauvinist religious nationalism of the Hindutva variety are only too apparent now.

Take, for instance, the following conversation between Sandip and Nikhilesh, reported by the former:

> 'though we have shouted ourselves hoarse, proclaiming the Mussulmans to be our brethren, we have come to realise that we shall never be able to bring them wholly round to our side. So they must be suppressed altogether and made to understand that we are the masters. . .'.
>
> 'If the idea of a United India is a true one', objects Nikhil, 'Mussulmans are a necessary part of it.'
>
> 'Quite so', said I, 'but we must know their place and keep them there, otherwise they will constantly be giving trouble.'[30]

We in our own times have heard much about the wisdom of being politically 'realist', whether in terms of keeping Muslims or Christians 'in their place', or in justification of the Indian atomic bomb.

Through his strictures concerning the 'impotent man', Sandip links up his political-realist creed with a basic notion of hard, aggressive masculinity. And here once again we have more recent echoes. Nathuram Godse, for instance, in his last speech before the court which sentenced him to death for the murder of the Mahatma, repeatedly accused Gandhi of effeminacy. Godse contrasted him with Savarkar, the real founder of the ideology of Hindutva, who he acknowledged as his principal inspiration.

But let us return to *Ghare-Baire*'s own times. The novel clearly points towards Rabindranath's Nationalism lectures of 1916–17, with their trenchant rejection of the 'endless bull-fight' between nation-states and incipient nationalisms threatening to become mirror images of each other, of the Social-Darwinist dogma that the 'unfit must go to the wall.' Sandip's fetishised 'world of reality' as the 'market of real things' is now expanded, with a verbosity and rhetoric

---

[30] *Home and the World*, p. 120.

which are often burdensome but which on occasion manage to hit their mark with remarkable prescience: an endless

> greed of wealth and power . . . [that] can never come to any other end but a violent death . . . Those who have made the gain of money their highest end are unconsciously selling their life and soul to rich persons or to combinations that represent money. Those who are enamoured of their political power and gloat over their extension of dominion over foreign races gradually surrender their own freedom and humanity to the organisations necessary for holding other peoples in slavery.[31]

For Nandy, Rabindranath's *Nationalism*, along with *Ghare-Baire* and two other novels that he takes up (*Gora*, and the much later *Char Adhyay*), constitute the testimony to a fundamental rejection of the modern West by their author, as contrasted to the indigenous 'civilizational' values of plurality and 'toleration encoded in various traditional ways of life.' Many passages can be found in Tagore that support Nandy's reading, and indeed, they dominate his writings in the early 1900s. His initial Swadeshi enthusiasm had led him then to a fairly unqualified justification of the varna system, in the essay entitled *Brahman* (1902). The Santiniketan ashram he started around that time initially even had caste-segregated meals. But I consider it indispensable, when looking at a man who wrote so voluminously and for so long, to remain attentive to the discipline of temporal-historical context. Nandy fails to give adequate weight to the fundamental shift in many of Rabindranath's perspectives that accompanied his disillusionment with Swadeshi, around 1907–8.[32] Unlike many then—or later—his rejection of political nationalism did not involve an espousal of what in effect amounts to cultural nationalism.

---

[31] Tagore, *Nationalism* (New York, 1917; reprinted Connecticut, 1973), pp. 44–5, 141–4.

[32] Nandy does recognise that Rabindranath had once been more Brahmanical in his values, and that 'It was after 1905 that he became open to an inclusive concept of India'. I do not think this is precise enough in pinpointing the change, and find it impossible to accept the further assumption that 'Tagore's political concerns did not change' over the quarter century that separates *Gora* from *Char Adhyay* (1934). (Nandy, *The Illegitimacy of Nationalism*, p. 10.) Such an assumption allows Nandy to ignore the temporal sequence of the three novels, discussing the first (*Gora*) last.

In his essay *Nationalism in India* (1916), Tagore did occasionally relate the caste system to what he thought had been the Indian experiment 'in evolving a social unity within which all the different peoples could be held together, yet fully enjoying the freedom of maintaining their own differences.' But he went on to add that India had rightly 'recognised differences, but not the mutability which is the law of life', and so had 'set up boundaries of immutable walls', a 'magnificent cage of countless compartments.' The essay went on to bluntly call for the removal of 'the state of affairs . . . brought about entirely by the domination in India of the caste system, and the blind and lazy habit of relying upon the authority of traditions that are incongruous anachronisms in the present age.'[33] All this, of course, did not make of Rabindranath an uncritical 'Westernist' or 'Modernist'. The point is that—like Gandhi, too, at least part of the time— he tried to remain aware of the contradictory dimensions of both indigenous tradition and modernity.

Ghare-Baire is at times even sharper in this regard, with the novel format allowing greater concreteness. In a magnificent passage, inexplicably left out of the English version, Nikhilesh sees in the Harish Kundu–Ponchu episode an epitome of the connections between rural poverty, landlord exploitation, and the power of the high-caste-religious establishment:

> I recalled, then, Ponchu, caught in the toils of poverty and fraud—it seemed as if he embodied all the poor peasants of Bengal. I saw Harish Kundu, bloated of body, ever faithful in his rituals, with all the marks of proper piety on his forehead . . . One will have to fight till the end this monstrosity of greed and power, which has fattened itself through sucking the blood of the dying, and burdens the earth with its sublime immovability—while below it lie all those who starve, remain blinded by ignorance, worn down by endless toil. This is the task that has remained postponed for century after century . . .[34]

Another passage in the novel goes even further, towards a rejection of the hierarchical organisation of society that in nineteenth-century orthodox Hindu discourses was often termed *adhikari-bheda*—a

---

[33] *Nationalism*, chapter IV, pp. 135, 137–8.
[34] *Ghare-Baire*, p. 483. My translation.

rejection through the affirmation in theory of equal rights for all. Nikhilesh recalls sadly how Bimala had once brushed aside as a joke his suggestion, made while thinking about Ponchu, that they both devote themselves to the eradication of poverty in the country:

> Though Bimala comes from a poor home, she has queenly assumptions . . . She thinks that the lower orders . . . are bound to have their woes, but they hardly feel it as wants. In Bimala's blood there is that arrogance which traditionally has cut up Indian society into infinite layers, in which every level has had the sense of being at least superior to the level beneath it, and has gloried in that petty superiority. She has the true tradition of Manu in her. While in me it seems that the blood of Guhak and Ekalavya still flows: I cannot thrust away as lowly those who today are situated below me in society. My Bharatvarsha is not made up purely of the bhadralok. I see clearly that it is India that declines and dies, when those below us suffer and die.[35]

Gender in nineteenth-century bhadralok discourses had been the major site where this debate between adhikari-bheda and equal rights had manifested itself.[36] In an interesting exchange in 1884 in the pages of the Bengali monthly *Nabyabharat*, for instance, it had been argued that women could not be taken to be inferior to men, as there should be equal rights for all. To this had come the retort that such a notion of equality was inadmissible. Every being had a claim to specific powers (*adhikar*), but these were necessarily differentiated. Otherwise a horse would have the right to sit at table, and the bhadralok would not be able to ride on the shoulders of palanquin-bearers.[37]

Ghare-Baire resumes that debate, in terms of conjugal relations and the sharply opposed conceptions of masculinity in Sandip and Nikhilesh.

---

[35] *Ghare-Baire*, p. 467. My translation: the English version leaves out some passages.

[36] I owe this point to Tanika Sarkar. For a discussion of *adhikari-bheda*, see my *Writing Social History*, chapter 7, and *passim*.

[37] Siddheswar Roy, 'Samaj-samanyay', *Nabyabharat*, Jaishtha 1291/May–June 1884; Sadananda Tarkachanchu, 'Pratibad', ibid., Asar 1291/June–July 1884).

IV

Sandip's aggressively masculinist and instrumental conceptions of realism and power extend beyond peasants, Muslims, and camp followers like Amulya. They relate, above all, to women and to Nature. 'I have found that my way always wins over the hearts of women . . . This power which wins these women is the power of mighty men, the power which wins the world of reality.'[38]

In a subsequent interior monologue, Rabindranath makes Sandip link up patriarchal domination with ruthless conquest over the environment in a manner that sounds utterly contemporary:

> We are men, we are kings, we must have our tribute. Ever since we have come upon the Earth we have been plundering her, and the more we claimed, the more she submitted. From primeval days have we men been plucking fruits, cutting down trees, digging up the soil, killing beast, bird, and fish . . . it has all been grabbing and grabbing and grabbing—no strongbox in Nature's storeroom has been respected or left unrifled. The one delight of this Nature is to fulfill the claims of those who are men . . . Likewise, by sheer force of our claims, we men have opened up all the latent possibilities of women. In the process of surrendering themselves to us, they have ever gained their true greatness.[39]

The counterpoint, throughout the novel, comes in passages where Nikhiesh describes his own relationship with Nature, and with Bimala and other human beings: quiet, contemplative, non-masterful, eager to respect the autonomy of the Other. Two conceptions of masculinity are in conflict, conceptions necessarily involving alternative constructions of womanhood. Here, I think, lies the real core of *Ghare-Baire*, and yet gender has figured surprisingly little in readings of the novel.[40]

[38] *Home and the World*, pp. 47–8.
[39] Ibid., p. 116.
[40] I see now that I had bypassed the question of gender entirely in my discussion of the novel in my *Swadeshi Movement*, op. cit. For Nandy, Bimala is important as embodying a primacy of 'motherliness' over 'conjugality', which is associated in his reading with the basic civilisational dichotomy between modern-Western and Indic values. She is therefore no more than the site, or 'battlefield on which two forms of patriotism fight for supremacy'. (*Illegitimacy,*

Sandip's conquest of Bimala takes the form of lavish, excessive praise and apparent adulation, placing her on a pedestal as virtual symbol of motherland and religion, calling her 'mokshirani', queen-bee of the entire patriotic hive. She does not really come into any public arena, it may be noted; she does not address meetings or join demonstrations, for instance, but is repeatedly assured by her lover that everything in the movement is happening because she is its inspiration. The strong erotic note, displacing the mother-figure with would-be mistress, and sheer crudeness of the manoeuvre is Sandip's alone, but otherwise there remains an affinity with the ways by which Swadeshi nationalism simultaneously exalted and subordinated womanhood. The bhadralok woman was revered as figure of motherliness and selfless service to the family. She was made to embody the 'mother'-land, but she remained at home (a few exceptional figures like Sarala Devi apart), serving the cause by sacrificing foreign luxuries, admiring, usually from behind the curtain, the patriotic oratory of male leaders. (Bimala emerged from the veil, but that had been made possible only by having a modernist husband who had urged her to do this for years.)

We have seen Gora expound the more usual version of the woman-on-a-pedestal theme integral to the ideology of the home/world disjunction. Sandip has shifted it to a crudely erotic register, but, by locating this in a Swadeshi politician, Tagore is surely suggesting that in both forms the woman is being kept within her 'proper' sphere—as mother, housewife, or subordinated mistress—precisely through the rhetoric that apparently exalts her. Both, though in very different ways, represent versions of a masculinist game of power. *Ghare-Baire*, then, in effect places a strong question mark against what, since Partha Chatterjee, has been commonly described as the 'nationalist resolution of the woman's question'.

Coming to such an understanding, it must be emphasised, had not been easy for Rabindranath. The novel needs to be located within a fairly long and difficult transition—more difficult, probably, for the author than the break with chauvinistic Hindu nationalism.

I began with an essay of Rabindranath dated April 1902, indicating how far he had been prepared then to go along with orthodox views

concerning women. As with the conjoint political transition, *Gora*
marks the beginning of a change through intense internal debate—
a process, however, which with respect to gender perhaps remains
incomplete in that novel. The two friends, Gora and Benoy, endlessly
argue about the true nature of womanhood. For the major part of the
novel Gora aggressively upholds a home/world type of disjunction as
authentically national, and also as a thing of beauty and grace by itself.
Benoy is much more critical, and even suggests at one point a homo-
logue between the confinement of women to purely domestic functions and the bhadralok tendency to categorise peasants and other
plebeian folk by their service to their social superiors alone.[41] The
conversations of the two Brahmo girls, Sucharita and Lalita, go much
further. The latter, in a bold act of rebellion, flouts convention to
travel alone at night with a man who is not her kin (Benoy), to avoid
participation in a play being staged for the British magistrate who has
just sent Gora to prison.[42] But the men still seem quite far from any
recognition of the autonomous subjectivity of women. Even Benoy,
by implication, seems to be thinking primarily in terms of the way
bringing women a bit out of pure domesticity could improve men:
'If we become capable of seeing women outside our domestic needs,
the beauty and plenitude of our country would become more evident
for *us*' (my emphasis).[43] Love for Sucharita makes Gora realise the
incompleteness of his earlier patriotic vision, which had excluded
women other than as figures of motherhood. Yet the same passage has
him exalting 'the woman who, deserving of worship herself, has
revered unfailingly the least deserving among us.'[44] The figure of
Anandamoyee, quintessentially maternal but free of all social taboos

---

p. 14). He does not refer at all to the near-contemporary 'Streer Patra' and the
other *Sabuj Patra* short stories.

[41] *Gora, RR,* IX, pp. 78–80.

[42] Elsewhere, Lalita explicitly rejects the home/world disjunction: 'You [men-
folk] think that you'll do the work of the world, while we do your work. That
wont happen. We too will either do the work, or remain a burden on you.' Ibid.,
p. 94. My translation.

[43] Ibid., p. 79. My translation.

[44] Ibid., pp. 243–4.

and prejudices, helps in a way to smooth over an unresolved debate. Gora's final peroration denouncing all sectarian barriers remains silent about gender.

The big change in Rabindranath's views on gender seems to have come a few years after his break with most other aspects of Swadeshi nationalism, achieved through the 1907–8 essays and *Gora*. In his 'Women's Lot in East and West' (*Modern Review*, June 1912), referring to Russian 'Nihilists', he was still expressing a fear that women in Europe might soon 'appear as Furies of destruction', and went on to declare: 'We are quite happy with our household goddesses and they too have never told us that they are very unhappy.' Indian widows then seemed to him happier than European spinsters, for they had the chance of rendering 'loving service' to other members of the joint family. And the wives, in traditional systems everywhere, had reigned as 'queen-bees' over the 'hives' to which the male 'worker-bees' brought honey. The metaphor is important, for it would be used again in *Ghare-Baire*, but with a very different, clearly pejorative, intent. It is Sandip who uses the metaphor, seducing Bimala through flattery as preparations for getting money from her on false, patriotic pretences. A passage towards the end of the novel vividly demonstrates the shift in Tagore's views regarding the lot of Hindu widows, too. Nikhilesh, on the eve of leaving his ancestral home, feels nostalgic about the childhood he has shared with Mejorani, his sister-in-law, who had come as a bride to the house at the age of nine, lost her husband soon, and lived on in the joint family without a break since then. He expresses a desire to return to those days. The sister-in-law replies, 'with a deep sigh': 'No, brother, never again a life as a woman! Let this one life be sufficient for what I have had to endure, I cannot stand any more.'[45]

What can explain this change, the first literary expression of which came through the sudden outburst of *Sabuj Patra* stories, particularly 'Haimanti' (Jaishtha 1321/May–June 1914), 'Bostomi' (Asar 1321/June–July 1914), 'Streer Patra' (Sravan 1321/July–August 1914), 'Aparichita' (Kartik 1321/October–November 1914), 'Payela Nambar'

---

[45] *Ghare-Baire*, pp. 539–40.

(Asar 1324/June–July 1917), and 'Patra-o-Patri' (Paus 1324/December 1917–January 1918)?

As the Swadeshi wave receded around 1908–9, scattered reports in contemporary newspapers indicated a revival of public interest and debate on issues concerning women: notably, widow-marriage, child-marriage, exorbitant demands for dowry.[46] The official *Report on Native Newspapers* between late February and mid-April 1908 indicate an intense controversy about the pros and cons of the widow-marriage which Asutosh Mukherjee, Calcutta High Court Judge and Vice-Chancellor of Calcutta University, had just arranged for his daughter. This was followed by a number of other widow-marriages in well-known families, including two within ten days in Mukherjee's own locality of Bhowanipur, in South Calcutta.[47] Mukherjee was of course something of a loyalist, and many of the newspapers which supported him—like the *Bengalee* of Surendranath Banerjea—were Moderates in their nationalism. And yet the easy equation of indigenist rejection of reform with nationalist purity breaks down once again. The critics of Mukherjee included the Extremist *Sandhya*, but also the loyal *Bangabasi*, and the orthodox Bharat Dharma Mahamandal leaders who denounced him were simultaneously engaged in organising a loyalist deputation under the Maharaja of Darbhanga to the Viceroy, Lord Minto.[48]

Meanwhile the steady accumulation of statistics through decennial Census Reports was providing a growing mass of material for anyone who cared to write or agitate about the conditions of Bengali women.

[46] The issues were of course interconnected. Child-marriage, usually to much older husbands, added to the number of young widows, whose suffering and alleged openness to possibilities of immoral conduct had figured prominently in all reformist arguments from Vidyasagar onwards. The social obloquy heaped on parents with daughters still unmarried after the onset of puberty led to the acceptance of harsh dowry terms set by parents of bridegrooms.

[47] *Report on Native Newspapers* (Bengal) for the weeks from 29 February to 18 April 1908. The Bhowanipur widow-marriages were reported by *Bengalee*, 8 March 1908.

[48] *Sandhya*, 25 February and 12 March 1908; *Bangabasi*, 14 March 1908; *Nabasakti*, 13 March 1908—in the relevant numbers of *Report on Native Newspapers* (Bengal).

The 1891 Census reported that one in three of Hindu women in Bengal were widows; that of 1911 found only 3% of girls unmarried in the 15–20 age-bracket.[49] There were many signs also that, despite the many nineteenth-century bhadralok reform endeavours, practices like the ban on widow-marriage or lowering of the age of marriage were actually becoming more widespread among upwardly mobile sanskritising groups. Dowry, too, was spreading downwards, replacing bride-price among lower castes: the 1901 Census found 42 out of 51 listed castes paying dowry.[50]

And then there was that further bit of Census data, one among several that U.N. Mukherji used in May–June 1909 to build what proved to be a remarkably influential and enduring bulwark of an emerging anti-Muslim Hindu-nationalist discourse about the 'dying Hindu'. Only one in eight among Bengali Muslim women was a widow, according to the 1891 Census. The demographic panic which Mukherji whipped up through a selective use of Census material linked incipient communal ideology with elements of social reform. It was directed mainly towards some kind of sanskritising move from the top to improve the conditions and status of lower castes so that they did not break away from the Hindu fold. But there were also occasional references to the taboo against widow-marriage restricting Hindu population growth and leading to elopements with Muslims.[51] The resultant discursive amalgam was far-reaching enough to evoke echoes in unexpected quarters, including in Rabindranath's *Gora*, where the character who comes closest to being the authorial voice, the non-sectarian Pareshbabu (father of Lalita), suddenly refers to Hindus facing extinction because of their stubborn adherence to obsolete traditions.[52] The combination, however, was also highly unstable, and capable of extension in quite different directions. *Gora's* central thrust was firmly anti-communal, while conversely, by the mid-1920s, social reform was being displaced by the issue of alleged

[49] Dagmar Engels, *Beyond Purdah? Women in Bengal, 1890–1939* (Delhi, 1996), pp. 41, 43.

[50] Ibid., p. 50.

[51] U.N. Mukherji, 'A Dying Race', serialised in *Bengalee*, 1–20 June 1909: see particularly 2 June.

[52] *RR*, IX, pp. 309–10.

abductions of Hindu women by Muslims in developed Hindu-communalist discourses.[53]

Scattered newspaper references to issues related to gender reform suddenly became a flood for a few months in early 1914, in the context of the sensational Snehalata case. A sixteen-year-old North Calcutta girl in a poorly-off Brahman family, Snehalata burnt herself to death on 30 January, two weeks before her marriage. It seems this was because she had realised her parents would be ruined by the excessive dowry the groom's family was demanding from them.[54] Judging from the flood of letters, articles and editorials in newspapers and periodicals that followed, middle-class public opinion was fairly unanimous that excessive dowry demands needed to be curbed—but there the agreement ended. Two rival meetings were organised in Calcutta to express divergent, relatively reformist, and conservative views on how the admitted evil of dowry could be fought. A College Square meeting, mainly of students, on 13 February tried to set up an Anti-Marriage-Dowry League of young men prepared to take a vow not to demand dowry when marrying.[55] Some letters and articles went much further, suggesting efforts to raise the age of marriage, and more basically to try to end the stigma attached to girls who remained unmarried (and the social obloquy heaped on their parents). *Modern Review* added that if more girls remained spinsters 'it would be necessary to educate them as would enable them to be economically independent, if necessary.'[56] There were even a few suggestions that

[53] The above paragraph summarises an important and complex argument developed in Datta, *Carving Blocs*, op. cit., chapters I, IV, and *passim*.

[54] *Amrita Bazar Patrika*, 7 February 1914, gave some details about the immolation, on the basis of proceedings in the Coroner's Court on 6 February. A fuller account was published in *Bengalee*, 13 February, according to which Snehalata's father, Harendrachandra Mukherji, was a petty broker from Faridpur, with one brother a doctor in Mymensingh, and another a zamindari agent in Muktagaccha in the same district.

[55] *Amrita Bazar Patrika*, 14 February 1914. The meeting, said to have been attended by a thousand young men (*Bengalee*, more sympathetic to the cause of reform, claimed next day that 5000 had been present), was chaired by the Brahmo nationalist leader Krishnakumar Mitra, and had among its speakers Ramananda Chatterjee, editor of *Modern Review*.

[56] Notes (The Extortion of Dowries), *Modern Review*, March 1914.

priests ought to boycott marriages associated with dowries, and Hindu laws be amended 'to bestow on the daughter a share in the parental property equal to that of the son.'[57]

That conservative opinion had become alarmed by the reopening of a range of social-reform issues threatened by the Snehalata case is indicated by parallel efforts to channel the sense of shock into safer, indeed recuperative, channels. A rival meeting, held on 14 February (to be followed by another on similar lines on 24 February, attended by 'many well-known Pandits'), also condemned dowry, but as a modern innovation associated with the spread of commercialised values, and went on to suggest earlier marriages, so that brides would have less problems adapting to their husbands' families.[58] Conservatives followed the standard strategy of elevating Snehalata to the pedestal of heroic martyrdom—her act was even described as akin to the *jauhar* practised by Rajput women 'from the days of Alladin' [*sic*][59]—after which the dangers involved in the suggestions of reformers could be outlined. This was done with exceptional clarity in an *Amrita Bazar Patrika* editorial of 24 February. An anti-dowry vow by unmarried young men might lead them to disobey their parents, which would never do. 'A Hindu will never agree . . . that the marriage of Hindu girls should not be made compulsory', while postponing marriage unduly might lead to girls insisting on 'choosing their own husbands. The parental control over the marriage of their children will necessarily be gone, and a Brahmin girl might secretly marry, say, a husband of the carpenter caste.' Age, gender, and caste hierarchies were all felt to be under threat.

There was nothing particularly unique about the Snehalata case,

[57] Letter from S.D. Mazumdar, *Amrita Bazar Patrika*, 27 February 1914.

[58] *Amrita Bazar Patrika*, 16 February, 25 February 1914. The editor of this daily, Motilal Ghosh, was prominent at these two meetings, perhaps in part as an incident of his lifelong rivalry with Surendranath Banerjea, editor of the somewhat pro-reform *Bengalee*. Several of Surendranath's close associates had been prominent in the College Square meeting.

[59] This was at a meeting of the Kalighat Peoples' Association on 15 February, where Snehalata was described as 'our very meek infant Snehas, having no idea of women's suffrage.' *Amrita Bazar Patrika*, 20 February 1914. Periodicals like *Modern Review*, it may be added, had been carrying news fairly often of the suffragette agitation in Britain.

and in fact several similar incidents were reported in its wake, as well as fairly often over the succeeding years.[60] That it was not exceptional in a way could have added to its impact. What it managed to do was bring into centre-space again the question of reform in gender relations, which had been submerged for a time by the rise of revivalist forms of nationalism. Despite the sympathy lavished on the 'martyr', it also helped expose the crudities of social conservatism in matters of family life and gender.

On 10 February 1914 an editorial in *Bengalee* made a direct appeal to Tagore. Snehalata's martyrdom, it declared, 'requires to be sung, storied and carried from mouth to mouth. We hope it will wake up Rabindranath's lyre and provide ample inspiration to his muse.' The *Sabuj Patra* stories started coming out in a couple of months' time: surely this was not a coincidence. There even seem to be a few direct references. In 'Streer Patra' the rebellious wife Mrinal reports the common reaction of many men to cases of women setting fire to themselves. 'They started saying "It has become a fashion among girls to die by setting their clothes on fire." You [her husband and in-laws] said "All this is play-acting." . . . maybe so, but why is it that what gets burnt is always the saris of Bengali girls, and never the dhoties of the brave men of Bengal?'[61] The Berhampur College joint letter published in *Modern Review* (April 1914) referred to instances of the neglect of illnesses of 'young daughters-in-law in respectable well-to-do families . . . The result was that the unfortunate girls died and

---

[60] A letter published in *Amrita Bazar Patrika*, 13 February 1914, reported a similar suicide in Dinajpur by another Kulin Brahmin girl. Girijasankar Bhattacharya and four other teachers of Berhampore College mentioned the immolation of Nibhanani, soon after Snehalata, in a long joint letter entitled 'The Dowry System: Its Effect and Cure', *Modern Review*, April 1914. In 1917 an article in *Bharati*, a monthly associated with the Tagore family, pointed out that the suicide rate among women in Calcutta was four times that of men: Dagmar Engels, op. cit., p. 54. A *Modern Review* article of February 1920 was still referring to an 'increasing suicide mania among Bengali young girls.' It did not forget to mention the Snehalata case, and also described how a particular house in North Calcutta had become locally infamous as 'daughter-in-law killing house' (*bau mara bari*): Sundari Mohan Das, 'The Causation and Prevention of Suicide among Girls and Women', ibid.

[61] (*RR*, Vishwabharati Edition), volume 23, p. 259. My translation.

their fortunate husbands brought some extra thousands to the family fund.' 'Haimanti', published just a month later, is partly built round an identical scenario.

But Tagore's *Sabuj Patra* stories go much beyond the possible context I have been outlining. What is remarkable about them is not the sympathetic depiction of the woes of women: that had been quite a standard theme for long, and the trope of unjust suffering bravely but patiently borne was eminently open to paternalist appropriation. More striking is a tone of extreme anger, expressed for instance in the 'Streer Patra' passage I have just quoted, going along often with a considerable degree of male guilt and auto-critique. But middle-class male guilt had been an important element in the constitution of the nineteenth-century social reform project focused upon the 'women's question' from Rammohan down to the 1880s, when it had been swamped by conservative-nationalistic moods. Rabindranath's short stories—and, I argue, *Ghare-Baire*, on a slightly different but very significant register—are not a mere resumption of that interrupted project. The new note is the effort to depict figures of independent-minded, autonomously-acting, rebellious women—an effort which simultaneously adds a new dimension to the theme of male guilt.

'Streer Patra' stands out from all the others in being written in the voice of a woman at the height of a total, uncompromising rebellion. Mrinal has just left her husband's house forever, the joint-family home which had been comfortable enough, but where she could never be anything more than *mejobau* (wife of the second brother), never a full-fledged human being. She recalls how she entered the house the first time, 'while all the skies were weeping to the tune of wedding music'—a striking image of the woes of patrilocality from the point of view of women. She traces back the roots of her rebellion, very significantly, to her intelligence, which had refused to internalise the many forms of subservience, and which had for long expressed its defiance through the secret writing of poetry: 'Whatever might have been its worth, there the walls of your *andar mahal* [women's quarter] could not reach.' Then Bindu, the helpless relative-by-marriage she had befriended, through whose eyes she had first become aware of her beauty, had been married off to a madman.[62] Refused shelter when

[62] There is an interesting note of sisterly solidarity here, at least—and, just possibly, a hint of a lesbian attraction.

she tried to run away, Bindu killed herself by setting her clothes on fire. That was when 'the mejobau of yours died.' Mrinal has left No 27, Makhan Baral Lane never to come back, and the letter ends in deliberate, defiant inversion of the standard, humble way a Bengali wife at that time was supposed to end a letter to her husband or elder: 'From Mrinal, who is torn off the shelter of your feet.'[63]

Women striking out for freedom in unexpected and unconventional ways figure prominently in many of the other near-contemporary stories. There is the mature teacher (and possibly political worker) who has refused marriage in 'Aparichita'; a wife who suddenly leaves both her husband and a would-be lover in 'Payela Nombor'; the daughter of a low-caste woman who defies social taboos to marry the son of a rich higher-caste merchant in 'Patra-o-Patri'. The other crucial feature is that, 'Streer Patra' apart, most of the *Sabuj Patra* stories are narrated through the persona of a series of self-critical, yet ineffective, men, who witness with amazement and a deep sense of guilt the affirmations of the women. The note of male auto-critique is clearest in 'Haimanti', where the wife is ill-treated when her in-laws discover her father was not as rich as they had thought. Her own total integrity adds to her problems. Doctors are not called for when she falls ill, her father is not allowed to take her home. Haimanti dies, and her mother-in-law is planning a second marriage for her son when the story ends. Her husband understands everything, feels deeply guilty, yet does literally nothing. It is precisely through this depiction of ineffectiveness that Rabindranath is able to make a statement of remarkable power which goes considerably beyond the limits of nineteenth-century male guilt and extends into a much broader critique of the culture underlying such injustice and inaction. It is a statement, moreover, that leaps across decades to seem, today, utterly relevant:

> All I had to do is just to leave with my wife. Why did I not take such an obvious, simple step? Why, indeed! If I am not to sacrifice my true feelings for what people regard as proper, if I was not to sacrifice my dearest one for the extended family, then what about the ages of social indoctrination running in my blood? What is it there for? Don't you know that on the day the people of Ayodhya demanded the banishment of Sita, I was

---

[63] My translations. I have been greatly helped in this brief discussion of 'Streer Patra' by Tanika Sarkar.

among them? Those who sang the glory of that sacrifice, generation after countless generation, I was one of them too.[64]

The *Sabuj Patra* stories—and, above all, 'Streer Patra'—evoked much conservative anger. The Extremist leader Bepinchandra Pal even attempted a 'revised' version called 'Mrinaler Katha' (Mrinal's Story). Here Mrinal's leaving home is depicted as a temporary aberration. She has a brief affair with a poet in Puri and then learns that Bindu had not really killed herself, and instead is now reconciled to her fate. Mrinal now begs to be allowed to come back to her husband, and the story ends with a letter signed: 'Mrinal, ever in the shelter of your feet.'[65] It seems likely that the attacks on Bimala for slandering the Sita image through adulterous passions may have had something to do with the fact that her creator had just published stories like 'Streer Patra' and 'Haimanti'.[66]

It is the theme of male auto-critique—though in a significantly different register—that allows us now to rejoin *Ghare-Baire*, and, specifically, Nikhilesh. Unlike the male narrator of 'Haimanti', he had been actively reformist and had tried for years to persuade Bimala to come out of her seclusion, to join him in constructing a new kind of conjugality grounded in the recognition of the equality of men and women. He refuses to surrender his principles even at the moment of greatest challenge—when he realises that Bimala is falling in love with Sandip—though the broken cadences of his interior monologue

[64] 'Haimanti', trans. Kalpana Bardhan, op. cit., p. 95.

[65] 'Narayan', Sravana 1324/July–August 1917. Pal's version is summarised in Asok Kumar Sarkar, *Sabujpatra o Bangla Sahitya* (Calcutta, 1994), pp. 56–7, which also refers to another parody of 'Streer Patra': 'Mrinalini Debi', 'Streer Prakrita Patra' (The Genuine Letter of the Wife), *Aryavarta*, Aswin 1321/September–October 1914.

[66] But Rabindranath seems to have had some unexpected supporters, too. In Magh–Falgun 1321/January–February 1915, a story entitled *Streer Patra* was published in a subordinate-caste woman's journal, *Mahishya Mahila*, depicting the sorrows of a wife whose husband had married again. The journal, connected with a 'Sanskritising' kind of caste movement, was usually quite conservative on family and gender issues. It had, however, written bitterly the previous year about the way some were acclaiming the immolation of Snehalata as an act of *jauhar*. 'Bangali Kumarir Jahar-vrata', *Mahishya Mahila*, Magh–Falgun 1320/January–February 1914.

indicate the depth of his inner struggle against the temptation to draw upon the resources of conventional patriarchy:

> 'My wife—and so, forsooth, my very own! If she says: "No, I am myself"—am I to reply: "How can that be? Are you not mine?" '[67]

In conventional terms, clearly, Nikhilesh is a failure, both in his politics and in the battle with Sandip over Bimala. He realises that he is so even when, at the end of the novel, Bimala prepares to come back to him—for that happens only because Sandip has been exposed so utterly. But it is important to explore exactly where and why he fails. Through such an exploration we may perhaps understand why Rabindranath deliberately created a situation where the reformer's initiative—which has full authorial sympathy—rebounds on himself, so that the freedom which Nikhilesh gives Bimala ends in all-round tragedy.

It would be entirely superficial, of course, to construe Nikhilesh's problem as mildness, a lack of 'manly' personality: that would involve an acceptance of Sandip's approach to life. Nikhilesh's apparent mildness really indicates enormous inner strength, grounded in a determined, sustained effort to respect, through an alternative kind of masculinity, the autonomy of the Other. There is an interesting affinity here, it might be suggested, between Nikhilesh and Paresh in *Gora*. Paresh is described by his adopted daughter Sucharita as a man who 'never displays his strength' by imposing his will on others, 'but an enormous strength lies easily hidden within himself'. Sucharita in the same passage compares Paresh with Gora, with whom she is in the process of falling in love: 'Gora's own desire and will has such power, is so enormously important for him! By forcibly expressing his wishes, he can bend others to his will.'[68] Maybe in some ways Sandip has a bit of Gora within him, but in a degenerate form—minus his sincerity and genuine patriotic fervour.

The alternative model of masculinity which I think Rabindranath tries to project through Nikhilesh attains clarity precisely through recognition of its own limits. What Nikhilesh realises, and recognises as his failure, is that his effort has, after all, been incomplete. It has

---

[67] *Home and the World*, p. 64.

[68] *Gora* (*RR*, Centenary Edition), IX, p. 280. My translation.

failed to give sufficient imaginative heed to the autonomous subjectivity of Bimala:

> 'I had been decorating Bimal so long with ideals that have been precious
> for me . . . But Bimal is what she is; she does not have to become the mis-
> tress of all virtues and beauty just because I want her to be so. Why should
> the Creator act according to my commands?'[69]
> 'I feel today that there had been an element of oppression, of power,
> in my relations with Bimal. I had tried to mould her into a model of what
> seemed seamlessly perfect to me. But a human being's life cannot be cast
> into a mould . . .'[70]

Through Nikhilesh, I would like to suggest, Rabindranath is seeking to reaffirm the basic values of nineteenth-century male reformism—
grounded at its best in notions of equal rights—and at the same time
recognise its inadequacy. In that honourable, but limited reformism,
even the phrase *stri-swadhinata*, so much in use in the 1860s and
1870s, had really meant the 'freeing' of women by benevolently
motivated men, some improvements in conditions and status—but
not really the emancipation of women as fully autonomous human
subjects. What had been lacking was what Rabindranath, in Swadeshi
and post-Swadeshi times alike, had come to foreground as a supreme
value: *atmasakti*, the need for autonomous self-development. Reform
had often been overdependent on foreign support and patronage—
the toadyism of some Brahmos like Panubabu and Baradasundari that

---

[69] *Ghare-Baire*, p. 448. My translation: I find the English version here
(p. 65) inadequate.

[70] Ibid., p. 546. My translation. It needs to be noted, however, that this power
element in Nikhilesh is far more subtle and nuanced than has been depicted in
a recent interesting conjoint study of the novel, and Satyajit Ray's film version,
by Nicholas Dirks. It is difficult to recognise Nikhilesh—of the novel, at least—
in Dirks' ascription to him of a 'relentless and imperious desire to shape Bimala
in the image of his own modern God . . . to shape her in his own terms (he
compels her to submit to this plan).' The essay attributes wrongly to Nikhilesh
the key decision, made entirely by Bimala herself, to come out before Sandip.
Nicholas Dirks, 'The Home and the World: The Invention of Modernity in
Colonial India', in Robert A. Rosenstone, ed., *Revisioning History: Film and the
Construction of a New Past* (Princeton, 1995), pp. 53, and 46; for Bimal's decision, see *Ghare-Baire*, pp. 420–1; *Home and the World*, p. 32.

Rabindranath so mercilessly pilloried in *Gora*—and plagued by sectarian narrowness.[71] Above all, it had been at its best for, not by, women.

It is within this context that we can begin the difficult task of trying
to situate and understand Bimala. She is given a privileged position
in the narrative structure, for, alone among the novel's protagonists,
she looks back on what has already happened in a process of remem-
brance coloured by knowledge of the eventual tragic outcome. Bimala
remains a complicated figure, more open perhaps to sharply opposed
readings than do the others.

The novel begins with a beautifully crafted passage where Bimala,
after the tragedy, seems to enter a mood that reinvokes the values of
maternity in a kind of womb-inversion:

> 'Mother, today there comes back to mind the vermilion mark at the part-
> ing of your hair, the sari which you used to wear, with its wide red border,
> and those wonderful eyes of yours, full of depth and peace . . .'

She recalls the way her mother had served food to her father:

> 'a beauty which passed beyond outward forms . . . transcended all de-
> bates, or doubts, or calculations: it was pure music.'[72]

The passage seems to support the kind of anti-modern reading of
Ghare-Baire and Tagore that Ashis Nandy has tried to develop, and
this is the only point where Bimala, and the question of gender as a
whole, enters his discussion. For him, 'in Tagore's world, motherliness questions the dominant consciousness' of what he would like to
call 'the principle of egalitarian hierarchy.' In contrast to the 'organising principle of the Indic civilization', the latter gives absolute priority to 'conjugality over maternity'.[73]

But Bimala then, in effect, begins to deconstruct her own initial

---

[71] Sectarianism could reproduce within the confines of the 'reformed' community many of the constraints of orthodoxy: this, again, is a theme central to
Gora. But Nikhilesh's reformist values, and their limits, do not come from any
particular religious affiliation, and this allows the problem in *Ghare-Baire* to be
posed more sharply, independent of religious differences between Brahmo and
Hindu.

[72] *Home and the World*, pp. 17–18. ❧

[73] *The Illegitimacy of Nationalism*, see pp. 41, 42, 49.

response. She recalls that she has failed to respond emotionally to her husband's constant insistence on equality in their relationship—'that was my woman's heart, which spontaneously expresses its love through worship' (*puja*). But the reader cannot fail to recognise soon that it is precisely such spontaneity that has made Bimala open to the wiles of Sandip. And, immediately after this passage, Bimala recognises that changes in her own lifetime have made unreflective devotion no longer a matter of 'simple prose': 'What had been as simple as breathing now requires rhetoric for sustenance.' 'Poetry' has become necessary now to justify the beauty of the wife's devotion and the widow's austerity—'A separation has taken place between truth and beauty. Can truth be recuperated today by mere insistence on beauty?'[74] At a more general level, too, I think Kalpana Bardhan makes an important point when she draws attention to the way the heroines of *Ghare-Baire* and the *Sabuj Patra* stories are childless wives. For Mrinal in 'Streer Patra', it is the relationship with Bindu that becomes the point for open anti-patriarchal rebellion, whereas motherhood could have tied her down more firmly to her husband's family.[75] Sisterhood, or relating to someone in a sisterly manner, seems in fact to be more crucial than maternalism in these stories. One recalls Bimala's relations with Amulya, through which she becomes aware of the real nature of Sandip.

Spontaneity, 'my woman's heart'—perhaps Rabindranath's intent through Bimala is precisely to question this 'naturalness', the absence of autonomous self-development through reason and strenuous effort: the need for atmasakti, once again. Bimala is very different from Mrinal, who preserves and cultivates her inner autonomy through the secret writing of poetry, or for that matter from the other heroines of the *Sabuj Patra* stories. Perhaps the point can be clarified through another look back at *Gora*, this time at the sub-plot woven around Sucharita's aunt Harimohini. Her's had been the miserable lot of a woman in a traditional family: child-wife, cooking all day with little

[74] *Ghare-Baire*, pp. 408–9. My translation: some important passages have been omitted in the English version.

[75] 'The energy and attention that nurturing requires, tends to diffuse and sublimate the oppression and frustration in conjugal life.' Bardhan, op. cit., Introduction, p. 16.

or no time for eating her own meals, and then widowed and pushed out to Benaras by in-laws. But when Paresh helps her to regain a kind of 'sansar' or household of her own, Harimohini soon begins to reproduce the contours of a similarly oppressive domesticity, seeking to impose numerous constraints on Sucharita, trying to get her married off without bothering to ask her consent. In a context, and through a persona, utterly different from Bimala, here already is the emphasis on the need for women's self-development for genuine women's freedom, and the insufficiency of even the best-intentioned male reformist benevolence.

But how far did Rabindranath's vision concerning the autonomous self-development of women really extend? The women in the *Sabuj Patra* stories, 'Streer Patra' apart, all have a certain externality about them: they are portrayed from the outside, as it were, through the eyes of amazed, ineffectual men. There are similarities of pattern here with the unforgettable figure of Damini in the novel just preceding *Ghare-Baire, Chaturanga*: she, too, retains an element of mystery for the other three (male) protagonists.[76] Even Mrinal is a figure caught at the moment of rebellion: no attempt is made to portray what she might be able to make of her independent life. Artistically extremely effective, such retention of externality might also be related to a certain authorial recognition of limits in portraying the freed subjectivity of women.

Recognition of the autonomy of the Other, of course, does not preclude having preferences among the many forms through which such autonomy might manifest itself. Rabindranath certainly did not like some of the forms that women's emancipation could take, and indeed had already started taking, in Bengal in his lifetime. Remarkably ahead of his times, in some ways, from the post-Swadeshi phase onwards—notably in introducing coeducation in Santiniketan in the early 1920s, within a residential set-up—he seems to have retained an aesthetic, almost physical, revulsion to the figure of the politicised activist woman. He would express this in quite extreme form in the

[76] One could also mention in this context another of the *Sabuj Patra* stories, 'Bostomi', where Tagore, using his own persona, narrates a tale, apparently based on real life, of a strange encounter he had with an utterly unconventional Vaishnava *sanyasini*, who repudiated husband and religious preceptor alike.

novel *Char Adhyay* (1934), written at a time when women had joined revolutionary-terrorist groups as comrades-in-arms. (One might recall the reference to the Russian Nihilist women in his 1912 article.)

But the dominant note in *Ghare-Baire*, surely, remains Nikhilesh's agonised determination to respect the autonomy of Bimala. Autonomy as a moral value, combined, however, with the other central theme in Tagore, the need for self-development, atmasakti, becoming worthy of true independence through one's own efforts—including, crucially, a cultivation of the intellect.

In an essay written twelve years after *Ghare-Baire*, Rabindranath argued that the field of work for men and women in society was fundamentally the same. There were some unredeemable physical differences, among which he mentioned the natural pressure on women to be mothers, for men to work outside their homes—but he was quick to add that these had been greatly exaggerated. 'Women have been enfolded into the stereotypes of mother and housewife . . . Then came an earthquake in the West which has shaken up this age-old structure of discrimination . . . We will have to recognise the common humanity of women as well as men, beyond all differences . . .'[77] And in 1936, in what was perhaps his last essay on the specific question of women: 'All over the world women today are coming out of the confines of their households into the open arena of the world . . . Let us hope for a new age in the building of civilization . . .' He ended with an appeal to women 'to open their hearts, cultivate their intellect, pursue knowledge with determination. They have to remember that unexamined blind conservatism is opposed to creativity.'[78]

V

We have been reading men's texts about women, and, in particular, the writings of someone indisputably quite exceptional. What about the voices of women themselves?

An early and unusual abundance of publications by women becomes evident in Bengal from around the 1860s, in the wake of the

[77] *Nareer manushyatva* (The Humanness of Women), 15 Baisakh 1335/April 1928, in *RR*, XIII, pp. 24, 28.

[78] *Nari* (Woman), Agrahayan 1343/November–December 1936; ibid., pp. 379–80.

conjoint spread of print and vernacular production. Largely ignored in the earlier historical literature about the 'Bengal Renaissance' and the debates around that category, nineteenth-century women's writings are now being studied intensively by scholars with feminist affinities. There has been relatively little work on equivalent material in the early twentieth century, and it will be obvious that the subject is much too vast to be tackled in this essay.[79]

I would still like to end with two instances of womens' writing roughly contemporaneous with *Ghare-Baire*—a newspaper article and a forgotten play. I came across them in an entirely serendipitous manner and find them interesting partly because of their location in utterly different social mileus.

Atmasakti, a weekly with a radical reputation, published on 28 November 1923 a rejoinder to some socially conservative statements by a leading Bengali woman novelist, Anurupa Devi.[80] It came—or so at least the weekly claimed—from Kusumkumari Dasi, a peasant woman of Kaivarta caste, and was written in very colloquial Bengali. The agriculturist section of the Kaivartas—'Hele', instead of the 'Jele' fishermen—had been engaged in a sanskritising kind of upward mobility effort for a generation prior to the 1920s, claiming the title of 'Mahishya', and simultaneously imposing stricter high-caste standards on their women. But there were dissident voices, it seems: I have already mentioned the reference to 'Streer Patra' in the *Mahishya Mahila* of early 1915.[81]

Kusumkumari, in 1923, went much further, and had the audacity to criticise a well-established high-caste woman writer for her

[79] One exception, about whom there is a considerable secondary literature, is Begum Rokeya (1880–1932), pioneer of Muslim women's education in Bengal, author of an Utopia where women are on top (*Sultan's Dream*, 1905), as well as a novel and essays quite remarkably feministic for those times. See Sonia Nishat Amin, *The World of Muslim Women in Colonial Bengal, 1876–1939* (Leiden, etc., 1996), chapter VII, as well as the discussion of Rokeya's novel *Padmaras* (1924) in Datta, *Carving Blocs*, pp. 217–19.

[80] Anurupa Devi was the grand-daughter of Bhudev Mukhopadhyay, the distinguished late-nineteenth century ideologue of Hindu conservatism. In her novel *Poshyaputra*, Anurupa made a character declare that Bhudev's *Paribarik Prabandha* deserved to become the Manusamhita of present times. Jnanesh Maitra, *Nari Jagriti o Bangla Sahitya* (Calcutta, n.d.), p. 194.

[81] See above, f.n. 67.

conservatism. The novelist had apparently praised the orthodox norms set by Manu, and justified the seclusion of women as giving them protection and a comfortable life free from arduous outdoor labour. 'Didi is a rich man's daughter, a rich man's wife', came the blunt rejoinder—'She probably doesn't know how much wives in our kinds of households have to work—cleaning and husking paddy, occasionally even helping to till land . . .' Kusumkumari went on to describe the sufferings of upper-caste child-widows in her village and expressed regret that, through imitation of Brahmins and Kayasthas, her own community was also giving up the practice of widow-marriage. As for the 'Arya-dharma' of Manu—'I am a Kaivarta girl, I am not an Arya. . . . Weren't Aryans the people who came from outside India and grabbed the lands of non-Aryans like us? Their dharma for us is in many ways the dharma of conquerors . . .'[82]

My second example comes from a much more exalted social context. *Debottar Vishwanatya* (1915) was an allegorical play written by Sarajubala Dasgupta, daughter of Brojendranath Seal, the distinguished intellectual, philosopher, and friend of Tagore. Sarajubala was connected by marriage with the family of Chittaranjan Das, and in 1915 had recently returned from England, having done a course on kindergarten education. Britain, and Europe generally, had been going through a phase of considerable labour militancy at the time of her visit (1912–13), as well as of suffragette agitation.[83] The impact of both is evident in her play, which the Imperial (now National) Library Catalogue describes as 'A metaphysical drama on socialism depicting the struggle of capital and labour.' It begins with the eviction of peasants from land by a city entrepreneur who had bought the estate off their indebted paternalist zamindar in order to start a factory there. Dinu Morol, who had tried without success to organise peasant resistance, becomes a powerful leader of dispossessed peasants-turned-proletarians. A scientist, whose inventions have helped

[82] Kusumkumari Dasi, *Nareer Svatantra* (The Autonomy of Women), *Atmasakti*, volume II, n.37, 28 November 1923. It may be noticed that she calls herself 'Kaivarta', not 'Mahishya'.

[83] Sarajubala married Chittaranjan's brother Basantaranjan, and, after his death, Das's widowed brother-in-law Saratchandrachandra Sen. Subodhchandra Sengupta and Anjali Basu, eds, *Sansad Bangali Caritabhidhan* (Calcutta, 1976), p. 546.

the capitalist entrepreneur to displace workers by machines, comes over to the side of the rebellious labourers, and the class struggle builds up into a vividly described general strike.[84] Then, in a resolution reminiscent of several near-contemporaneous allegorical plays by Rabindranath,[85] tensions get diffused when the king gets rid of his evil minister. A sanyasi suddenly appears, and king and capitalist both accept his suggestion that they act from now on as trustees of their subordinates.

But what, significantly, is left unrecuperated is a most striking feminist dimension. During the run-up to the strike there was already a woman weaver who complains that union leaders never think of women's problems, of child-care and of preserving their dignity. Male workers belong to 'that same race of cannibalistic men, always greedily staring at us . . . O Hari, you too are a man, you are the God of men . . .'[86] Then Kamini, daughter of Dinu, takes up and develops this theme. She rejects Dinu's command that she marry the scientist's son to cement the alliance between labour and knowledge. Kamini chooses the zamindar's son instead. What is much more significant, she makes it clear to him that this has to be a totally different kind of relationship, one that will try to solve the contradiction of love that needs to be entirely voluntary and therefore open to change, and the permanence required for the sake of children. Her partnership with her lover will be on the basis of complete equality, it will have no formal grounding in religion or law—the only condition being that a part of their independent incomes from labour would be left apart as a trust ('devottar'—hence the play's title) for their possible child. Sarajubala makes no attempt whatsoever to tone down the vehemence of her heroine's rejection of marriage, 'which binds down by force men and women—in a bondage without any affinity. Only an age-old custom, a kind of blind force . . .'[87]

[84] 'Mills, factories, markets in all cities are closed. . . . No trams on the roads, even trains have stopped running. The wealth of mahajans, the ingenuity of scientists, the activities of entrepreneurs, the skills of artisans—everything has come to a halt . . .' Sarajubala Dasgupta, *Debottar Vishwanatya* (Calcutta, 1322/ 1915), p. 155.

[85] *Achalayatan* (1911), *Muktadhara* (1922), *Raktakarabi* (1926).

[86] *Debottar*, pp. 96–7.

[87] Ibid., p. 120.

The post-Swadeshi years, and more specifically the mid-1910s, do seem to have been marked by considerable iconoclastic writing, both about, and by, women. *Debottar*, it should be noted, was almost exactly contemporaneous with Sailabala Ghosh Jaya's *Sheikh Andu* (serialised in *Prabasi*, 1914–15). This was a daring depiction of passion across lines of both religious community and class that brought together, though only briefly, the Muslim chauffeur Andu and Jyotsna, widowed friend of his employer's daughter.[88]

But how did such unconventional writing about gender relate to nationalism? Foreign rule is irrelevant to Sarajubala's play and Sailabala's novel, while the emancipatory potential concerning gender that is evident in the *Sabuj Patra* stories and in *Ghare-Baire* is clearly related to Rabindranath's critical self-distancing from nationalism in the post-Swadeshi era. Yet it will not do to conceptualise the relationship of nationalism to stri-swadhinata in solely antagonistic terms. *Ghare-Baire* itself contains a tremendously evocative passage where Bimala recalls how, even before the coming of Sandip, the sudden dawn of Swadeshi had brought a message of freedom also for a housewife like herself.[89] And conversely, it is tempting to suggest that the shifts and experimentations in thinking about women during the post-Swadeshi decade could have flowed back, just a little, into the next wave of mass anti-colonial struggle during 1919–22.

Certainly Non-Cooperation–Khilafat was significantly different from the Swadeshi days, so far as the active participation of women was concerned. Not only did women now join demonstrations and picketing: at the initiative of the women relatives of Chittaranjan Das they even started courting arrest in Bengal at the height of the movement, in winter 1921–2.

[88] Jnanesh Maitra, p. 245; P.K. Datta, 'Impossible Loves: The Implications of Narrative Recuperations in Sailabala Ghosh Jaya's *Sheikh Andu* and Begum Rokeya Hossein's *Padmarag*', in *Studies in Humanities and Social Sciences*, volume v.i, 1998.

[89] 'My sight and my mind, my hopes and my desires, became red with the passion of this new age. Though, up to this time, the walls of the home, which was the ultimate world to my mind—remained unbroken, yet I stood looking over into the distance, and I heard a voice from the far horizon, whose meaning was not perfectly clear to me, but whose call went straight to my heart.' *Home and the World*, p. 26.

Let me end with a contemporary account of a Calcutta street scene, taken from the *Amrita Bazar Patrika* of 2 February 1922. A meeting had taken place the previous day at College Square, defying a police ban, and attended by some three to four thousand people. Speeches were made by Hemaprava Majumdar, Binodini Sarkar, 'a Gurkha lady, and two other Bengali ladies—As the ladies were making their speeches, the sergeants went on belabouring the people with lathies.' In the classic Gandhian manner, the crowd refused to be provoked into violence, but stood its ground and refused to disperse. Hemaprava was herself hit on the wrist by a lathi while trying to protect a boy. She then told the police 'that the audience would not disperse at the police violence, but if the police withdrew she would dissolve the meeting as the business was finished'. The police obeyed her command, shifted to one side, and only then did the crowd disperse, in a disciplined manner.

Here we see women, very much out of the 'home' and in the public, political space, providing leadership in a nationalist assertion of autonomy over that space in the face of state violence. Straightforward inspiration, total detachment, a definitive resolution through the home/world divide: none of these formulas appear adequate for grasping the shifting, complicated, dialectical relationships between nationalism and the women's question.

CHAPTER VI

Postmodernism and the Writing of History*

RECENT YEARS have witnessed a somewhat ambiguous coming together of philosophy and history, as the truth claims of both come under trenchant scrutiny through a linguistic-cum-literary turn which has tried to invert the traditional primacy of logic over rhetoric. What has brought philosophy and history closer is the common critique directed at them. Emanating from new forms of literary theory, this critique seeks to blur genre distinctions between literature, philosophy, and indeed all disciplines, and grants to literary criticism, in Habermas's words, 'an almost world-historical mission' to seek out and destroy the metaphysics of presence everywhere.[1] Herein lies one major constituent of what, conveniently, if vaguely, have come to be called postmodernist moods.

I use 'moods' advisedly, for postmodernism, as is well known, not only eludes but rejects precise definition or systematisation. Part of

*Earlier versions of this essay have been presented as the Sudhir Bose Memorial Lecture at the Department of Philosophy, St Stephen's College, Delhi, March 1998, and published in *Studies in History*, 15,2, n.s., 1999. I have benefited greatly from the very helpful criticisms and comments during the discussions that followed my lecture, and, while finalising this version, from the suggestions of Aditya Sarkar.

[1] Jurgen Habermas, *The Philosophical Discourse of Modernity* (Frankfurt, 1985; trans. Polity, Cambridge, 1987), p. 192.

the problem is that even a very preliminary and partial *tour de horizon* reveals an enormous variety of intellectual trends and historical contexts that have helped to constitute these moods. There has been the transition, rooted in the development of linguistics, from structuralist to poststructuralist positions, from Saussure's arbitrary nature of the sign to the Derridaean universe of *differance* and free-floating signifiers. The accompanying swing towards more or less extreme forms of epistemological and ethical relativism have been strengthened by tendencies of quite different origin: in particular by the significant revival of interest in Nietzsche. Habermas in fact locates in Nietzsche the fountainhead of two intellectual currents, one pointing towards Foucault, the other towards Derrida. The relentless reduction of all ideals, motives, and institutions to the workings of the 'will to power' eventually grounds that striving in the power to create meanings. The counterpoint then can only come from a will to illusion, and so art becomes man's genuine metaphysical activity, stimulating an aestheticisation of life that enthrones 'taste . . . as the organ of a knowledge beyond true or false, beyond good and evil.'[2] Nietzsche had combined a rejection of Christian morality with a regrounding of ethics in aesthetics, and the desire to go beyond truth and falsity implied a denigration of at least the conventional forms of rationalism. Significantly, his *Untimely Meditations* had included a powerful critique of history.[3]

But today's critiques of Enlightenment rationalism also have connections with other, on the whole more nuanced, intellectual streams.

[2] Habermas, op. cit., pp. 95–6.

[3] Thus Nietzsche's *On the uses and disadvantages of history for life* (1874) used a series of evocative analogies—rather than logic—to condemn the contemporary 'surfeit' of history. Animals and children are happy, since they live without the burden of deep memories. '. . . a man seized by a vehement passion, for a woman or for a great idea . . . forgets most things so as to do one thing, he is unjust towards what lies behind him'—while 'a man who wanted to feel historically through and through would be like one forcibly deprived of sleep.' With characteristic elitism, Nietzsche went on to suggest that history, while dangerous for 'the impotent and indolent . . . dancing mob', could be helpful, in a deliberately selective and partial manner, for 'the man of deeds and power, to him who fights a great fight . . .' Friedrich Nietzsche, *Untimely Meditations*, ed. J.P. Stern (Cambridge, 1983), pp. 62–4, 67.

In particular, one needs to recall the later developments within Frankfurt School Marxism during its New York exile, culminating in Adorno and Horkheimer's *Dialectics of Enlightenment*. There are interesting paradoxes here, for Marxism is often condemned today for being an allegedly inextricable part of the 'Enlightenment project', while perhaps the most substantial philosophical arguments against postmodernism have been coming from the last representative of the Frankfurt tradition, Jurgen Habermas. Terms like 'Enlightenment rationalism'—as well as of Marxism's relations with it—may be in need of greater refinement than is often allowed within the rather homogenised polemics of much postmodernism.

Critics have found much in postmodernism that appears inconsistent, perhaps even incoherent: yet the sweeping advance of such moods in recent years is undeniable. Perhaps contexts here can be more important than inherent strength of argument. Three aspects seem particularly crucial.

Virtually all forms of postmodernism have been marked by a near-obsessive concern with power. Extended to realms far beyond authoritarian rule and class exploitation—the two forms prioritised in conventional liberal and Marxist criticism—power is seen to be all-pervasive and yet decentred. It penetrates to the very pores of everyday life, can become deeply internalised, and is all but irresistible, since 'effective' resistance tends to produce new forms of power. The counterpoint, if any, is felt to lie in the local, fragmentary, fleeting, marginal—as well as, sometimes, in survivals of the pre-modern or pre-colonial. Assumptions of, or quests for, 'totality' (including strivings for overall social transformation) then become the cardinal enemy, most notably in Lyotard, who has famously defined the postmodern as 'incredulity towards meta-narratives.'[4] The links here with

---

[4] Among the meta- or grand narratives characteristic of modernity, which postmodernism needs to discard, Lyotard mentions specifically 'the dialectics of Spirit, the hermeneutics of meaning, the emancipation of the rational or working subject, or the creation of wealth.' The alternative, for him, lies in a 'pragmatics of language particles. There are many different language games—a heterogeneity of elements. They only give rise to institutions in patches—local determinism.' J.F. Lyotard, *The Postmodern Condition: A Report on Knowledge* (Paris, 1979; Manchester, 1992), Introduction, p. xxiv.

repeated frustration of hopes for radical transformation are obvious enough. Nazi triumph in a country that had seemed to many to have been on the brink of socialist revolution, the growing loss of faith in the Stalinist Soviet Union, the spectacle of the 'culture industry' in advanced capitalist countries effectively co-opting workers—all these underlay the pessimism of the later Frankfurt School and found expression through its pioneering critique of the Enlightenment. The experiences of more recent years hardly need retelling: the ebbing of radical hopes once centred in Maoist China, Vietnam, May 1968, or the Prague Spring, and finally, of course, the collapse of the Soviet Union. And there is also the striking fact that many of the Parisian intellectuals who figure so prominently in any narrative of postmodernism had gone through spells within the French Communist Party.

Beyond this experience of defeat and disillusionment, the attractions of postmodernism, particularly in literary and artistic expression, have resided also in its evident resonances with many features of today's vastly transformed world. Globalisation—polite term for the new forms of triumphant world capitalism—is associated obviously with pressures for uniformities and homogenisation that often seem oppressive. But our times are characterised also by diversity, difference, a welter of conflicting ethnic identities, fragmentations of the self. In the postmodern imagination, correspondingly, Matthew Arnold's *Dover Beach* gets displaced by the international airport lounge, to draw upon the analogy suggested by a feminist critic.[5] Again, postmodernism's sense of a crisis of representationality—of it having become difficult to demarcate image from reality, surfaces from depths and foundations (which may not, perhaps, exist)—has clear connections with today's communication revolutions and forms of consumerism. For Baudrillard, consumer objects have become a

---

[5] Postmodernism, she suggests, tends towards 'decentering consciousness itself', and finds 'no universal ground of truth, justice or reason . . . no longer origin, author, location of intentional agency . . . no ethics, no aesthetics because existence itself is aestheticised, and no ideology because no "truth"—at best provisional consensus, pragmatism, interpretative communities.' Patricia Waugh, *Stalemates? Feminists, Postmodernists and Unfinished Issues in Modern Aesthetics*, in Philip Rice and Patricia Waugh, eds, *Modern Literary Theory: A Reader* (London, etc., 1989, 1992), p. 341.

network of floating signifiers, inexhaustible in their ability to incite desire, a world of simulacra where the contrasts between the imaginary and the real get increasingly undermined.[6] And indeed today leaders are made and unmade through their television images, vast amounts of liquid capital speed across continents on computer screens, and unprecedented masses of information are stored or transmitted not through tangible physical objects like manuscripts or books, but across the mysterious cyberspace of the internet. Not surprisingly, Frederic Jameson, the not-unsympathetic Marxist critic of postmodernism, has found in it the central 'cultural logic of late capitalism'.[7]

What remains much more controversial is the precise quality of response of various postmodernisms to an undoubtedly much-transformed world—the political implications of the stances they have adopted. The question is valid and relevant particularly because enough of the language of 1960s radicalism has persisted within the bulk of postmodernism, making most of its spokespersons insist upon theirs being 'political interventions' of invariably 'oppositional' or 'transgressive' kinds. Critical commentaries have sometimes tried to distinguish between more nonconformist, even utopian, and 'commercial or 'coopted' brands of postmodernism.[8] Despite the radical rhetoric, the 'coopted' elements do seem to predominate, on the

[6] Mark Poster, ed., Jean Baudrillard, *Selected Writings* (Stanford, 1988), Introduction, pp. 2–3, 6.

[7] Frederic Jameson, 'Postmodernism, or the Cultural Logic of Late Capitalism', *New Left Review*, 146, July–August 1984. Jameson's line of argument has been extended and enriched by David Harvey, *The Condition of Postmodernity: An Enquiry into the Origins of Cultural Change* (Cambridge Mass and Oxford, 1990). Harvey explores the interconnections between a wide range of postmodernist moods and the post-1973 transition in global capitalism from Fordist-Keynesian strategies to 'flexible accumulation'.

[8] Thus E. Ann Kaplan writes about 'what may be called a "utopian" postmodernism (which moves in a Derridaean direction)', as distinct from 'a commercial or "coopted" one (which moves in a Baudrillardian direction).' E. Ann Kaplan, ed., *Postmodernism and Its Discontents* (London, 1988), Introduction, p. 3. Even Alex Callinicos' much more aggressive and unqualified polemic at times tries to distinguish Deleuze, Derrida and Foucault, with their 'partial insights', from Lyotard and Baudrillard. Alex Callinicos, *Against Postmodernism: A Marxist Critique* (Oxford, 1989,1992), p. 3, and *passim*.

whole. Postmodernism often seems to swim, even wallow, in the fragmentary and chaotic currents of change, in celebratory ways.[9] Precisely here, Jameson has suggested, lies the crucial distinction between modernist and postmodernist forms of art, despite many anticipations and similarities (e.g. in the moves away from realist representational conventions) which make dubious the exaggerated claims to absolute novelty that are often heard today. Modernism had often shocked contemporary established tastes—one recalls the classic stereotype of the alienated artist dying in poverty like Van Gogh, immortalised only afterwards. Postmodernist art, in contrast, tends to get immediately institutionalised, for the economic urgency of producing ever more novel-seeming goods has imparted an increasingly structural function to aesthetic innovation and experimentation. Correspondingly, postmodernism tends to discard the sharp distinction between 'high' and mass commercial culture and hostility towards the 'culture industry' which had once been common to most varieties of modernism. The alienation of the subject has been displaced by the fragmentation of the subject, Jameson concludes, making the possibilities of effective resistance far more problematic.[10]

A serious qualification might seem in order at this point to the generally negative assessment of postmodernism I have been outlining, in terms of the new spaces it has created for a range of undoubtedly oppositional trends: feminism, above all; critiques of modern scientific technology and related ecological concerns and movements; exposures of colonialism, focused, following Said, on its cultural-literary dimensions. Along with the collapse of older transformational hopes and resonances with the changed, post-1970s world of globalised capitalism, these constitute a third kind of contextual appeal for postmodernism. The contexts relevant here include the upsurge in feminist movements and theories from the 1970s, the growing importance of environmentalist or Green activism, the new centrality of problems of non-white immigration, race and ethnic conflicts in metropolitan countries, and a novel importance attached to some expatriate Third World intellectuals within First World academia. The last constitutes, it has been cogently argued, much of the explanation for the

[9] David Harvey, op. cit., p. 44.
[10] Jameson, op. cit., p. 66.

sudden prominence of yet another variety of 'post-' theories —
postcoloniality.[11]

For many of these new tendencies, the 'man' of European humanism is felt to be irremediably white and male, complicit with, indeed
inseparable from, both patriarchal and colonial structures. Through
a convenient though somewhat homogenising shorthand, 'Enlightenment rationalism' has become the central polemical target. Attacks
on the Enlightenment are of course nothing new, and can if we like
be traced back through Romanticism to Rousseau. But certainly
twentieth-century developments have put unprecedentedly troubling
question-marks against the easy faith, common for long to bourgeois
liberals and most Marxists, in the benefits of man's conquest of nature
through scientific technology.[12] For some varieties of feminism,
again, as well as for the bulk of the critics of 'colonial knowledge',
the universalist claims and conceptions of individual rights associated
with the Enlightenment are in need of total repudiation. Enlightenment Reason appears to them as no more than the destructive, and
ultimately self-destructive, Reason of Western Man. Problems remain, however, as to whether any emancipatory project can really
afford such a total and homogenised rejection—problems perhaps
most acute, as I shall briefly argue in a subsequent section, for feminism,[13] as well as for societies where bourgeois-liberal institutions and
values are weak or non-existent.

[11] 'When exactly . . . does the "post-colonial" begin?'. . . I will supply here an
answer that is only partially facetious: When Third World intellectuals have
arrived in First World academe.' Arif Dirlik, 'The Postcolonial Aura: Third
World Criticism in the Age of Global Capitalism', *Critical Inquiry*, 20, ii, Winter
1994. For another, pioneering critique, see Aijaz Ahmad, *In Theory* (London,
1992; Delhi, 1993), chapter v.

[12] Here, as in much else, the Frankfurt School were pioneers. Already in his
doctoral thesis of 1930, Horkheimer had related the Renaissance view of science
and technology to political domination, mastery over nature as interrelated to
mastery over other human beings. He came to feel subsequently that Marx had
dangerously overemphasised labour as man's principal mode of self-realisation—
the 'production paradigm', which Habermas too rejects. Martin Jay, *The Dialectical Imagination* (California, 1973, 1996), pp. 257–9.

[13] For an exceptionally nuanced analysis of feminism's necessarily ambiguous
relations with postmodernism, developed through a critique of Lyotard, see Seyla
Benhabib, 'Feminism and the Question of Postmodernism', in *Situating the Self:*

It will be evident that I can only touch on a few of the themes I have indicated in this rapid conspectus. My central concern is about postmodernism's impact on the historian's craft. I intend therefore to focus primarily on postmodernist questionings of history, in terms of their validity, as well as impact on historical practice. This will be followed by a briefer look at critiques of Enlightenment rationalism and colonial discourse, and some discussion of the simultaneous questionings and prioritisations of identity that have been characteristic of much postmodernism. I want to argue a case for two general propositions. There are aspects of postmodernism which can, and at times demonstratively have, proved not only unavoidable and relevant, but extremely fruitful for historical practice: mine is not an argument for a return to the old certainties, unmodified. At the same time, these benefits can be obtained only through a simultaneous struggle against many of the built-in thrusts within postmodernism. These include, notably, the rejection of all forms of universalism as necessarily homogenising, accompanied by an absolute valorisation of the 'fragment'; a pervasive 'culturalist' turn; and the retreat from— indeed, the theoretical rejection of—all programmes of transformation that seek to go beyond the purely specific or the fleeting. An uncritical adoption of such postmodernistic assumptions and values as the latest intellectual fashion, an unreflective floating with the tide, has produced, amidst incessant claims to novelty and transgression, a truly depressing quantum of banality and dangerous conformism.[14]

Gender, Community and Postmodernism in Contemporary Ethics (Cambridge, 1992), chapter 7. I came across Benhabib's essay after completing the St Stephen's College lecture and the Studies in History article, and am happy to discover a considerable convergence of views between us.

[14] Commenting on my paper, Ania Loomba has suggested that a distinction between 'post-structuralism' and 'postmodernism' might be helpful for clarifying my position. The first would refer to sets of tools and methods open to usages with widely varied intellectual and political implications, including in particular many feminist deployments that have proved very helpful. The second would relate to moods on the whole accommodative of late-capitalist pressures that need to be resisted. I am tempted by this distinction, but perhaps it needs to be complicated a bit further. I am not sure how far a methods/values disjunction is entirely tenable: thus poststructuralist methods and assumptions do seem to lean towards some philosophical and political affinities more than others. Distinctions might still remain necessary within both poststructuralism and postmodernism.

II

Criticism of (all, or most) modern history-writing has been one of the more ubiquitous elements in anti-modernism from Nietzsche onwards. The charges today are very wide-ranging, and it might be an useful exercise to try to distinguish between the various strands more precisely than is common, proceeding from the less to the more significant.

There is first the strategy of reducing opponents to straw figures, and here 'positivism' has become the great buzz word. The several different—not to say contradictory—usages of that term[15] get blithely ignored in the blanket assertion that all history-writing (indeed, sometimes all 'Western thought' or philosophy), prior to the great contemporary moment of postmodernist Revelation, has been guilty of positivism, and, more generally, of a truly remarkable degree of epistemological naivete.

Two Indian examples may suffice: from a literature scholar, and from a leading member of the Subaltern Studies group:

Tejaswini Niranjana has described 'Western philosophical notions of reality, representation and knowledge' in the following manner: 'Reality is seen as something unproblematic, "out there"; knowledge involves a representation of this reality; and representation provides direct, unmediated access to a transparent reality.'[16] It would surely be difficult to think of any philosopher, even the crudest advocate of materialism and reflection theory, who has been that naive.

And here is a very recent account, by Gyanendra Pandey, describing how 'contributors to *Subaltern Studies*' have 'moved on also to critique the givenness of history and historical categories'. The polemical targets here consist of alleged views about history as 'just

[15] Positivism, of course, was associated originally with Comte, and therefore with generalisation and systematisation on a colossal scale. By the inter-war years, it was being used more to refer to the Logical Positivists of the Vienna Circle, empiricist critics of metaphysical system-building. A term that has been employed to describe thinkers as far removed from each other as Auguste Comte and Karl Popper should obviously be used with greater care.

[16] Tejaswini Niranjana, 'Translation, Colonialism and the Rise of English', in Svati Joshi, ed., *Rethinking English: Essays in Literature, Language, History* (New Delhi, 1991), p. 125.

something "out there", waiting to be recovered', as well as an 'auto-matic presumption of "authenticity" for particular kinds of historical sources and evidence (eyewitness accounts, private letters and diaries, and so on) . . .'[17] I am puzzled: surely testing sources for degrees of authenticity have been integral to 'positivist' historical procedures ever since the era of Ranke? As for assumptions of unproblematic, total objectivity, the claim notoriously made by Lord Acton on the first page of the *Cambridge Modern History* a hundred years ago was actually given up by most historians several generations back.[18] I can recall being told about the differences in this respect between the old and the new Cambridge History series by my undergraduate teachers in the late 1950s.

Notable in polemic of this kind is the use of single quotes, as well as capitals, in a rather elementary rhetorical ploy, to suggest that op-ponents are guilty of crass simplification and homogenisation in their deployment of the impugned categories. Postmodernism, with its insistence on overthrowing generic distinctions between literary and other discourses, has often been very helpful in exposing the rhetorical strategies within other people's writings: such passages, by no means infrequent, indicate a remarkable blindness to one's own. The point is worth making only because it leads on to something much more substantial. A polemic that so drastically simplifies its Other is pecu-liarly open to the danger of homogenising itself. Critics of what are described endlessly as the 'grand narratives' of Reason, Enlighten-ment, Progress, Orientalism, Colonial Discourse (quite often in the singular, it may be noted), etc., surely are often engaged in construct-ing grand narratives of their own, merely inverting the value judge-ments. We shall shortly encounter several such examples of continu-ity-through-inversion.

---

[17] Gyanendra Pandey, 'Subaltern Studies: From A Critique of Nationalism to a Critique of History', paper presented at a seminar on Problematising History and Agency: From Nationalism to Subalternity, University of Cape Town, October 1997, pp. 4–5.

[18] 'So far as truth can be known to mortal men, so far as learned, impartial judgement can be final, we have it here'—the covers of the Cambridge Modern History volumes, published around the turn of the nineteenth–twentieth cen-tury, used to carry this assertion of Acton.

At *this* level, Lawrence Stone's rejoinder to charges of crude positivism, through a simple recall of his own historical training in the 1940s, appears sufficient.[19] But Stone's further implicit suggestion that there is not much else in the linguistic-cum-postmodern turn worth consideration has evoked less support, and understandably so.[20] For underlying anti-positivist polemics there are the traces of a much more significant, broader pull towards relativistic positions which cannot be dismissed so readily as irrelevant. Relativistic questionings of an external reality independent of consciousness or perceptions have been a recurrent feature of both Western and other philosophical traditions. Such probings can have undeniable value, as critiques of unwarranted, commonsensical certainties.[21] Though theoretically discarded a long time back, implicit assumptions of 'facticity'—history as consisting of absolutely certain facts or events, free of value judgements—do creep into much everyday historical writing and teaching, and predominate particularly at the level of elementary textbooks. It remains fairly easy to forget that a historical 'fact' becomes that only within a particular narrative framework, and so always implies not absolute objectivity or givenness, but choice, value, construction.[22]

One needs to emphasise, at the same time, that paradoxically a totalised critique of reason might actually undercut the capacity of

[19] Lawrence Stone, 'History and Postmodernism', *Past and Present*, 135, May 1992.

[20] See, for instance, Raphael Samuel, 'Reading the Signs', *History Workshop Journal*, 32, Autumn 1991.

[21] Even the Marxist Antonio Gramsci felt that the philosophical discussion of the 'reality of the external world . . . is certainly not pure futility, even for a philosophy of praxis . . .' He even suggested that the commonsensical, unquestioning belief in the objective existence of the external world could have religious origins, and therefore is not free from problems. Antonio Gramsci, *Selections from the Prison Notebooks*, eds Hoare and Smith (London, 1971), pp. 440–2.

[22] Gyanendra Pandey therefore is not entirely flogging a dead horse, though the claim to originality in this regard on behalf of 'Subaltern Studies' remains rather absurd. One could recall E.H. Carr's well-known instance in his *What is History?*: Julius Caesar crossing the Rubicon is normally taken to be a significant historical fact—but so many have crossed that stream before and since.

reason to be critical.[23] All statements then become indistinguishable, from the point of view of relative probability or dubiousness, and we are left free to pick and choose, on grounds of pragmatic utility, aesthetic appeal, or sheer dogmatic belief. What gets strengthened are precisely tendencies, otherwise rightly critiqued by postmodernism, towards instrumental rationality and dogmatic authoritarianism.

Relativistic pulls are nothing new, but there is an important, specific quality in the postmodern turn in that direction. This has been provided by Derrida's efforts to level the generic distinction between literary and other uses of language on the grounds that all texts without exception abound in rhetorical tropes. Deconstruction reveals hidden rhetorical surpluses even in philosophical, historical, scientific or other texts that by claim or authorial intent are non-literary. Questions of truth, in the sense of approximations to actual happenings, then become as irrelevant as they normally are for imaginative literature: distinctions between a history text and a historical novel threaten to disappear.

Once again, there is a need to distinguish between an often valuable focus on language and rhetoric that has been part of a wider 'literary turn' and which actually much precedes Derrida, and extensions of such moves towards a total rejection of genre distinctions. Thus, already in 1978, Hayden White's *Tropics of Discourse* had tried to probe the tropes implicit in E.P. Thompson's *Making of the English Working Class*, while simultaneously rejecting 'radical scepticism': 'I have never denied that knowledge of history, culture and society was possible.'[24]

Two types of rejoinders have been suggested to the overthrowing of genre distinctions and its extreme-sceptical corollaries. The first, reminiscent of arguments against earlier types of philosophical

[23] An important point made by Thomas McCarthy in his Introduction to J. Habermas, *The Philosophical Discourse of Modernity*, p. xvii.

[24] Hayden White, *Tropics of Discourse: Essays in Cultural Criticism* (Baltimore, 1978), p. 23. The problem with that text by White had consisted, rather, in an over-neat, highly schematic, framework of tropes allegedly embedded in historical writings—an approach that recalls the constraining dimensions of some varieties of structuralist analysis.

relativism, proceeds through extreme examples of the ethicopolitical perils implicit in assertions of the equal validity, or its reverse, of all representations. Stephen Greenblatt, for instance—who combines to my mind in an exemplary manner a brilliant deployment of the best in postmodernistic techniques with acute awareness of its dangerous pulls—cites a particularly horrific account of European colonial barbarism in Java (left by a seventeenth-century East India Company trader) to pose the question as to what difference it would make if the referentiality of this narrative is declared to be a matter of indifference. He finds this quite unacceptable in circumstances like these, and concludes that 'the poststructuralist confounding of fiction and non-fiction is important but inadequate'.[25]

I find more convincing the second type of argument, formulated by Habermas, as this confronts directly the new element in postmodern relativism—its denial of genre distinctions in language-use. Rhetorical elements, Habermas grants, are inseparable from all deployment of language. One could add that deconstruction is helpful in so far as it can make historians much more aware, than they traditionally have been, both of the language games they are playing (consider for example the common use of the authorial 'we', implying reader-complicity), as well as of the rhetorical elements in the representations they use as their sources. But is the place and role of rhetoric identical across all genres? And is it necessarily always the same kind of rhetoric: i.e. is there not a certain danger of essentialising that term, too? Habermas suggests a necessary distinction between the dominantly self-referential language-use in poetry and imaginative fiction, and languages of everyday life and academic disciplines where 'the rhetorical elements, which are by no means expunged, are tamed, as it were, and enlisted for special purposes of problem-solving.' There is, then, a continuum, but with significant distinctions, with rhetoric playing different roles in specific contexts of communicative action. Derrida, Habermas argues, has permitted 'the capacity to solve problems to disappear behind the world-creating capacity of language'.[26]

I have been reviewing, so far, some of the current epistemological

---

[25] Stephen Greenblatt, *Learning to Curse: Essays in Early Modern Culture* (London, 1990), Introduction, p. 15.

[26] Habermas, op. cit., pp. 205, 209.

doubts about history-writing. But equally if not more prominent have been attacks focused on history's alleged special complicities with power. At its simplest, this sometimes takes the form of sweeping assertions that the 'historians' history' has been bound up with the modern 'nation-state project', and hence incorrigibly 'statist'. '[. . . a]ll histories since the nineteenth century have been national histories', Gyanendra Pandey argues, due to the 'historian's privileging of the viewpoint of the state.'[27] There are several assertions here that demand unpacking. Histories dealing with states or nations are not necessarily statist or nationalist, any more than research on communalism is inevitably communal. The political implications of a historical account are conditioned primarily by the values, approaches and choices made by the writer, not by the subject or kind of source material (which, for many areas, might have to be primarily official). It is possible to use non-official, popular, oral material for deeply statist or conservative purposes, and vice versa. A second confusion is the tacit collapsing of all forms of nationalism into purely political, statist projects, ignoring the ample evidence for forms of cultural nationalism that have actually been anti-statist in various romantic-populist ways. And of course such arguments brush aside all manner of oppositional histories, notably the rich traditions of radical, socialist or Marxist, and feminist history-writing prior to the present unique moment of Subalternist redemption.

More serious are critiques of history deriving from Lyotard's distinction between a pre-modern fluid, free, popular universe of narrativisation in the form of storytelling, and the abstract world of modern, professionalised, 'scientific' discourses (including, of course, history) that perpetually seek legitimation through argument and debate, which try to rule out discourses they think they can prove to be false, and which are therefore allegedly intolerant and bound up with power. There are echoes of Nietzsche here, but also a much more unambiguous valorisation of the pre-modern. Conventional or commonsensical notions about the relative status of myth and history, and the value or otherwise of verificatory procedures, are sought to be inverted. That hypotheses in science, or in disciplines like history, try

[27] Gyanendra Pandey, 'The Prose of Otherness', in David Arnold and David Hardiman, *Subaltern Studies VIII* (Delhi, 1994), pp. 190, 193, 214.

to remain open to the possibility of being falsified (or at least shown to be less probable than other propositions), paradoxically becomes the ground for charges of dogmatic, power-laden imposition. Conversely, the pre-modern, 'popular', sometimes the non-Western, is homogenised and construed as somehow totally free of internal power structures. That mythic narratives may have often been transmitted by specialised groups, not necessarily unconnected with power, is never considered even as a possibility. As so often in postmodernist writings, the argument proceeds fundamentally through suggestive analogy and metaphor, and also often latches on to current romantic valorisations of the 'popular' and the 'primitive'. These positions in fact are often deeply 'Orientalising', for they tacitly assume non-Western traditions to have been popular in an undifferentiated, essentialised manner, ignoring the presence within most of them of well-developed, classical or high-cultural elements.[28] Pre-modern narrative for Lyotard becomes a way of 'consuming' the past, as contrasted to its 'storage, hoarding and capitalisation in science and scientific thought'—an 'accumulation' inseparable from questions of power and domination. Why myths or fables, which after all are also 'stored', in the sense of being retold across generations, should be declared analogous with immediate consumption or use-value is left unexplained.[29] A comparison with Walter Benjamin's brilliant insights about the changing forms of storytelling, their connections with the evolution and eventual decline of artisanal production, and their fate in the age of mechanical reproduction immediately reveals the extent of impoverishment that a homogenised binary polarity can produce

[28] Benhabib has brought out this 'Orientalising' dimension of Lyotard's construction of pre-modern narrative knowledge with exceptional clarity: 'Lyotard constructs the epistemology of narrative knowledge in such a way that the only appropriate attitude to adopt towards it is the standpoint of the curator of an ethnological museum of the past . . .' This might appear to be an attitude of respect, 'a gesture of solidarity with the oppressed', but actually we are condemning 'the subjects of this episteme to ahistoricity. We do not interact with them as equals . . . You cannot respect the "otherness" of the other if you deny the other the right to enter into a conversation with you . . .' Benhabib, 'Feminism and the Question of Postmodernism', in *Situating the Self*, pp. 233–4.

[29] Lyotard, *The Postmodern Condition*, op. cit, p. xii.

within what, at first sight might appear a not dissimilar problematic.[30] And the possible consequences of such arguments seem particularly worrying when one has to confront, as in India recently, modern productions of 'myths' like that of the Ramjanmabhumi that claim inherent superiority over history-writing by virtue of unexamined claims that they are 'popular'.

Some curious notions about the relationship between history and myth have become rather widespread today. It is often assumed that academics exploring the domains of myth, popular memories, oral traditions and histories conceived outside the professional guild are doing something new and courageous, challenging through their choice of themes alone the presuppositions of modern, statist, positivist historiography imported from the West. Actually, historians have been working with such material for a very long time, in a venerable tradition going back through Michelet to Vico. Myths, again, are by no means immune from statist readings, as for instance in Hemchandra Raychaudhuri, who uses puranic king-lists to construct a narrowly-political narrative of ancient Indian history with an evident nationalist slant. Similar mythic material can produce histories of a very different sort, when, say, Marc Bloch studies medieval legends of the king's touch curing disease, or when Romila Thapar works on ancient lineages. The substantial point relates to whether all procedures for verification or criteria of (relative) validity—which of course may well be diverse and subject to change—should be abandoned altogether, which seems to be the implication of Lyotard's conclusion that 'All we can do is gaze in wonderment at the diversity of discursive species, just as we do at the diversity of plant or animal

[30] Walter Benjamin, 'The Storyteller', and 'The Work of Art in the Age of Mechanical Reproduction', in *Illuminations*, ed. Hannah Arendt (New York, 1969). Benjamin often seems to be engaged in a critical dialogue with Nietzsche, and through that with a series of themes which have later become characteristic of postmodernism. See for instance the famous aphorism with which Benjamin concludes his essay on the 'Age of Mechanical Reproduction': 'Man kind['s] . . . self-alienation has reached such a degree that it can experience its own destruction as an aesthetic pleasure of the first order. This is the situation of politics which Fascism is rendering aesthetic. Communism responds by politicizing art.' Ibid., p. 242.

species.'[31] An eschewing of analytical or critical thrusts in favour, presumably, of a strictly hermeneutic approach that uses only the categories already present in the myths could amount to a simple re-telling, or at best the unearthing of new myths in quite conventional, folklorist-antiquarian (indeed, 'positivistic') fashion. Paradoxically, the often valuable tools of postmodernist language-analysis are being deliberately eschewed here. And it is important to recognise that efforts to work on mythic material for analytic exercises need not mean its abolition, or necessarily result in reductive denigration of its value. Such an attribution, by yet another paradox, implicitly equates the worthwhile with the factual—in inverted continuity with positivistic assumptions.

For Lyotard, and indeed for much recent postmodernism, 'modern' or 'scientific' discourses are objectionable and inevitably power-ridden primarily because they are 'foundational', grounded in grand or meta or master narratives—among which, very often, Marxian ones become the preferred targets for polemic.[32] The projected alternative is 'local knowledge', a valorisation of the 'fragment', and here the two strands of the postmodernist critique of history—epistemological doubt and the charge of exceptional entanglements with power—often come together. Yet it remains unclear why the local, fragmentary or fleeting should be immune from either of these charges. That knowledge of particulars can be somehow direct and certain, while generalisations are dangerous, is paradoxically a classically positivistic position put forward, for instance, many years ago by Karl Popper. Once again, some varieties of postmodernism fall into the same errors they repeatedly discover in their opponents.[33]

[31] Lyotard, op. cit, p. 26.

[32] Thus for Lyotard, 'everywhere the critique of political economy [the sub-title of Marx's Capital] and its correlate, the critique of alienated society, are used in one way or another as aids in programming the system.' In another move that has become characteristic of much postmodernism, he refuses to draw distinctions between varying forms of Marxism, even those as different as Stalinism and the Frankfurt School. Heidegger's notorious pro-Nazi inaugural speech as Rector of Freiburg-in-Bresgau can then be brushed aside as just one more 'unfortunate episode in the history of legitimation.' Ibid., pp. 13, 37.

[33] Frederic Jameson has made some caustic comments about the 'latter-day transmogrification of these same quite unphilosophical, empirical and anti-systemic positivist attitudes and opinions into heroic forms of resistance to

The problems are even more acute with respect to the question of power. For surely one of the more obvious features of today's world is that the local is becoming less and less immune from the operations of wider, indeed global, power structures; and that globalised capitalism simultaneously produces homogenisation and difference—as when multinationals encourage a degree of products differentiation to suit ethnically diverse markets. In an important critique of theories of postcoloniality, Arif Dirlik has argued that the cult of the fragment tends to confound ideological metanarratives with the actualities of power. Fragmentations in the first might actually further the consolidation of the second, for the (purely theoretical) rejection of global structures can produce a pattern of complicity through silence.[34] For 'rejection' can mean two very different things—'opposition to', and 'denying the existence of'—and postmodernist writing is often replete with such ambiguities and slippages. The complicity noted by Dirlik has become particularly obvious in some of the writings of Gyan Prakash, a recent recruit into Subaltern Studies who carries his rejection of 'foundational historiography' to the point of a condemnation of any effort to write modern history in terms of the development of capitalism. 'How is it possible', he asks, 'to write such a narrative, but also contest, at the same time, the homogenisation of the contemporary world by capitalism?'[35] How, it is tempting to respond, does one contest something without talking about it? The roots of this strange formulation—as I have elaborated elsewhere, and will touch on briefly later in this essay—lie in the now fairly common total bifurcation of the domains of power and resistance, in a crucial move away from the immanent critiques of structures that had been the strength of Marxian dialectical approaches.[36]

---

metaphysics and Utopian tyranny.' 'Actually Existing Marxism', in *Polygraph* 6/7: *Marxism Beyond Marxism?* (1993).

[34] Arif Dirlik, 'The Postcolonial Aura: Third World Criticism in the Age of Global Capitalism', *Critical Inquiry*, 20 ii, Winter 1994.

[35] Gyan Prakash, 'Writing Post-Orientalist Histories of the Third World: Perspectives from Indian Historiography', *Comparative Studies in Society and History*, 32, 1990.

[36] See my 'The Decline of the Subaltern in Subaltern Studies', in Sumit Sarkar, *Writing Social History* (Delhi, 1997), p. 90, and *passim*, for an elaboration of this point.

Superficially considered, many of Foucault's themes might seem to resemble or anticipate Lyotard's, and the impact of postmodernism does often take the form of either easy transitions from the earlier to the later thinker, or eclectic amalgams of both (with which, even less consistently, elements of Derrida might also get added). In a famous essay, Foucault grounded his distinctive critique of usual histories on a reading of Nietzsche, while of course 'power/knowledge' became increasingly central to his concerns, particularly, as he has explained in a partly self-critical interview, after the experiences and failure of May 1968. And 'local' is important too, both in the emphasis upon multiple, decentred forms of power, and the valorisation of local, fragmented—so to say offbeat—resistances (about and within prisons, for instance).[37] But the implications of Foucauldian ideas for the historian's craft have been very different from those being produced nowadays by Lyotard, and even the fiercest of critics of postmodernism might find it difficult to deny their immensely productive qualities. One need recall only the pioneering, specific studies of the histories of an immense range of power/knowledge regimes—asylums, hospitals, prisons, barracks, schools, factories, the history of sexuality as bound up with techniques of self-formation. Foucault has permanently expanded the range of historical studies of power relations beyond the conventionally defined 'political' and 'economic', into the pores of everyday life. Feminism, notably, has often felt empowered by some of his writings, even though directly feminist concerns are not very obvious in Foucault. After Foucault, again, many themes in modern Indian history for long considered conventional and somewhat boring—colonial administration, army, medicine, education— suddenly take on new interest and excitement as possible sites for examining the 'micro-physics' of power/knowledge. In significant contrast to Lyotard, Foucault's sustained theoretical critique of conventional histories in 'Nietzsche, Genealogy and History' was able to open up important, if controversial, questions that can stimulate

[37] Michel Foucault, 'Nietzsche, Genealogy, History' (1971), and the important interview, *Truth and Power*, published in the *Power/Knowledge* collection (1977). Both are included in Paul Rabinow, ed., *The Foucault Reader* (Harmondsworth, 1986).

research. There is no surrender, here or elsewhere in Foucault, to the temptations of mere aesthetic contemplation or rhetorical display.[38]

Yet major problems remain, for the ultimately Nietzschean thrust of Foucault's work both stimulates, and produces tensions difficult to resolve. The rejection of totalisation leads to 'a plurality of irregularly emerging and disappearing islands of discourse'[39]—, or, after Foucault has shifted from 'relations of meaning' to 'relations of power'—to distinct, incommensurable regimes of power/knowledge.[40] Yet certain tacit, underlying epochal patterns persist from *Madness and Civilisation* right through Foucault's writings. Repeatedly, dates around 1500, 1650, and 1800 become points of rupture—broadly, the familiar moments of Renaissance, absolutism, bourgeois revolution. One might go so far as to suggest that an unacknowledged, residual Marxism helps to give Foucault's specific analysis of discursive or power/knowledge shifts some of its effectiveness and precision— unlike the more sweeping denunciations of the whole of Western Reason that Nietzsche and many of today's postmodernists have indulged in. Where Foucault himself moves in that direction, other problems emerge. Thus 'Nietzsche, Genealogy and History' calls for

[38] Foucault in that essay rejected conventional histories for their assumptions of linear development, teleology (a 'monotonous finality'), and pretensions to 'an apocalyptic objectivity'. Such claims, he argued, assume a 'suprahistorical perspective', and see 'a history whose function is to compose the finally reduced diversity of time into a totality fully closed upon itself . . .' Following Nietzsche's 1874 essay, he condemned 'monumental history', dedicated to the exaltation of national pride. The purpose of the 'genealogy' Foucault suggested as alternative would be 'not to discover the roots of our identity, but to commit itself to its dissipation.' But the genealogy of Foucault is very different indeed from any easy play with fragments. It has to be 'grey, meticulous, and patiently documentary', dependent on 'a vast accumulation of source material . . . it corresponds to the acuity of a glance that distinguishes, separates, and disperses, that is capable of liberating divergence and marginal elements . . .' 'Nietzsche, Genealogy and History', in *Foucault Reader*, pp. 76, 86–7, 95.

[39] Habermas' description of the early work of Foucault, *Philosophical Discourse of Modernity*, Lecture IX, p. 251.

[40] In his *Truth and Power* interview, Foucault proclaimed his shift from 'the great model of language (*langue*) and signs, . . . to that of war and battle . . . relations of power, not relations of meaning'. *Foucault Reader*, p. 56.

a 'history without constants', a rigorous historicisation that would recognise that words, for instance, could change their meanings in different times and contexts. Yet Foucault also asserts in the same essay that 'in a sense, only a single drama is ever staged . . . the end-lessly repeated play of dominations', flowing from the will to know-ledge producing the will to power.[41] The banished 'suprahistorical' seems to be making a comeback, through what amounts to an essentialisation of 'power'. Charles Taylor, in a fine essay, poses a third set of questions. Foucault repeatedly presents himself in 'un-masking' roles, constantly talks of power or dominance—but how far is this logically reconcilable with his Nietzschean thrust towards a complete relativism of values, which threatens to leave us with totally distinct and homogenised epistemes-cum-regimes of power, incom-mensurable truth-effects bound up with corresponding structures of domination? Are categories of 'power' and 'illusion'—implying, pre-sumably, a lack of freedom and distance from truth or reality—con-ceptually maintainable without some possibility of standards of truth and freedom which have not been totally relativised?[42] And finally, as Taylor also mentions, there is the problem of Foucault's accounts of the disciplinary regimes of modernity often becoming 'terribly one-sided', divested of contradictory tendencies. The overwhelming emphasis on all-pervasive power/knowledge leaves little scope for effective counter-points. This profound pessimism, I have already suggested, has been in fact a recurrent feature of much postmodernism. In Foucault, its personal-political roots seem particularly clear: not only the aftermath of 1968, but also his experiences as an intellectual

[41] *Foucault Reader*, pp. 85, 87.

[42] Charles Taylor, 'Foucault on Freedom and Truth', in D.C. Hoys, ed., *Foucault: A Critical Reader* (Oxford, 1988), reprinted in *Studies in Humanities and Social Sciences*, Indian Institute of Advanced Study, Shimla, Winter 1995. Christopher Norris has made a similar point, noting a 'curious disjunction in Foucault's work between his passionate (intensely ethical) commitment to ex-posing . . . sources of oppression and his resolute refusal—on Nietzschean grounds—to acknowledge any truth-claims, principles or values that could equip that project with a normative basis.' Christopher Norris, 'Culture, Criticism, and Communal Values: On the Ethics of Enquiry', in Barbara Adam and Stuart Allan, eds, *Theorizing Culture: An Interdisciplinary Critique after Postmodernism* (London, 1995).

within the French Communist Party with its long-continued rigidities, with which, significantly, he began the sketch of his intellectual evolution in the *Truth and Power* interview.

A brief look now at the ways postmodernism has been influencing the practice of professional historians would reveal a similar pattern of potentialities and major limits. The initial phase of the linguistic (or semiological) turn, associated with the brief moment of structuralism and intense dialogues with social anthropology, helped to broaden enormously the domains of history by stimulating historians to search for the meanings of all manner of 'signs' in hitherto little-explored remains of the past. The paths pioneered, already from the 1930s, by the founders of the Annales tradition, Marc Bloch and Lucien Febvre,[43] became well trodden in what amounted to an era of major breakthroughs in social history.[44] If signs were recognised to be everywhere, however, poststructuralist questionings soon appeared to render all interpretations or meanings doubtful. Yet, as a generally critical assessment of postmodernism by a socialist historian has pointed out, 'the curious effect of these iconoclastic questions has been to greatly enlarge the potential field of scholarly enquiry.' The rhetoric of history has become an important field for investigation, historians have become much more aware of the need for probing the historicity of the categories they are using, 'sources' have taken on unexpected dimensions when read 'textually'.[45]

Perhaps I might be permitted a personal reference at this point.

---

[43] In his essay 'A New Kind of History', written in 1949, Febvre had insisted on the need to fashion history 'even without written documents if none is available'—from 'Words, signs, landscapes, titles, the layout of fields, weeds, eclipses of the moon, bridles, analysis of stones by geologists and of metal swords by chemists, in a word, anything which, belonging to man, depends on man, serves him, expresses him and signifies his presence, activity, tastes and forms of existence.' Peter Burke, ed., *A New Kind of History: From the Writings of Lucien Febvre* (London, 1973), p. 34.

[44] For perhaps a slightly over-celebratory account of that moment, see my 'Social History: Predicaments and Possibilities', Presidential Address, Modern Indian History section of the Indian History Congress, 1984; reprinted, *Economic and Political Weekly*, June 1985.

[45] Raphael Samuel, 'Reading the Signs II: Fact-grubbers and Mind-readers', in *History Workshop Journal, No. 33, Spring 1992.*

Despite my profound disagreements with the bulk of postmodernism (which must have become obvious), I cannot but acknowledge the ways in which it has influenced—I think, improved—my own historical practice. When I started research on Ramakrishna in the mid-1980s, I had looked at the record of his conversations, the *Ramakrishna-Kathamrita*, primarily in terms of its (fairly obvious) authenticity as a source. Finding traces in the *Kathamrita* of a learned literate knowledge/unlearned oral wisdom binary, I had seen it as evidence of the liminal moment when a rustic and nearly illiterate Brahman becomes the guru of highly educated bhadralok. I thought that I could use this source directly, as a kind of record or reflection of traces of village culture and religion on the one hand, and bhadralok life on the other. I came to recognise subsequently that the polarity I had noticed was also, indeed primarily, an authorial construct. Our only information about Ramakrishna comes from his bhadralok devotees, whose texts simultaneously illuminate and transform. This is not necessarily a disadvantage, for it was not a perhaps unapproachable Ramakrishna-by-himself, but rather the saint as constituted in the gaze of the late-nineteenth century urban bhadralok, which was the historical phenomenon I needed to investigate. But this shift in perspective was dependent on a degree of strategic distancing between representation and what it claimed to represent, and here postmodernism has been and remains a major stimulus.[46]

Postmodernism is benefiting historical practice also through its critique of over-simple unilinear and teleological models. Here there is important common ground with the achievements of feminist history in the West, which, from the 1970s onwards, has been problematising monolinear assessments of phenomena like the Renaissance and the French Revolution.[47] In my own field I have come to

[46] Sumit Sarkar, 'Kaliyuga, Chakri and Bhakti: Ramakrishna and His Times', in *Writing Social History*, pp. 283–8. I have attempted a similar exercise in the essay on Vidyasagar, included in the same volume, with the biographical texts about the reformer. The value of such strategic distancing is evident in much recent social-historical work. For a fine example, see Sarah Maza, *Private Lives and Public Affairs: The Causes Celebres of Pre-Revolutionary France* (California, 1993).

[47] An early landmark here was Joan Kelly-Gadol's 'Did Women Have A

feel, increasingly, that a single-track vision which collapses all developments of late-colonial South Asia into a colonial/anti-colonial binary is not only simplistic but at times positively harmful. Processes that cannot be shown to have 'contributed' to the 'freedom struggle' then tend to get ignored or condemned. It should be obvious that many of the essays in this volume, as indicated also by its title, seek to break some of these silences.

But postmodernism, I am equally convinced, can be helpful for history only if one simultaneously retains the ability to draw distinctions: guards, indeed struggles, against many of its inbuilt thrusts. Let me confine myself to two examples.

In recent years, a group of (mainly Italian) historians, among whom Carlo Ginzburg is the best known, have been developing a genre which they like to call 'microhistory'. At first sight this might seem similar to postmodernist valorisations of the local and the fragment, echoes of which have already become familiar in Indian history-writing.[48] Ginzburg's famous *The Cheese and the Worms* based itself on an admittedly isolated, fragmentary happening—the testimony extracted by the Inquisition from a single, quite exceptionally radical North Italian miller. It is unlikely that historians will unearth many Menocchios in the sixteenth century.[49] Such concentration on specifics, the subsequently elaborated microhistory argues, is helpful in enabling historians to remain constantly aware of the constructed nature of all phases of their research—aware, that is to say, not just in prefatory programmatic declarations, but through the course of investigation and writing, since the texts they are using remain manageable in number and can be investigated in minute detail. But Ginzburg immediately adds that what distinguishes microhistory 'is the insistence on context, exactly the opposite of the isolated contemplation of the fragmentary . . .' The emphasis upon the 'constructive'

Renaisance?', in Bridenthal and Koonz, eds, *Becoming Visible: Women in European History*.

[48] Gyanendra Pandey, 'In Defence of the Fragment: Writing about Hindu–Muslim Riots in India Today', *Economic and Political Weekly*, Annual Number, 1991.

[49] Carlo Ginzburg, *The Cheese and the Worms* (1976; Penguin, 1982).

elements involved in all research has to be combined with an 'explicit rejection' of the extremes of postmodernist scepticism. Italian micro-history has been given its distinctive quality by this 'cognitive wager',[50] a phrase that aptly combines a necessary recognition of uncertainties with a determination to avoid any closure of meaningful historical practice. In another essay, Ginzburg has elaborated this point through three vivid metaphors. Positivistic facticity looks upon evidence as an open window, while for relativists it is like a wall: both share the assumption of an unmediated relationship between evidence and reality, in affirmation or in denial. The more appropriate analogy would be a distorted glass: thorough analysis of its patterns of dis-tortions is indispensable, but that itself demands the rejection of 'a purely internal reading of the evidence, without any reference to its referential dimension.'[51]

My second instance is from the literary historian I have cited already, Stephen Greenblatt, founder of the so-called New Hist-oricism.[52] Stylistically, Greenblatt's writings might appear to ap-proximate to postmodernism at its best. There is a primary focus on high-cultural texts, unexpected transitions, startling asides that are apparently playful, and quick passages between different representa-tional forms—as when the essay on Thomas More (with which *Renaissance Self-fashioning* begins) moves easily to and from Holbein's painting *Ambassadors, Utopia,* and the *Dialogue of Comfort* written by the ex-Chancellor awaiting execution. The point here is not rhe-torical display but a skilfull exploration of the Renaissance in terms of the varied, often agonised, trajectories of intellectuals moving from service to the Church towards new, attractive yet dangerous, courtly careers. The richly ambiguous term 'self-fashioning' provides the key analytical category, for it implies both self-making (and so connects

[50] Carlo Ginzburg, 'Microhistory: Two or Three Things that I Know about It', *Critical Inquiry*, 20, Autumn 1993.

[51] Ibid., 'Checking the Evidence: The Judge and the Historian', *Critical Inquiry*, 18, Autumn 1991.

[52] 'So-called' because Greenblatt appears unhappy with the term, and has spent some time indicating how, for him, it stands for almost the reverse of dic-tionary meanings of historicism. 'Resonance and Wonder', in Stephen Green-blatt, *Learning to Curse*, op. cit.

with the traditional glorifying accounts of 'Renaissance Man'), and dressing up for others—ambiguities, Greenblatt suggests, which may have a lot to do with the new importance of theatre in Elizabethan and Jacobean England.[53] Postmodernist techniques here have enabled exceptionally nuanced studies of power and identity—but a necessary component in that achievement is Greenblatt's simultaneous awareness of their problems and limits. *Learning to Curse* is replete with such qualifications, in particular, as we have seen, about the dangers of extreme relativism. Even while brilliantly transgressing generic borders, Greenblatt remains wary of a total blurring of distinctions between literary criticism and historical research. This, he hints, can produce shoddy work in both, unless special efforts have been made to acquire the specific disciplinary tools: 'boundaries, provided they are permeable and negotiable, are useful things to think with.' And Greenblatt seems particularly relevant when he points to certain continuities between conservative and radical positions in English literary studies, in terms of a recurrent assumption that literary criticism can by itself constitute an effective act of political intervention. There is a need, Greenblatt concludes, 'to eschew an aestheticized and idealized politics of the imagination'[54]—an excellent description of much postmodernism.

But if postmodernism has helped to stimulate some of the best ongoing work in history, its uncritical, dogmatic, and purely polemical applications have had often, to put it mildly, extremely unfortunate consequences. The debate around Marxian social history in Britain can provide us with a convenient glimpse of this other, on the whole much more prominent, face of postmodernism.[55] The principal polemical target has been what may be called the Thompsonian moment of the 1960s and 1970s, which produced an exceptionally rich variety of creatively Marxian social history with a worldwide

[53] Stephen Greenblatt, *Renaissance Self-fashioning: From More to Shakespeare* (Chicago, 1980, 1984), chapter I, and *passim*.

[54] *Learning to Curse*, op. cit, pp. 5, 166.

[55] Much of this debate has taken place in the pages of the British journal *Social History*. For a more detailed account, with references, see my 'The Relevance of E.P. Thompson, in *Writing Social History*, op. cit., chapter II, particularly pp. 72–6.

impact (including, one needs to recall, an influence on Subaltern Studies in its first, radical 'history-from-below' phase). This was closely associated with generous dreams of democratic and humane forms of socialism, and so a retention of broadly Marxian horizons went along with sharp criticism of orthodox Marxist practice and theory.

In a move reminiscent of the tirades against positivism, the two specialists on nineteenth-century British labour history who have headed the attack, Gareth Stedman Jones and (much more aggressively) Patrick Joyce, have repeatedly sought to reduce the richness of this moment to the economistic rigidities of the cruder kinds of orthodox Marxism. For Joyce, all Marxism stands condemned because of its totalising nature, for being part of 'the modernist "grand narrative" project'—where, invariably, 'if society was the system, or the machine, class was the motive force . . . which drove the machine.' The mechanical analogy is of course almost ludicrously inappropriate,[56] as are the frequent efforts to convey an impression of heroic struggle against allegedly Thompsonian–Marxist domination of the historical 'establishment'. Marxism, even at moments of high academic influence, never became the kind of talisman for quick upward mobility that some forms of postmodernism seem to provide today.[57]

As with regard to positivism, again, polemical simplification tends to produce continuities via inversions, in effect substituting allegedly

[56] Patrick Joyce, 'The End of Social History?', *Social History*, 20, i, January 1996. The mechanical analogy is inappropriate not only for historians of the order of Thompson, Christopher Hill, and Eric Hobsbawm, but also for a host of Marxist historians in many parts of the world, including India. (One need only recall D.D. Kosambi.) The reductionist polemic, incidentally, has been extremely common, though in several different forms. Thus the cultural theorist Robert Young's otherwise interesting *White Mythologies: Writing History and the West* (London, etc., 1990) contains critical discussions of Lukacs, Sartre, Althusser and Jameson but remains remarkably silent about virtually all Marxian professional historians, with Thompson earning literally half a line for his 'casuistical device' . . . of 'taking refuge in a rejection of theory altogether' (p. 94).

[57] Geoff Eley and Keith Nield have pointed out that postmodernists are often guilty of 'misremembering how embattled the presence of Marxism in academic history has actually been.' 'Starting Over: The Present, the Postmodern, and the Moment of Social History', *Social History*, 20, iii, October 1995.

economistic with linguistic-cultural reductionism. Here Patrick Joyce unwittingly confirms, with almost uncanny precision, Ginzburg's point regarding the affinities between positivism and extreme relativism. For him, the 'challenge of postmodernism to history' consists in 'its invitation to question the idea of a clear distinction between representation and the "real".'[58] Disregard for mediations can clearly take two opposed forms, Ginzburg's open window, or wall—and passage from the one to the other is often unexpectedly easy. Thus Patrick Joyce's *Visions of People: Industrial England and the Question of Class, 1848–1914* argues from an alleged absence of a distinct class language to the total irrelevance of class analysis for understanding nineteenth-century Britain, thus tacitly assuming, some critics have argued, an unproblematised, reflection-theory-like linkage between social relations and political consciousness. There is also a disabling assumption of purity, an expectation of clear disjunction between domination and resistance: a feature that recurs often also in Subaltern Studies.[59] But contestations normally occur '*within* the dominant language', not in some pure domain of resistance immune from hegemonic values.[60]

The postmodernist turn, finally, has sometimes taken the form of a tacit return, in effect, to fairly conventional, 'elitist', studies of poli-

[58] Patrick Joyce, 'The Imaginary Discontents of Social History: A Note of Response to Mayfield and Thorne, and Lawrence and Taylor', *Social History*, 18, i, January 1993.

[59] Stedman Jones and Joyce find working-class consciousness absent, and therefore class analysis irrelevant, in nineteenth-century Britain, as labour discourses frequently used not any clear-cut language of class, but an older, radical-populist idiom demarcating 'producers' from 'idlers'. An assumption that class must be 'pure' in order to exist then becomes the ground for an easy rejection. Somewhat similarly, a counterposing of Bengal jute labour to the highly abstract model of labour–capital relations with which Marx began his analysis in *Capital Volume I* enabled Dipesh Chakrabarty, in his early work, to postulate a total disjunction between metropolitan and colonial labour conditions, trade-union forms, and culture: *Rethinking Working-Class History: Bengal 1890–1940* (Princeton, 1989). For the importance of assumptions of 'purity' in Partha Chatterjee's work, see my *Writing Social History*, chapter 3.

[60] This is Marc W. Steinberg's criticism of Joyce, in 'Culturally Speaking: Finding a Commons between Post-structuralism and the Thompsonian Perspective', *Social History*, 21, ii, May 1996.

tical-institutional or intellectual history, because texts most amenable to literary readings are much more abundant at such social levels.[61] Joyce's readings of language, again, have been critiqued for their frequent slide into assumptions of transparency: the insistence on the indeterminacy of meanings, it seems, gets applied mainly in polemic alone.[62] The intervening 'Thompsonian' moment in social history had been richer, arguably, in potential, even in the handling of language. Interesting suggestions have been made recently about the possibilities of further elaboration of its many insights, through a critical dialogue for instance with Habermasian notions of changing 'public spheres'.[63] But it seems that some forms of postmodernism—in sharp contrast to the richness, say, of Greenblatt—can discard one set of simplified certainties only through embracing another.

III

I have indicated that despite the familiar problems of homogenisation and excessive claims to novelty, the polemic against the Enlightenment around which many forms of postmodernism converge has had productive consequences through the opening up of discursive spaces for ecological critique, feminism, and anti-racist cultural values. One could raise, it is true, a caveat about temporal priorities here. Feminism, notably, for reasons internal to its own development, anticipated many of the more fruitful aspects of what today passes under the postmodernist banner. Since the archives produced by governments and other overwhelmingly male-dominated institutions tend to say little directly about gender, feminists had to turn their attention to literary and non-conventional sources, and explore even familiar material for rhetorical strategies and hidden meanings. A 'literary

[61] A point elaborated by Raphael Samuel, op. cit. See also David Mayfield and Susan Thorne, 'Social History and Its Discontents: Gareth Stedman Jones and the Politics of Language', *Social History*, May 1992.

[62] Steinberg, op. cit.

[63] Geoff Eley, 'Edward Thompson, Social History and Political Culture: The Making of a Working-class Public', in Kaye and McClelland, eds, *E.P. Thompson: Critical Perspectives* (Oxford, 1990); Eley, 'Nations, Publics and Political Cultures: Placing Habermas in the Nineteenth Century', in Craig Calhoun, ed., *Habermas and the Public Sphere* (Cambridge, Mass, 1993).

turn', in other words, was eminently necessary for much feminist history. Feminism, more generally, has needed to develop thoroughgoing critiques of the patriarchal assumptions embedded in linguistic and other forms of representation. The questioning of representations, further, has been accompanied by that of identities so often assumed to be 'natural', homogenised and stable.

The real issue, however, is not the allocation of priority or determination of direction of influence. It concerns the enabling nature of the *total* repudiations that have been so common in postmodernism: whether, for example, effective responses to the ecological devastation being caused by scientific technology do not have to be drawn most often from alternative notions and applications of science itself.

The relations between postmodernism and feminism have been particularly complicated, and indeed demand separate and extensive discussion on a scale not feasible here. Let me confine myself to two very general comments. First, feminism has both contributed to, and benefited from, contemporary postmodernist criticisms of an undeniably male-centred Enlightenment Reason, modernity and liberal humanistic 'universalism'. Feminist historians, for instance, have revealed the crucial role of Jacobins during the French Revolution in the suppression of incipient women's movements. They have explored the ways in which women were deliberately excluded from the new public spaces being created by the Revolution in the name of the equal rights of 'man'.[64] Feminism necessarily has to insist on the historical presence of forms of oppression and subjectivities other than class, and here there are evident convergences with postmodernist theorisations about multiple sites of power and the decentring of homogenised notions of subjecthood. Yet, secondly, wholesale rejections of Enlightenment humanism do not always mesh with feminist perspectives. For feminism—particularly, one might add, in countries like India—might well need to seek the extension, rather than the theoretical undermining, of notions of individualised rights from which women, like other subordinated groups, have often been excluded. Nostalgic valorisations of pre-modern or pre-colonial 'communities' also tend to be deeply problematic from consistently

[64] The pioneering work here has been Joan B. Landes, *Women and the Public Sphere in the Age of the French Revolution* (Ithaca, 1988).

feminist standpoints, since so much in such traditions has been deeply and most oppressively patriarchal. Hence the perspectives of Habermas about modernity as not exhausted, but unfinished, have proved attractive for some feminists, despite that thinker's near-blindness regarding questions of gender.[65] Some recent empirical research on late-eighteenth-century France has moved in a similar direction. Feminists, it is suggested, need to relate to the Enlightenment and the French Revolution as 'rebel daughters'.[66] And exceptionally rich intellectual fare is being provided by ongoing debates about the ambiguous implications of postmodernism among feminist political philosophers like Seyla Benhabib, Nancy Fraser, and Judith Butler.[67]

It hardly needs to be stated that the critique of 'Orientalising' colonial discourse has been the principal conduit for the entry of some postmodernistic moods into South Asian literary-cultural studies and historiography—despite Edward Said's own ambivalent positions concerning postmodernism.[68] Radically inclined intellectuals in the

[65] Some of the most effective critiques of postmodernism have in fact been coming from feminist thinkers in recent years. See, particularly, Patricia Waugh, *Stalemates?* op. cit.; also Marsha Hewitt, 'The Regressive Implications of Postmodernism', in Ralph Miliband and Leo Panitch, eds, *Socialist Register, 1993* (Merlin, London, 1993), and Martha Nussbaum, 'Human Capabilities, Female Human Beings', in Nussbaum and Glover, eds, *Women, Culture and Development* (Oxford, 1995). Hewitt, it may be noted, has raised a pertinent point about the wholesale decentering of agency and subjecthood: 'Why is it, exactly at the moment when so many of us who have been silenced begin to demand the right to name ourselves, to act as subjects rather than objects of history, that just then the concept of subjecthood becomes "problematic"?' Miliband and Panitch, op. cit., p. 85.

[66] Sarah Melzer and Leslie Rabine, eds, *Rebel Daughters: Women and the French Revolution* (New York, 1992).

[67] See, for instance, Linda J. Nicholson, ed., *Feminism/Postmodernism* (New York/London, 1990); Judith Butler and Joan Scott, eds, *Feminists Theorize the Political* (New York/London, 1992); Joan Wallach Scott, *Gender and the Politics of History* (revised edition, Columbia, 1999); and Seyla Benhabib, Judith Butler, Drucilla Cornell, and Nancy Fraser, *Feminist Contentions: A Philosophical Exchange* (New York/London, 1995).

[68] An early review of *Orientalism*—by James Clifford—emphasised Said's oscillations between Foucault and Auerbachian humanism. *History and Theory*, 19, 1980. The point has been elaborated more recently by Aijaz Ahmad in *In Theory*, chapter v.

discipline of literary, and particularly English, studies have responded enthusiastically to Saidian critiques, for in their field unproblematised assumptions about the 'humanist' value of European literature, abstracted from ethnic, gender, or class determinants, still tend to dominate academic establishments. The exposure of the colonial complicity of European knowledge of the Orient, and indeed of the bulk of modern Western culture in general—not excluding many literary classics—has consequently seemed a liberation. There had been many earlier critiques on similar lines of specific texts, but an overall, easy-to-apply, general framework was both new and attractive. (It is considerably less novel for Indian historiography, dominated on the whole by anti-colonial nationalist assumptions—though even there the earlier critiques had been much more economic and political than cultural.)

Some qualifications are still required. The Saidian turn, involving a major shift in anti-colonial discourses from politico-economic to cultural registers, has exacted a high price in terms of the near-oblivion of earlier kinds of analysis of imperialism. For many today, the long and honourable history of critiques of colonialism from within Western intellectual and political traditions—primarily Marxist, but also occasionally liberal—appears forgotten. Hobson, Hilferding, Rosa Luxemburg, Bukharin and Lenin may never have existed. Culturalism has also produced tendencies towards extrapolation from specific historical contexts, as when Said feels tempted to trace Orientalism back to Aeschylus or Dante. This is to make Orientalism into a characterological essence, disregarding ample evidence about similar ethnocentric elements in virtually all cultures. Such analysis runs the danger of ignoring precisely the things that make modern Western cultural arrogance so exceptionally oppressive: its links with very material forms of imperialist economic and political power, for the understanding of which a narrowly literary critique is hardly adequate.

More is involved, then, than a forgetting of earlier critiques, many of which are certainly quite dated today. Much more important is the absence of effort, within Saidian and/or postmodernist frameworks, at developing effective analysis of contemporary globalisation, neo-colonialism, and the world as dominated by multinationals. It is surely significant that the endless denunciations of Enlightenment rationality have remarkably little to say about one of its most indisputable products: the ideology of the 'free market' that reigns virtually unchallenged today on a truly 'universal' scale. And, even within cultural criticism, the rather easy exposure of one instance after another of collusion with colonial power/knowledge, endlessly confirming one's own politically correct values, can soon become tediously predictable.

Whether in admiration or criticism, many today see in Subaltern Studies the major locus for postmodernism within South Asian scholarship, and of course Subalternist historians—notably Dipesh Chakrabarti, Gyanendra Pandey, and above all Partha Chatterjee—have been quite central to formulations of theories of 'postcoloniality'. Subaltern Studies, which had attracted little attention outside India in its initial radical and populist 'history-from-below' phase, is today a significant part of a kind of postmodernist counter-establishment—more precisely of that section within it which conjoins anti-Enlightenment polemic with critiques of Eurocentrism and colonial knowledge. I have written much about such matters already, tracing the shifting trajectory of Subaltern Studies from a starting point not too distant from Thompsonian social history, through the insertion of Saidian colonial discourse analysis by Chatterjee in 1985, to the current rejection of 'Enlightenment modernity', growing 'culturalism', and valorisations of the 'fragment'. It does not seem entirely unfair, however, to suggest that despite such obvious affinities, relatively little of the richer dimensions of postmodernism have entered the project so far—a few exceptions apart. There has been, rather, a continuous adherence to a fundamentally binary model, the positing of power and resistance in distinct domains, in and through repeated shifts in the meanings of the two poles. This is very reminiscent of the less impressive kinds of postmodernist interventions in Western historiography, where a similar disjunction of domains has been repeatedly assumed: in Patrick Joyce, for example. I find its South Asian manifestations to be equally problematic, on a whole range of themes. Binary models seem peculiarly prone to the temptation of substituting one kind of homogenisation by another, bypassing the moment of radical decentering. Much more interesting work, critically and creatively appropriating at times select aspects of postmodernist thinking—Foucault, above all—has been going on in South

Asian scholarship outside the Subaltern Studies project, despite the latter's enormously high profile in the West.[69] What makes the Subalternist variant particularly troubling is the possibility of slides towards indigenist or culturally-nationalist positions. The original elite/subaltern dichotomy had been unmistakably (though flexibly) grounded in Marxian class-analysis. Ranajit Guha's *Elementary Aspects of Peasant Insurgency in Colonial India*, for instance, began with the subjection of the peasant to the 'triumvirate' of colonial state, landlord, and money-lender.[70] The Saidian turn led to power getting increasingly identified with colonial discourse, through which Enlightenment rationalism supposedly established cultural domination, colonising indigenous minds—at least English-educated middle-class ones. In so far as analysis of such domination went beyond the purely discursive, institutional embodiment came to be sought through the highly generalised category of the 'modern nation-state', in both its colonial and postcolonial forms. The retention of the nation-state as main polemical target allowed an apparent maintenance of links with the original critique of 'elite nationalism', a residual radical or oppositional ambience expressed through continuities with anti-statist language. But the reasons underlying such critique had changed quite fundamentally. The polemical target was no longer the state as related—in however complex or mediated ways—to class rule, exploitation, and forms of surplus appropriation, but rather the modern state as embodying Western (mainly rationalist) values—against which indigenous communities need to be valorised while being more-or-less abstracted from internal power relations. For meanwhile, the counter-point has also shifted from 'subaltern', through 'peasant' and 'peasant community', to 'community' in general, occasionally even defined in religious terms. The implicit criterion of judgement has

[69] Examples would include Javed Majeed, *Ungoverned Imaginings: James Mill's 'History of British India' and Orientalism* (Oxford, 1992); C.A. Bayly, *Empire and Information: Intelligence-Gathering and Social Communication in India, 1780–1870* (Cambridge, 1996); Radhika Singha, *A Despotism of Law: Crime and Justice in Early Colonial India* (Delhi, 1998); and Singha, 'Settle, Mobilize, Verify: Identification Practices in Colonial India', *Studies in History*, 16 ii, July–December 2000.

[70] Ranajit Guha, *Elementary Aspects of Peasant Insurgency in Colonial India* (Delhi, 1983), chapter I, and *passim*.

become authenticity, indigenous origin, no longer any vision of egalitarian social change.[71]

Very recently, there have been some signs that the valorisation of certain kinds of identity politics is tending to displace the critique of colonial knowledge as the central thrust for Subaltern Studies. A presentation made in October 1997 by Partha Chatterjee entitled 'A Brief History of Subaltern Studies' omitted all reference to it, moving, after a critical account of the early history-from-below phase, straight into what it describes as the 'three ongoing social and political debates' that Chatterjee now considers most vital—about identity politics around religious community, gender and caste.[72] The topicality of these themes for South Asia today is indisputable, and the opening-up of recent Subaltern Studies volumes to feminist and Dalit scholars is certainly a welcome change. Some questions may still arise about the ways in which caste, gender, and particularly religious identities are being explored within the Subalternist ambience.[73] I feel that identities tend to get conceptualised in unduly 'culturalist' terms, in ways that excessively prioritise questions of authenticity and origin.

Identities have been a crucial concern for many varieties of postmodernism too, and it seems appropriate to end with a glance at the field of possibilities and problems here. In an important essay, Charles Taylor has traced a tension within post-Enlightenment thought going back to the times of Kant, Rousseau and Herder, between a politics of universalism, emphasising equalisation of individual rights and entitlements, and a politics of difference, based on claims that the

---

[71] The preceding two paragraphs are a highly summarised version of my 'Decline of the Subaltern in Subaltern Studies', in *Writing Social History*, chapter 3, along with the as-yet unpublished 'From Subalternity Towards Cultural Nationalism: The Trajectory of Subaltern Studies', paper presented at a conference on 'Problematising History and Agency: From Nationalism to Subalternity', University of Cape Town, October 1997.

[72] Partha Chatterjee, 'A Brief History of Subaltern Studies', paper presented at the seminar on Problematising History, op. cit.

[73] I expressed my sense of disquiet with the ways religious identity, more precisely communalism, was being studied within Subalternist or anti-modernist frames in 'The Anti-Secularist Critique of Hindutva: Problems of a Shared Discursive Space', *Germinal*, volume I, 1994. See also Datta, *Carving Blocs*, chapter I, and *passim*.

authentic 'identities' of distinct groups or communities be recognised, often through differential treatment. Abstract universalism, from the point of view of the second tradition, tends to get associated with the imposition of homogenised uniformities.[74] Yet the rich discussion that ensued from Taylor's paper has repeatedly indicated that this disjunction cannot be erected into a binary opposition. For all forms of universalism are not necessarily or equally hostile to recognition of difference. Historically, universal rights have often been extended or actualised in and through democratic struggle for *differential* treatment of underprivileged groups—labour, women, ethnic minorities—the whole history, in fact, of the evolution of social welfare interventions and affirmative action procedures.[75] The balance sought in our own Constitution between legal equality and reservation would be just one obvious instance among many.

One needs, further, to move from what amounts to essentialised notions of universalism and difference, towards their contextualisation in specific historical situations. Both have been open to appropriation by widely varied groups at different times. The radical intellectual located in the contemporary West is often rightly indignant at the ways in which the universal so often gets tacitly collapsed into the modern, white, and male. But we cannot afford to forget that the slogan of universal equal rights had emerged in late-eighteenth-century France as a weapon against the established special privileges of dominant minorities of nobles and clergymen, and that in the twentieth century, too, oppressed groups have rallied often enough under universalist banners: in South Africa against apartheid, to mention only one striking instance.

[74] Charles Taylor, 'The Politics of Identity', in Amy Gutman, ed., *Multiculturalism: Examining the Politics of Identity* (Princeton, 1994).

[75] See, particularly, Jurgen Habermas' contribution to the debate around Taylor's essay: 'Struggles for Recognition in the Democratic Constitutional State', in Amy Gutmann, op. cit, pp. 113–19. A recent essay draws on contemporary Australian experience to argue that 'rejection of universal ethics and overarching national political programmes renders . . . defence of multiculturalism ineffective . . . diversities . . . have actually been most successfully defended by appeals to generalisable interests.' Boris Frankel, 'Confronting Neo-Liberal Regimes: The Post-Marxist Embrace of Populism and Realpolitik', *New Left Review*, 226, November–December 1997.

Postmodernist handlings of problems of identity tend to swing between two sharply opposed poles that yet have much in common.[76] Its total rejection of universalism, in culturally-relativist ways, may valorise ethnic or other community identities as incommensurable and internally homogenised—distinct species, which we can only contemplate in wonder, to apply Lyotard's analogy. At the same time, the process of fragmentation might get extended further, till all identities become problematic and fleeting, myths of pure, self-enclosed cultures made authentic by origin are destabilised, and we enter Homi Bhabha's influential (if often difficult to comprehend) world of hybridity. I would not like, however, to press this contrast too far. As in many recent novels, the questioning of boundaries might go along with an overwhelming concentration on, precisely, problems of identity. Thus Bhabha's hybridity rejects arguments of authenticity, but the very metaphor it uses reinscribes, in a way, what might be an excessive focus on the question of origins. The language used makes it difficult to take adequate cognisance of developments going so far beyond origins that the nature of the initial impetus might become rather unimportant.

The more important question, for my argument, relates to the implications of what is widely felt to be a general shift from the politics of class and class struggle to that of identity. Postmodernism has contributed greatly towards the valorisation of this change, helping to constitute a situation where the labour struggles that still take place fairly often in many parts of the world, for instance, get very little media or intelligentsia attention. One might begin by posing the question why identity politics are so often thought to exclude themes of class, since the latter, in strict logic, is surely also a kind of identity. This is so particularly when class is looked at from the point of view of consciousness, felt solidarities and commonalities of action— which on the whole is the way that has proved most fruitful within Marxian historical approaches (Thompson being the most obvious example). Is the shift towards identity then no more than additive,

[76] See, for instance, Aijaz Ahmad's comments on 'identitarian-particularist' and 'globalising-hybridist' forms of postmodernism as opposite poles that still share important commonalities. 'Politics, Literature and Postcoloniality', in *Race and Class*, 36, iii, January–March 1995.

and therefore welcome in an unproblematic manner? Surely it is only drawing belated and necessary attention to aspects generally neglected in conventional Marxism: sites of power other than productive relations, and crosscutting solidarities of gender, ethnicity, religion and caste that can emerge in resisting them?

I think more is involved in this transition than the purely additive, and this becomes clear once one recalls the *transformative* vision embedded in the classic Marxian conception of class. The proletariat, for Marx, has the potential, unique among all other classes, for abolishing itself ultimately through revolution, instead of becoming a new putatively permanent ruling class in the way the bourgeoisie had replaced the feudal lords. The proletariat becoming the 'universal' class was no doubt a very distant, perhaps utopian, ideal, but it has repeatedly conditioned the practice of Marxian movements through efforts to go beyond affirmations of narrow class identity—even though much everyday class politics has obviously been confined to winning recognition for specific demands. That indeed had been one original meaning of hegemony: building working-class leadership through broad alliances, as contrasted with merely sectional demands. To recall for a moment some nearly-forgotten figures and texts: Lenin's *What is to be Done?* had contrasted 'trade union' to 'socialist' consciousness, and Gramsci had refined that distinction through his language of 'economico-corporative' and 'hegemonic' moments.[77] The Marxian project, then, has envisaged transformation through the self-transformation of an 'identity' of a very specific kind.

Dominant patterns of thinking today tend, in important contrast, to emphasise, overwhelmingly, valorisations of resistance, not total change, and the more or less permanent recognition of difference. This makes ample sense in certain contexts. Contemporary Western

[77] Discussions of hegemony in recent years have tended to concentrate overwhelmingly on the question of power or domination operating not just by sheer coercion but through the successful production of internalised consent. The counter-hegemonic stresses equally present in Gramsci have been eclipsed, one might suggest, by ideas derived much more from Althusser and Foucault. How distant that other meaning of hegemony has become is indicated by the discussion of that term in Jeremy Hawthorn's generally very helpful and balanced *Glossary of Contemporary Literary Theory* (London, 1992). Here that other meaning is almost totally omitted.

discourses of ethnicity and multiculturalism focus on immigrant, clearly distinct minorities, many of them relative newcomers for whom 'hegemonic' aspirations are evidently irrelevant. Much more generally, though, transformative aspirations today have been not only abandoned as unrealistic but often found guilty of the sins of universalism and teleology.

It is this *theoretical* repudiation that needs to be emphasised, for otherwise it could be argued that there have been not dissimilar moves in recent years away from transformative programmes also among the bulk of what remains of the traditional, Marxist or socialist, Left, and that nothing more radically anti-capitalist appears at all feasible to-day.[78] Conversely, some kinds of non-class identity politics surely can help to bring about substantially radical changes: feminism, for instance; or in the Indian context subordinate-caste movements.[79] The vicissitudes of the latter, however, are a reminder of the need to simultaneously affirm, and yet partially transcend, sectional identities. From Phule down to today's politics of reservations, moments of united struggle against high-caste domination have been repeatedly dissipated through fragmentation. Where postmodernism is debilitating is in its insistence on the absolute separation of the particular or fragmentary from any more general perspectives—without which a politics of hegemony makes little sense, and resistance, or the winning of 'recognition', displaces transformative horizons.

Fragment, culturalism, the rejection in principle of strivings for global change: these key thrusts of postmodernism feed into and reinforce each other. Thus, in narrowly culturalist or discursive terms, the break-up of master-narratives through the emphasis on fragments might well appear, and indeed often is, emancipatory. Things begin to look more complicated and ambiguous once one starts exploring the practical effects of analogous fragmentation on oppositional movements: the break-up of working-class solidarities, for instance, as the old kind of concentration of labour in big factories gives place to forms of capitalist production at once transnational and apparently decentralised. Culturalism, again, valorises certain ways of conceptualising minority or marginal groups and not others, in terms primarily

[78] This is the important point raised by Rohit Wanchoo in the discussion following my paper at St Stephen's College.

[79] Neeladri Bhattacharjee raised this question at the St Stephen's discussion.

of threats to cultural 'authenticities'. Questions of poverty or economic exploitation—which might be as much or more central to the
everyday lives of immigrants or ethnic-religious minorities—get less
attention, in a kind of mirror inversion of the earlier orthodox
Marxist habit of collapsing everything into class. In the end, there is
the danger of a purely aesthetic contemplation of difference. Involvement or interest in actual movements of the oppressed gets displaced
by romanticised depictions of exotic 'tribal' or 'popular' cultures, the
'wonder' of a Lyotard gazing at the diversity of a discursive species.

I would like to suggest, in conclusion, that the retreat from perspectives of radical change is integrally connected with the recurrent
tendency within postmodernism to conceptualise processes and categories—modernity, the modern state, 'sites' of power, history itself—as free of internal tensions. Counterpoints are sought always
outside these sites, and consequently end up in valorisations of resistance alone: quite often, it seems, the more fragmentary and ineffective
the better, the objects ultimately of aesthetic contemplation and
pleasure. This whole approach stands in contrast to the stress on
immanent critique, the search for possibilities of change rooted in
contradictions within structures, which is roughly what classical
Marxism had meant by dialectics. The precise, confident formulations of dialectics within those traditions stand discredited today, and
in the main rightly so: not only the 'laws of historical development'
of Stalinist Marxism, but perhaps also the assumption that Hegelian
dialectics could be taken over easily as rational kernel from the idealist
shell of notions of the Absolute Idea. Yet one still stands in urgent
need, I think, of more many-sided and nuanced approaches than
much of postmodernism allows. Nor need rejection of teleology be
equated necessarily with a complete jettisoning of hopes and efforts
for change towards a more liveable, just, and humane world—if only
because such surrender so quickly becomes synonymous with opportu-
nist accommodation under cover of a residual radical rhetoric.

Ginzburg, we have seen, has written about an epistemological
'wager': maybe we need some such combination of clear-sighted analysis of realities so often dark and dismal, with a determination to
struggle on against the tides. This language of 'wager' might helpfully
remind us of Lucien Goldmann's use of the same metaphor in his *The
Hidden God*. The immediate context there had been Pascal's wager

about the existence of God amidst the radical uncertainties produced by seventeenth-century science—the terrifying silence of infinite spaces—a wager felt to be necessary to preserve faith and ethical standards. But Goldmann had extended it, in an imaginative and deeply moving manner, to the question of a socialist future: implicitly acknowledged as no longer something guaranteed or inevitable, but no more—and no less—than a 'wager . . . [that] in the alternative facing humanity of a choice between socialism and barbarity, socialism will triumph.'[80] And perhaps Gramsci was hinting at something similar when, sitting in a Fascist prison cell amidst what must have seemed the collapse of all hope, he adopted as his own the motto: pessimism of the intellect, optimism of the will.

[80] Lucien Goldmann, *The Hidden God: A Study of Tragic Vision in the Pensees of Pascal and the Tragedies of Racine* (Paris, 1955; trans., London, 1964), p. 301, and *passim*.

CHAPTER VII

The BJP Bomb and Nationalism*

'A strange game. The only winning move is not to play it.'—
The computer about thermonuclear war in *War Games*, an
American anti-war film made in 1983.

ONE OF the frightening things about nuclear bombs is the way
their possession gets normalised. Not even four years have passed since the Pokhran and Chagai tests of May 1998, yet already the bomb has all but died as a significant media issue or topic
of everyday conversation. It is true that anti-nuclear public initiatives
have not entirely died down in the subcontinent. Organisations like
MIND (Movement in India for Nuclear Disarmament) and a significant number of other groups in many parts of India (and, though we
come to know little about it, Pakistan) do carry on at least sporadic
activities, and there was a big all-India conference in November 2000
in Delhi. But thousands had marched on the streets of many Indian
cities on Hiroshima Day 1998: there was a (considerably smaller)
march in Delhi in 1999 too, but in 2000 only an indoor meeting.
There is small consolation in the fact that pro-bomb tub-thumping
has also fallen into relative abeyance. Periodic 'explosion[s] of self-
esteem'[1] keep on getting staged on other, far from unrelated, issues—
above all Kargil—redolent with assumptions identical to those through

*Revised version of 'The BJP Bomb and Aspects of Nationalism', *Economic
and Political Weekly*, XXXIII, 27, 4 July 1998.
[1] *The Pioneer*, 12 May 1998.

which Pokhran had been hailed. And the media's lack of interest is perhaps more dangerous even than enthusiasm, for in effect—as happens so often nowadays—the crucial issues are being kept deliberately away from the public gaze and possible debate.

The curious thing is that not one of the arguments against India going nuclear in summer 1998 have become out-of-date or irrelevant: in many cases they have only been strengthened by subsequent developments. The plea that going definitively and openly nuclear would improve an allegedly worsening security environment sounds even more ridiculous today, after the Kargil incursion. It has become more obvious now that Pokhran has considerably worsened the Indian strategic balance *vis-à-vis* Pakistan (while it obviously remains irrelevant militarily in relation to China's far more numerous arsenal, except in its having provided a gratuitous provocation in a context of improving relations). All that has happened is that the BJP-led government has thrown away the obvious superiority that India always had over Pakistan in terms of conventional arms (due to its size and resources), for now Indian cities lie open to nuclear strike as much as do those of its neighbour. In effect, this situation has laid India, rather than Pakistan, open to nuclear blackmail. During the Kargil episode, India could not use the methods it had adopted in 1965, when communication links with Kashmir had been threatened—a strike across the Panjab plains—and had to fight on unfavourable terrain.

The other justification often offered in 1998—the hypocrisy of existing nuclear powers compelling poor innocent India to turn 'realistic'—also makes as little sense now as four years back. South Asia turning nuclear has clearly not helped world nuclear disarmament one little bit. If anything, it may have contributed to some extent to dangerously blatant retrogressive tendencies, most obviously in the USA, with senate rejection of the CTBT and efforts to revive 'Star War' programmes. The 'patriotic' argument had been that India, through turning nuclear, would become more independent and self-reliant: what has happened, as could have been (and was) predicted in summer 1998, is that it has become very much more dependent on the uncertain favours of the USA in economic and strategic matters alike. Occasionally, the new need to respond with alacrity to US pressures might bring a few real fringe benefits, like the cessation of the Kargil war and the possibility of real negotiations at long last over Kashmir. These mean, though, that the BJP in effect has managed to internationalise the Kashmir problem—which should bring cold comfort to our flourishing breed of armchair super-patriots.

Beyond, and far more vital than, all such debates around strategy lie the two key reasons why the nuclearisation of South Asia is an unmitigated and ever-deepening disaster. Weaponisation and the nuclear arms race (that the media doesn't talk about them is no guarantee at all that these are not accelerating all the time, quietly, in the interests of 'national security') can only imply enormous burdens on people who in the majority are so very poor, and cutbacks on already minimal social, health, and educational investments. Military experts of the stature of ex-Admiral Ramdas have pointed out that nuclear weaponisation is going to prove a far more expensive and complicated matter than has been officially admitted.[2] In their very effective and comprehensive critique of nuclear politics, Praful Bidwai and Achin Vanaik have calculated that additional expenditure required for even a very modest nuclear arsenal, not taking into account the probability of a major arms race, would amount to *c.* 3% of the Indian GDP. This is the cost of providing universal primary education to every Indian child of the 6–14 age-group. And a single Agni missile costs as much as 13,000 primary health centres.[3]

Such obscene expenditure of scarce resources on weapons of mass destruction, which everybody recognises in theory to be unusable, may not bother upwardly mobile wallowers in 'self-esteem' much. But one cannot discount the possibility that bombs and radioactivity—which unfortunately cannot be taught to distinguish between Hindu, Muslim, and Christian, rich and poor—might catch up with

[2] At a convention against nuclear weapons in Delhi on 9 June 1998, Admiral Ramdas explained that weaponisation involves not just the fairly easy fitting of warheads to missiles, but complicated systems of communications, command structures, fail-safe devices. The Indian armed forces, he emphasised with all the authority and expertise of decades of high military office, are totally unprepared for any of these drastic changes. As for civilian protection, has anyone noticed even a conventional air-raid shelter in Delhi?

[3] Praful Bidwai and Achin Vanaik, *South Asia on a Short Fuse: Nuclear Politics and the Future of Global Disarmament* (Delhi, 1999), p. 162.

them. For it needs to be emphasised that the danger of actual nuclear war, whether by intent or accident, in South Asia is very real, probably greater than at most times during the US–Soviet Cold War. Here we have a situation that is really new: two nextdoor neighbours with nuclear arms, with a history of mutual rivalry, three wars (or maybe three-and-a-half, if now we count Kargil) and capitals and major concentrations of population within a few minutes missile time from each other. There is little or no scope for hot lines and other devices that developed over the years between America and the Soviet Union for avoiding nuclear war through human or mechanical error.[4] The side losing out in a conventional 1965 or 1971-type conflict could be tempted to go in for a nuclear first strike. An Indo-Pak nuclear war is both unthinkable in terms of logic—a bomb dropped on Lahore will affect Amritsar—and made frighteningly possible by the folly of Pokhran. And, short of such worst-possible scenarios—going nuclear on a big scale—even peaceful uses of nuclear energy remain inseparable everywhere from the danger of accidents, radioactive leakages, and acute problems in the disposal of waste products. The Western media regularly exposes many such actual or near-disasters—in sharp contrast, one must add, to the Indian. Can we really assume that in this one area among so many, India has somehow attained a level of super-efficiency unequalled anywhere in the world?

All this is, or at least should be, obvious, and I do not want to go on reiterating arguments that have been elaborated so much better elsewhere.[5] In what follows, I intend to concentrate on two somewhat less-explored themes, which might also help me to connect the present essay with some of the themes I have been elaborating in other parts of this book. Pokhran, along with Chagai (which came as a slightly delayed response), have been acts of sheer folly. But was the BJP then being just plain stupid and irrational? One must also try to understand its logic within the terms of Sangh Parivar discourse in order to appreciate the full implications of what we have to confront today. And there is need, too, for some introspection. The 'euphoria'

---

[4] The time between missile launch and impact in an Indo-Pak nuclear war can be as little as three minutes—as compared to thirty minutes in the US–Soviet stand-off. Praful Bidwai, 'A Deadly Deterrence', *Times of India*, 19 June 1998.

[5] Most notably in Bidwai and Vanaik, op. cit.

or 'national consensus' around Pokhran was certainly very exaggerated. Yet it cannot be denied that support for the tests came also from quarters that have often been strongly critical of the Hindutva combine, as well as from large numbers of people who are not firm supporters of the BJP but generally uninterested in politics. Nor can the hesitations and ambiguities within the Left (and more generally, secular and democratic formations) be ignored. I would like to explore some of the things that might lie behind such attitudes: in particular a dangerously limited appreciation of the horrors of nuclear (indeed, all large-scale modern) war, and inadequate thinking about the more problematic aspects of nationalism.

II

Since the security threat arguments were so unconvincing, many in summer 1998 related the tests to the BJP desire to bolster its then-quite-unstable coalition, silence its troublesome allies, and perhaps go in if need be for a quick election where it might hope to get an absolute majority through sheer jingoism. The subsequent obvious link between the Kargil hype and the enhanced majority of the NDA in the late-1999 elections might be taken to confirm this possibility. But I feel that as an explanation it does not go far enough. India has had a succession of minority and unstable governments since 1989: why is it that only the BJP took the nuclear plunge? (We are being told now that even the 13-day first Vajpayee ministry had decided on testing.) One needs to recall and emphasise that, already in 1951, the Jan Sangh manifesto had proclaimed the need for India to go nuclear. On 26 February 1966, just before his death, Savarkar, the premier ideologue of Hindutva, had called on the Indian government to 'immediately equip India with nuclear weapons and missiles'. For him, that was the logical extension of the slogan he had proclaimed way back in 1942: 'Hinduise the nation and militarise Hinduism.'

Militaristic authoritarianism has been at the heart of the entire Hindutva project throughout. The RSS functions on the principle of *ek chalak anuvartita*, 'following one leader', who is nominated for life—on the model supposedly of the patriarchal Hindu joint family. Not accidentally, women are excluded from membership of this core training-cum-directing body. The theme of emasculation has been very central in Hindutva rhetoric—the allegedly puny and impotent Hindu who needs to be trained in aggressive martial qualities so as to match and overpower the virile Muslim—and it is significant that emasculation was the central charge that Godse made about Gandhi in his final speech in court.[6] For more than seventy years now, the RSS has concentrated on catching boys very young and instilling in them an unquestioning, total discipline: through paramilitary drill, carefully-devised games, a repertoire of simple stories, heavy doses of pseudo-history.[7] It has been, and remains a fundamentalism not of dogma—where eclecticism and fluidity is deliberately projected (a perennial oscillation between the 'Hindu' and the 'national' card, for instance, or, particularly today between 'tradition' and 'science', the temple and the bomb)—but of organisation.[8]

There is an intimate connection between this authoritarian, anti-democratic thrust and the suggestions made periodically from BJP or other Sangh Parivar quarters for replacing cabinets responsible to Parliament with a presidential executive, irremovable during its term of office. The point is not any abstract discussion of the merits and failings of the two forms, but the likely consequences in the specific Indian context. Concentration of executive powers with an elective president is bound to restrict the vital, federal, aspects of the Indian polity, and might produce a stark alternative between over-central-isation and tendencies towards separatism, with the two poles of course feeding each other. This will be so particularly because in India linguistic-cultural distinctions and identities often coincide with state boundaries—in significant contrast to the US situation. The presi-dential form is also conducive to highly personalised elections, and vastly enhances possibilities of media manipulation—the varied tech-niques of 'selling the president', so noticeable in American elections.

---

[6] Nathuram Godse, *May It Please Your Honour* (Pune, 1977).

[7] *Shakha*-recruits are asked, for instance, what they should do if their officer asks them to jump into a well. The correct answer of course is that they should do so immediately. One is tempted to suggest that the BJP wants the whole country to do the same.

[8] Tapan Basu, *et al.*, *Khaki Shorts and Saffron Flags: A Critique of the Hindu Right* (Delhi, 1993); W.K. Anderson and S.D. Damle, *The Brotherhood in Saffron* (New Delhi, 1987).

And recent history, globally, hardly provides much basis for preferring the presidential form. A deeply discredited Yeltsin could manage
to hang on to power in Russia for years, while Clinton, several times,
all but started wars against Iraq in an effort to divert attention from
personal scandals. It is difficult to imagine the head of a cabinet system of government getting away with such behaviour.

For a few days after Pokhran, when the euphoria was at its height,
Vajpayee briefly seemed to be getting projected as larger-than-life
supremo, holding aloft a Rajput or Sikh sword. That did not last, nor
is it very clear whether the commission set up to look into or review
the Constitution will suggest very substantial changes. But the danger
remains, for the Sangh Parivar has perfected the art of blowing hot
and cold, alternating aggressive suggestions or actions with apparent
retreats, but all the time working to shift the terms of discourse in
its favour. The trick is to gradually normalise what at first seems to
most people absurd, unthinkable: as the proposed wanton destruction of a particular mosque had appeared in the mid-1980s.

The phenomenon of regimes and military industrial cum scientific
establishments locked into a nuclear arms race threatening to become
mirror images of each other, almost interdependent, had been com-
mented on even in the US–Soviet stand-off, despite very real differences in ideologies, social systems, and degrees of aggressive behaviour.[9]
In the subcontinent, the virtual concordance between right-wing
fundamentalist or chauvinist forces in Pakistan and India has often
been extremely striking. One recalls for instance the Coimbatore
blasts, allegedly by the ISI, just at the moment when the BJP election
campaign seemed to be flagging in early 1998: or, just possibly, the
way in which the alleged discovery next year of a fringe Islamic group
as responsible for some blasts in churches was sought to be made into
an alibi for the Sangh Parivar in relation to the anti-Christian campaign.

The second, perhaps even more fundamental, way in which Pokhran

[9] This had been a recurrent theme in the writings of E.P. Thompson during
the years he had sacrificed historical research for full-time work as activist and
premier theoretician of the campaign for European Nuclear Disarmament. See
for instance his *Double Exposure* (London, 1985).

was geared to overall Sangh Parivar objectives was through vastly acclerating the processes of militarisation of culture and education. The 'national' cum 'Hindu' chauvinism very obviously stimulated by the bomb fosters unthinking, jingoistic, aggressively male mind-sets, for which the RSS has been systematically working for decades, and which are quite evident, to some extent autonomously, among significant sections of privileged, high-caste, upwardly-mobile Indians. The BJP understands—far better than do Left or democratic forces— the crucial importance of education, and so, while readily surrendering a number of apparently key ministerial posts to its coalition partners, it placed the Hindutva hardliner Murli Manohar Joshi in charge of human resources in both the central ministries it has constituted since 1998.

As with the bomb, the BJP has been moving very quickly indeed in education. For history, in particular, the prospects are extremely grim, as that has always been a prime Sangh Parivar target. The massively used textbooks of the National Council of Educational Research and Training came under attack, and in a matter of a few months, starting, significantly with the Indian Council of Historical Research, the major funding bodies for higher education were drastically packed with a combination of well-known Sangh supporters and venerable gentlemen whose knowledge and understanding of academic disciplines had stopped quite some time back. Protests by certain of its allies may have forced a temporary scaling-down in the agenda of open saffronisation that had been placed before the education ministers' conference in October 1998, but insidiously, it is becoming clear, the same programme remains at work. Thus, newspapers have carried reports of a University Grants Commission (UGC) circular asking for the introduction of courses on Vedic ritual and astrology in college and university syllabi. History, in particular, will be sought to be reduced once again to mere lists of kings, battles, and a selective parade of 'national heroes', abstracted from socio-economic and popular dimensions. The sorry state of Pakistani historiography, thanks to long periods of military rule, is one indication of what can happen if history gets compulsorily reduced to a patriotic-cum-communal drill—for which, once again, the bomb, combined with periodic clashes like Kargil, might be expected to create just the appropriate atmosphere.[10]

III

But why and how has the BJP managed to whip up support and even enthusiasm for the bomb from circles considerably wider than its usual supporters? Paradoxically, here, what might be considered some of the more positive aspects of recent Indian history, have turned into liabilities.

The subcontinent has, in the first place, never faced a really major modern war—in the sense of its cities being heavily bombed, large territories ravaged by battles, and compulsory military service. We have never had situations (unlike most other parts of the Eurasian land mass) where having had one or more near-relatives killed or injured in war has been the norm for a big section of the population. This happy absence—so far—has, however, contributed to a grossly insufficient awareness of the horrors of modern war, whether conventional or nuclear. In children's tales, school texts, and films alike, war is overwhelmingly presented as something heroic and 'manly'—totally abstracting modern warfare from the ways in which it is marked far more often by bestiality and cowardice: soldiers looting and burning civilian homes, raping defenceless women, and, above all, men who hide in underground bunkers and press buttons to make a distant city go up in flames. Can we recall an effective Indian anti-war film, I wonder, or even films comparable to that species of Western war comedy which, within limits, foregrounds anti-heroes, ridicules stupid generals and soldiers, and, occasionally, the grosser absurdities of jingoism? Disastrously, such attitudes towards war in general have spilled over into thinking about the qualitatively different question of nuclear weapons which can render humankind as extinct as the dinosaurs, make life itself perhaps impossible on earth, and which, even through nuclear tests (or inefficient peaceful use), can have genetic effects extending across many generations.

[10] I take up the question of the relations between Hindutva and history in chapter 9 below. Recent months have seen a major acceleration in such processes of the 'saffronization' of education.

The second paradox is related to the dominant rhetoric and— to a lesser but still important extent, practice—of Indian foreign policy till very recently. This has been anti-nuclear and pro-disarmament, and repeatedly rejected, as late as 1995–6, theories of nuclear weapons being essential for national security and effective or acceptable as deterrents.[11] Issues and demands which in many other parts of the world have had a radical, even subversive, content, formed part of official discourse here, and hence were bereft of oppositional attraction: respectable, taken for granted, almost dull. The various peace, solidarity and friendship organisations, which till the collapse of actually existing socialist regimes had been fairly numerous, tended to get a little too identified with one or other Communist Party, as well as sometimes with diplomatic and Indian official circles. One can recall occasional impressive demonstrations,[12] but sustained and autonomous mass anti-nuclear and peace movements have never really developed in India. There has been nothing comparable to, say, the campaign for unilateral nuclear disarmament in Britain in the late 1950s and 1960s, the massive youth protests and draft-burning in the United States during the Vietnam war, or the END in many parts of Europe during the second Cold War of the Reagan era. Awareness of the cataclysmic dangers of nuclear war remained on a low level, except among numerically small urban educated groups influenced by the radical youth culture and the protest and peace songs of the 1960s West—and it has probably declined over the years.

Lack of awareness often gets embodied in a strange insensitivity to language, a readiness to slip into the digits of so-called political realism[13] or realpolitik even on the part of many people on the Left.

[11] Praful Bidwai, op. cit., refers to statements to this effect by India before the World Court in 1995, as well as Foreign Secretary Salman Haider's speech at the Conference on Disarmament in 1996.

[12] Thus there was a 400,000-strong all-India peace rally in New Delhi in October 1982, and, on the occasion of the All India Peoples' Science Festival in 1987, the Delhi Science Forum published a most valuable collection, *Darkness of a Thousand Suns*. Sadly, one of the editors of that collection, C. Rajamohan, is today a notable nuclear hawk.

[13] For an effective critique of this dominant paradigm in International Relations, see Achin Vanaik, *India in a Changing World*, Tracts for the Times (New Delhi, 1995), as well as Bidwai and Vanaik, op. cit., chapter 8.

Take for instance the widespread assumption that there had been a satisfactory 'national consensus' on nuclear matters, before the BJP broke it, around what is called the 'open nuclear option': India should not go openly nuclear through testing and weaponisation but should maintain (and presumably go on quietly developing) its potential. That, it was argued, was necessary to fight 'nuclear apartheid', the collective monopoly over the bomb being maintained, selfishly and dangerously, by the five existing nuclear powers. Use of the term 'national consensus' to describe either the pre- or the post-Pokhran situation is in the first place highly dubious. There has been virtually no dissemination of relevant information, whether about the effects of nuclear weapons, or the costs of India's nuclear programme—or for that matter about how safe or efficient that programme is.[14] Whatever debate there has been about such matters has really been confined to a small minority, and a profound nuclear illiteracy seems to prevail even among many defence or security 'experts'. And while the behaviour of the existing nuclear powers—above all, of course, the USA—has often been atrocious, I have serious problems with the use of the term 'apartheid' in this context. Apartheid implies as its valorised Other a notion of equal rights. But should all states (and, by extension, perhaps any community or group seeking autonomy or statehood) have 'equal rights' to the bomb—which would obviously enhance enormously the possibilities of nuclear annihilation? Would India welcome a nuclearised Nepal or Bangladesh, for instance, or for that matter bombs in the hands of sundry dissident groups that most of us tend to describe as 'militant', 'extremist', or 'separatist'? Shouldn't Bodos, say, have the bomb too? The demand for equal rights to weapons of mass destruction is on a par, really, with a hypothetical equal right to murder, since so many murderers remain unpunished.

---

[14] The 'national consensus' argument—the content of which in any case changed overnight on 11 May from abstaining from tests to enthusiastic acclaim for them—was at its most absurd in the 'opinion polls' conducted by some newspapers during the brief media hype about Pokhran. One of them discovered a 91% endorsement of the bomb—on the basis of a sample of 2000 telephone subscribers in the metropolitan cities. Most people even in these cities do not have phones, and we were not told anything about how even the people who were rung up had been selected.

The only difference is that a murderer can kill one or two, the bomb will finish off millions, if not the entire world.

The problem lies in an insufficient appreciation of the qualitatively different nature of nuclear weapons, for it is being assumed that the bomb is not really all that different from a rifle or a gun which—total pacifists apart—is generally assumed to be good or bad depending on who is using it, and for what purpose. For far too many on opposite sides of national or ideological divides, the bomb remains terrible in the hands of others but fine for ourselves. Pacifism might be unpractical in a grossly imperfect and unjust world, though the nobility of that ideal should not be questioned. But it is widely agreed today that a nuclear war cannot be meaningfully 'won', and that 'deterrence' through nuclear weapons is a dangerous myth.[15] Nuclear pacifism, far from being unrealistic, therefore becomes today the only sane, rational and moral choice.

Phrases like 'nuclear apartheid' and 'keeping the nuclear option open' came into frequent use during the debate on the Comprehensive Test Ban Treaty (CTBT) in 1996–7. This was a debate in which those who tried to argue that the CTBT should not be rejected out of hand, notably Praful Bidwai and Achin Vanaik, found themselves in a small minority, at times even virtually blacked out from much of the media. Maybe I am very dense, and certainly can claim no expertise in this matter, but I must confess that I have yet to encounter an argument that makes it clear to me where exactly the CTBT is so terribly and specially discriminatory. Unlike the Nuclear Non-Proliferation Treaty (NPT), which was clearly discriminatory in that it allowed existing nuclear powers to retain and expand their arsenals while imposing restrictions only on non-nuclear countries, the CTBT does impose some verifiable restraints on all states, nuclear as well as

[15] The problem with deterrence is that sticking to a stable minimum level of nuclear armaments is extremely difficult, for you are always fearful that the potential enemy might be stealing a march on you, developing a first-strike capability of such dimensions as to be able to wipe out your capacity for retaliation. You therefore feel compelled to build more and better missiles, and so, what (just possibly) might have started as a sincere policy of minimum deterrence slides into a full-scale nuclear arms race—for of course your rival's fears and calculations have been exactly the same as yours.

non-nuclear. True, it still allows the more advanced nuclear states to go on improving their arsenals through sophisticated ways like computer simulation which late- or newcomers may not possess. It is clear, however, that in the absence of a CTBT, the upgrading and development of new generations of weapons (through underground tests, notably, which the CTBT bans) is bound to be far more unrestricted. The treaty, then, the fruit of negotiations which have been going on intermittently since 1958, is one big step forward.[16] The key point is that, in a grossly unequal world, any treaty that falls short of immediate and total nuclear—and maybe even universal—disarmament will have some unequal fall-outs, for it will leave more developed and sophisticated states with an advantage. (Even total disarmament may not end that advantage: technologically and scientifically advanced states like the USA would still be able to rearm much more quickly and effectively than, say, India.) No treaty, however perfect, can be expected to end the unequal economic, military, and scientific state of the world: *that* would require wholesale social and political transformation.

The 'all or nothing' standpoint from which India claims to have rejected the CTBT is in any case a very recent discovery of ours. Jawaharlal Nehru was the first world statesman to advocate a ban on nuclear tests, independently of other disarmament measures.[17] The Partial Test Ban Treaty of 1963 has been widely acknowledged as a significant, though limited, step away from the nuclear abyss, even though in a way it was as 'discriminatory' as the CTBT. It banned atmospheric but not underground testing, and at that time the more advanced nuclear states (USA, USSR, Britain) were obviously better prepared to carry on testing underground than latecomers into the nuclear club, France and China (the two countries which went on with atmospheric tests till 1980). As late as 1993, India co-sponsored

[16] Praful Bidwai and Achin Vanaik, *Testing Times: The Global Stake in a Nuclear Test Ban* (Uppsala, 1996).

[17] On 2 April 1954, after the American hydrogen bomb test at Bikini had killed a Japanese fisherman and 46 Pacific islanders, leading to worldwide indignation at the way atmospheric tests were poisoning the environment. Ibid., p. 34; *Darkness of a Thousand Suns*, p. 18.

with the USA a UN resolution urging negotiations on the CTBT, without making timebound disarmament by existing nuclear powers a precondition—the stand which it would take, rather suddenly, around late-1995, early-1996.

After Pokhran II, it is difficult to avoid the inference that this sudden Indian volte face was connected primarily with internal pressures for going openly nuclear through underground testing. The anti-US rhetoric used to justify rejection of the CTBT—and then to defend the Indian bomb—consorts very oddly with the obvious growing subservience to the West in every other matter, notably economic policies, precisely during the same years. It is significant, also, that after the tests several commentators known for their hawkish tendencies have started hinting that *now* India can sign the CTBT. Evidently, the whole point had been, not any principled struggle against nuclear hegemony or 'apartheid', but just a desire to join the club of the big bullies. Such great-power ambitions—absurd and peculiarly obscene for a country with such levels of mass poverty and illiteracy—provide the context also for the occasional attempt to locate Indian nuclear policy in the context primarily of China rather than Pakistan. Yet India has lived with a nuclear China since 1964, without having to surrender its border claims, and without—after 1971—any major conflict or sense of being seriously threatened. The China bogey, however, might prove helpful in justifying much heavier investment in nuclear armaments than would be plausible *vis-à-vis* Pakistan alone. And in any case our leaders are now busy developing a new language of an alleged post-Cold War South Asian 'power vacuum' which India somehow has an obligation to fill.

Hindsight indicates that the Left may have made a big mistake in going along with the opposition to the CTBT, at a time when it did have a chance of influencing major state decisions under the United Front regimes. That, and perhaps that alone, could have restrained subsequent BJP irresponsibility and blocked Pokhran II. The middle ground of the open nuclear option was inherently unstable, maybe even illogical,[18] and has now collapsed with the greatest of ease.

[18] Keeping the option open implied that there was no principled rejection of the bomb, only a question of expediency. If so, as hawks had been arguing for years, why not go ahead and become nuclear openly, particularly because

Inexplicably, the confusion within the Left on this question conti-
nues. In a welcome though belated shift, the CPI and the CPI(M) did
considerably stiffen their criticism of the BJP tests, subsequent sabre-
rattling, and talk of weaponisation. But undying hostility to the
CTBT still seems for them something like an article of faith. For the
Left, in particular, it should be amply clear by now that Indian opposition to the CTBT has not helped world disarmament processes,
nor obstructed US imperialist designs in the slightest. If anything, it
may have strengthened, slightly, the bitter opposition of US right-
wing forces to even this partial constraint.

The other way in which insensitivity about nuclear perils keeps
manifesting itself is in the praise lavished on the allegedly wonderful
achievements of Indian scientists in blasting bombs. We may leave
aside as less important questions about the real extent and originality
of this achievement, which at best can have only repeated what a number of other countries did forty to fifty years ago. The real point is
to ask why we should be asked to celebrate as our patriotic duty the
coming into operation of still more weapons of mass annihilation,
and what kinds of mind-sets and assumptions lie behind such expectations. Praise of this sort is an insult to the galaxy of eminent scientists,
from Einstein and Szilard through the Pugwash Conferences down
to Sakharov, who have fought against the bomb. The honour of
Indian science has been upheld, rather, by those scientists who have
protested, putting at risk sometimes their careers (several of them
work in laboratories funded by the DRDO), and facing on one occasion an assault by thugs of the Vishwa Hindu Parishad (VHP).

No doubt such praise for the marvels of Pokhran is coming most
easily from those who have already 'grown up and learnt to love the
bomb', to paraphrase the subtitle of *Dr Strangelove*. But one must recognise also a wider appeal, based on the assumption, common
among scientists and many others, that the progress of scientific
knowledge and technology is an end in itself, laudable even if totally
abstracted from human considerations and values. Such fetishisation
of science is not really effectively countered by the anti-science modes

---

a potentiality claimed for many years but never actualised would tend to seem
a bit like a bluff?

of thinking which have been projected in recent years by groups of small but influential intellectuals as part of a more general onslaught on post-Enlightenment 'Western' rationality. Like its fetishisers, this too takes science as a bloc and ignores the manifold ways in which scientific modernity has improved the human lot—by helping to dramatically extend life expectancy, for instance, even in a country like India. The point really is, as one article powerfully argued after Pokhran II, '*what* science are we talking about.'[19] There is a need to recognise that a fetishised science is above all an ideology, in the precise sense of being bound up, whether deliberately or not, with specific group interests. The arms race has been fuelled everywhere by combinations of political, military, industrial, and scientific interests, and nuclearisation of course vastly enhances the relative weight of the scientific component within such complexes. Tests and weaponisation, bluntly, mean a vast expansion of funding for certain branches of science and some defence establishments. It is not just a question of an abstract national interest, but very concrete matters of grants, promotion, patronage—and much of it kept conveniently under wraps, in India far more than in other democratic countries, for reasons of 'security'.

The problem lies not in rationality but in a reason that has turned irrational. For that, precisely, is what love of the bomb amounts to—and it is not at all surprising that celebration of the scientific achievement of Pokhran consorts perfectly with the most blatant forms of irrationality and superstition. The VHP, it may be recalled, even wanted a Shakti temple at Pokhran and was eager to sprinkle radioactive sand from there all over the country.

IV

Celebration of the BJP bomb is rooted, above all, in nationalism of a peculiarly unreflective kind. Once again, as with science, there is a need to distinguish, to discriminate: wholesale rejections of the modern nation-state, as indulged in by some intellectuals today, do not help. Such rejection in fact can go along with implicit forms of cultural nationalism, where the place of origin of ideas or institutions

---

[19] Rustom Bharucha, 'Politician's Grin, Not the Buddha's Smile', *Economic and Political Weekly*, XXXIII, 22, 30 May–5 June 1998.

become the basic standard of judgement. There are many nation-states in the world more technologically advanced than India who have not felt this desperate desire for the bomb. An over-general critique is radical only in appearance. By spreading the target too wide, to include all 'modern' states—or, within India, the entire Westernised middle class and high-caste elites, it actually risks providing an alibi for the precise political formation that has made India definitively nuclear today: the Sangh Parivar. Analysis must seek to combine exploration of wider affinities and linkages with firm recognition of where the precise responsibility has to be located.

With a history of two hundred years of colonial subjection, it is perhaps natural for many of us to ascribe a positive value to nationalism per se in third-world contexts: the 'bad' nationalisms being assumed to be those of the Western imperialist nations alone. Yet it is actually quite remarkable how much of courageous self-criticism and internal debate there was in the pristine years of Indian anti-colonial nationalism. That had seldom been the monolithic narrative of unquestioning, simple-minded anti-foreign thinking and action that is presented today in the bulk of elementary textbooks and media projections—dangerous oversimplifications that under BJP rule threaten to drown out alternative views of history as 'anti-national'.

Two aspects of this valuable but often forgotten internal debate appear particularly relevant. In different, sometimes contradictory ways, the major Indian thinkers of the early twentieth century, notably Tagore, Gandhi and Nehru, were deeply critical of aggressive, chauvinist, power-obsessed nationalism, whether Western or Indian (or for that matter Japanese). Rabindranath wrote a book entitled *Nationalism* where that term was used throughout in a pejorative sense.[20] Gandhi clearly felt that freedom would be worthless if it merely replaced white rulers by brown. Unlike cultural nationalists, then or now, the real problem for him was the immorality, not place of origin,[21] of industrial civilisation, whether in the West or

---

[20] Perhaps even more remarkable was the way in which he attacked what today would be termed by many 'political realism,' through the portrayal of Sandip in *Ghare-Baire* (1915–16). For a more detailed discussion, see chapter v above.

[21] Gandhi, as is well known, had no problem with acknowledging his indebtedness to Western thinkers like Ruskin, Thoreau, Emerson, and Tolstoy.

elsewhere. Predictably, he denounced the atom bomb unequivocally as the 'most diabolical use of science'.[22] In a different mode, Nehru, along with the Communist and Socialist Left, sought to impart an internationalist dimension to the Indian anti-colonial struggle.

The more fruitful and effective kinds of Indian anti-colonial nationalism, in the second place, seldom rested content with projecting the 'nation' in the abstract. Right from the times of Dadabhai Naoroji and R.C. Dutt, the poverty of the vast majority of Indians became central to nationalist critiques of colonial rule. Anti-colonial nationalism was eventually able to enthuse and mobilise millions because it had come to be increasingly associated with perspectives of social justice and a more egalitarian world: wiping the tears from the eyes of every Indian, in the memorable words of the Mahatma. There were great differences, at times sharp conflicts, between the alternative programmes that had emerged—Gandhian, Nehruvian, Left, Ambedkarite—but what remained common was a basic concern with the fate of those most numerous and most poor. The one great exception in this respect was constituted by the communal forces, and notably the Hindutva formation, in the writings and activities of which questions of mass poverty and exploitation have hardly ever figured.

After Independence these wider perspectives of anti-colonial nationalism came to be progressively attenuated, often reduced to official rhetoric or slogans for getting votes. Even populist rhetoric, however, helped to keep alive till recently a sense of guilt among Indian elites for being privileged and prosperous amidst people who, despite significant development and change, remain so terribly poor. The language of liberalisation that has come into vogue over the last decade or so, however, has largely shattered this residual populism. The coincidence in time between this change in dominant discourse and the rapid rise to power of Hindutva is surely too close to have been entirely accidental, though the possible linkages still await detailed explication.

The nationalism that strides so arrogantly across the political stage today is curiously bereft of inner content or meaning. The 'nation' nowadays often seems to mean not living human beings but a map and a flag, a geographical space with 'sacred' boundaries that must

[22] *Harijan*, 29 September 1946: cited in *Darkness of a Thousand Suns*, p. 7.

be maintained at all costs—even, it seems, with nuclear weapons that might in the process wipe out the people living within that space as completely as those outside. The object of fetishisation has moved from abstract 'people' or 'culture' to lines on a map: frontiers which in our case, incidentally, happen to have been entirely inherited from colonial times and were often drawn up with very little knowledge of conditions on the ground, by minor British officials like MacMahon for the China frontier and Radcliffe when India was partitioned. (The Chinese case is of course no better, for that rests on Manchu-imperial claims.)

The cult of sacred borders has spread so deeply that even the General Secretary of the CPI(M), if the newspaper report was accurate, felt the need to declare that his Party was 'opposed to even an inch of Indian soil being annexed by any country.'[23] And this at a meeting in Thiruvananthapuram to commemorate the 150th anniversary of the Communist Manifesto, that text of soaring internationalism which had proclaimed that workers have no country, only chains to break and a world to win. So much has changed on the Left, too: dare we recall today those weeks immediately after the October Revolution when Trotsky, as Commissar of Foreign Affairs, had published the secret treaties giving Constantinople and many other strategic advantages to Russia, and had declared them all 'torn to pieces and annihilated'—and when Stalin as Commissar of Nationalities had gone to Helsinki to proclaim the independence of Finland, a part of Tsarist Russia for more than a century? No doubt it is absurd to expect such utopianism anywhere today, but surely patriotism needs to be rescued from the fetishisation of maps and frontiers.

V

In the weeks and months just after Pokhran and Chagai, several delegations of Hibakushas (Hiroshima survivors) visited the subcontinent to express solidarity with anti-nuclear protests in India. For some of us, the first-hand accounts of that terrible August morning stirred memories of a book read a long time back, and all but forgotten during the years when nuclear war had seemed so safely distant from

[23] Hindu, 15 June 1998.

India: Robert Jungk's searing tale of Hiroshima after the bomb, *Children of the Ashes.*

The luckiest, Jungk writes, were those who were vaporised instantaneously, like the mayor of Hiroshima, turned into a 'little pile of ash' at the moment when he was explaining to his son the meaning of the Buddha's teachings. But larger numbers 'were condemned to long-drawn-out agonies, to mutilation, to endless sickness.' For many days after 6 August, Hiroshima became 'the site of movements repeated a hundred thousand times, of a million agonies that filled morning, noon, and night, with groans, screams, whimperings, and of crowds of cripples. All who could still run, walk, hobble, or even drag themselves along the ground were searching for something, for a few drops of water, for food, for medicine, for a doctor, for the pitiful relics of their possessions, for shelter. Or searching for the uncountable thousands who need no longer suffer, for the dead.'[24] The agony and tension has continued for many. Many still die every year of radiation-induced cancer fifty-five years after the Americans dropped those bombs on a country which had already started suing for terms of surrender.

The 'Little Boy' that destroyed Hiroshima has been far surpassed in size and destructive power by tens of thousands of bombs and missiles. Even some of the Indian ones claim to be considerably bigger.

Is it being unpatriotic or 'denationalised' to try to do what little one can to prevent our cities and peoples, all peoples, from turning into such a nuclear hell?

[24] Robert Jungk, *Children of the Ashes: The People of Hiroshima* (Harmondsworth, 1963), pp. 16, 18, and *passim.*

CHAPTER VIII

Christianity, Hindutva, and the Question of Conversions*

P OKHRAN BLASTS and vastly accelerated 'liberalisation' apart, it
seems likely that BJP-dominated rule at Delhi might come to be
remembered above all for the concerted campaign against Christians. The Sangh Parivar has always needed one or more enemy Others to consolidate into an aggressive bloc the 'Hindu community'
which it claims to represent and seeks to constitute. What is new is
that for a couple of years after coming to power at Delhi and prior
to the Gujarat genocide of 2002, Christians appeared at times to have
displaced Muslims as the primary target.

It started in Gujarat in 1997–8, the one state where the BJP has
on its own a stable majority, and spread to the adivasi areas of Orissa.
The widespread revulsion evoked by the sheer horror of the Staines
killings (23 January 1999) seemed to have produced a brief lull. But
then the attacks started again and came to be more and more widely
distributed. By August 2000 they had spread to a very big part of the
country: Uttar Pradesh, Haryana, Panjab, Madhya Pradesh, Andhra,
Karnataka, Tamilnadu, Goa . . . the list is growing. A recent Christian estimate places the number of recorded attacks since 1998 at 184,
while there have been 35 incidents in the first six months of 2000
alone.[1]

---

*Earlier versions of parts of this essay have been published as 'Hindutva and
the Question of Conversions', in K.N. Panikkar, ed., *The Concerned Indian's
Guide to Communalism* (Delhi, 1999) , and 'Conversions and Politics of Hindu
Right', *Economic and Political Weekly*, xxxiv, 26, 26 June 1999.
[1] *Frontline*, 7 July, 4 August 2000.

Efforts at absolving the Vajpayee government and the Sangh Parivar from responsibility have been frequent but unconvincing. For a long time we were assured that the incidents were no more than 'normal' criminal acts without ideological or religious motivations—and sometimes that they were products of quarrels among Christians themselves. By summer 2000 this was clearly becoming unbelievable, and then suddenly the hidden hand of Pakistan's ISI displaced pure criminality in official discourse. A few members of an utterly obscure Islamic sect were held responsible for the series of bomb blasts in churches in some of the southern states. Even if further investigation establishes such responsibility for the bomb attacks (which did stand out quite a bit from the other, far more numerous, incidents), it is surely stretching credulity much too far to believe that a tiny fringe group would have the capacity to organise such a concerted, countrywide anti-Christian campaign. Above all, there is the continuous flow of hate literature, with clearly identifiable Hindutva markers, being produced by a plethora of 'faceless, addressless front organisations of the Sangh Parivar',[2] as well as numerous statements by top VHP leaders.[3] But then such camouflage has been the RSS strategy throughout its 75-year-long history, setting up ever so often new, openly aggressive outfits which are controlled by its own cadres, but for which it (as well as the more 'respectable' Parivar members) can always deny responsibility.[4]

[2] Parvati Menon, 'An Assault on Christians', *Frontline*, 7 July 2000.

[3] To cite just a couple of statements among very many: after the gang-rape of four nuns in Jhabua, Madhya Pradesh (23 September 1998), B.L. Sharma, ex-BJP MP and current VHP leader, claimed that this was a result of the 'anger of patriotic youth against anti-national forces . . . the direct result of conversion of Hindus to Christianity by Christian priests.' And VHP general secretary Giriraj Kishore combined condemnation of the rape with the demand that 'foreign missionaries should be removed from the country.' *Hindu*, 29 September 1998; *The Times of India*, 1 October 1998.

[4] Thomas Blom Hansen's *The Saffron Wave* (Delhi, 1999) includes a case study of Pune illuminating this strategy, as elaborated primarily *vis-à-vis* Muslims. A Patit Pawan Sangh was set up in the city in 1967, with a primarily non-Brahman (Maratha) membership, apparently very different in composition and style from the Brahman-dominated RSS. A Patit Pawan activist described the RSS as characterised by 'silent work, no attack . . . typical brahmin style . . . our

The smokescreens may not be all that effective, but there is a need to recognise that the Sangh Parivar has been playing rather effectively upon one element of widespread 'common sense' that has a reach much beyond adherents of Hindutva. This is the issue of conversions, on which any anti-Christian campaign in India necessarily has to base itself. For, in partial contrast to Hindu–Muslim relations, between Hindus and Christians there are no memories of communal violence or Partition, nothing that really corresponds to issues like *go-korbani* or music before mosques that have sparked off so many riots at least since the 1890s.[5] It is not at all accidental that the so-called mild face of the BJP, namely Vajpayee, had recourse to this ploy when he visited Gujarat just after the Christmas burnings of churches in December 1998 and called for a 'national debate' on conversions, thus adroitly hinting that Christians are ultimately responsible for their own woes.[6]

There remains much confusion about this question of Christian

---

style is the other one, the Maratha.' A group of Patit Pawan members boasted to Hansen (30 January 1993) that 'Pune is more peaceful because they [the Muslims] are in minority and always beaten up.' Patit Pawan leaders however are invariably also RSS cadres, and Gopinath Munde, BJP leader in the Maharashtra Assembly, began his career in that front organisation. Hansen, pp. 124–5.

[5] Christian propaganda against 'idolatry' might seem to provide a similar issue, and no doubt there have been many instances, particularly in the colonial era, of such campaigns being very aggressive. But then so many Hindu reform movements have also condemned image worship, notably the Brahmos and the early Arya Samaj.

[6] And this, though the Director-General of the Gujarat police had declared categorically on 6 October 1998 that charges of forced inter-religious marriages and conversions by Christian missionaries in the Dangs adivasi belt of Gujarat were baseless, and the real 'serious danger to peace' was coming rather from Vishwa Hindu Parishad and Bajrang Dal activists. There have been many reports, in contrast, of tribals being rounded up in jeeps, taken to a Hindu ashram, given a purificatory bath (*shuddhikaran*) at a hot spring, and then being told that they were now no longer Christians but Hindus. Conversion by force requires the complicity of sections of the state apparatus, and it is clearly absurd to think that such support could come the way of Christian missionaries today, above all in the BJP bastion of Gujarat. For more detail, see Teesta Setalvad and Javed Anand, ed., *Communalism Combat*, October 1998, January 1999, as well as their extremely informative *Saffron Army Targets People of the Cross, Resources for Secularism 3* (Mumbai, September 1998).

conversions even among well-intentioned and progressive people.
While few hesitated to condemn the Staines murder, this could be
accompanied by something like a *sotto voce* 'but' about conversions—
as indicated by the oft-repeated argument that the doctor was not engaged in proselytisation. Even if he had been, would that have justified his being burnt alive with his children? Even Swami Agnivesh,
well-known champion of so many progressive causes, welcomed
Vajpayee's call for a national debate, and, while stating that 'individual freedom is the key to the modern outlook', declared he was
'indignant at conversions.'[7] Under the headline 'Gandhians blame
conversions, seek total ban', the *Indian Express* of 7 January 1999 carried a statement by two senior Gujarat Sarvodaya workers, one of
whom, the 82-year-old Ghelubhai Nayak, claimed that way back in
1948 Sardar Patel had sent him to the Dangs region to counter possible Christian conversions.

    In logic and law alike, one would have thought, there is little scope
for doubt or confusion here. Article 25 (i) of the Fundamental Rights
chapter in the Constitution defines the 'Right to Freedom of Religion' quite categorically: 'all persons are equally entitled to freedom
of conscience and the right freely to profess, practice and propagate
religion.' Propagation makes no sense at all without the possibility
of convincing others of the validity of one's religious beliefs and rituals. Freedom of choice, in religion or for that matter in politics or
anything else, and therefore freedom to change one's beliefs, is surely
in any case integral to any conception of democracy. Conversely, conversion by force or fraud is contrary to the basic principle of equal
freedom.

    Yet, in an admittedly specific and isolated judgement, a Supreme
Court judge defied common sense by declaring that the right to propagate does not include the right to convert, and it is pointless to deny
that doubts about this subject have come to be accepted as somehow
'natural' by many. But it is always the 'natural' that stands in need
of the most rigorous questioning, and I feel that a little historical
exploration might help. In what follows, I look first at the question
of conversions and its changing meanings and forms across time, trying to investigate when, under what conditions, and how it became

    [7] 'Why Fear a Debate about Conversions?', *Communalism Combat*, January
1999.

such a contentious issue. My closing section will come back to current events, and ask why the Sangh Parivar has chosen such a tiny minority as its prime target, and what developments might be helping to make such targeting appear plausible.

II

Let me begin by raising two preliminary questions, one of logic, the other of semantics.

What conditions, or widely held assumptions, are necessary before conversions can become a contentious issue, and arouse widespread and violent passions? Clearly, religious communities need to have become crystallised. They need to be seen as having firm and fixed boundaries, so that the crossing of borders becomes a dramatic, one-shot matter. But conversions become controversial on a qualitatively higher scale when relations between such crystallised religious communities come to be widely assumed to be inevitably conflictual. It is then that we have what in twentieth-century Indian English has come to be called 'communalism', for which developed 'community-consciousness' is a necessary, but not sufficient condition. This requires, not just the transition from 'fuzzy' to 'enumerated' communities (to which Sudipta Kaviraj drew attention in an influential essay), but the further assumption of inevitable and overriding[8] conflict of interests, such that, in a kind of zero-sum game, the gain of one community is thought to invariably involve the loss of the other.

It needs to be emphasised that this distinction between developed community consciousness and communalism is important precisely because tendencies exist that virtually equate the latter with any firmly bounded religious identity. These operate from two diametrically opposed points of view. P.K. Datta has made the perceptive point that communalism is distinctive among ideologies in its refusal to name itself.[9] There is rather the constant effort at identification with religious community, as well as, for Hindu-majoritarian communalists, with nationalism. Consider for instance the very term 'Hindutva'

---

[8] In the sense of being considered more vital than, say, anti-colonial struggle, economic development, or ideals of democracy or social justice.

[9] 'Unlike fascists, no one claims to be a communalist. . . . The nature of communalism encourages itself to be overwritten by other narratives.' Datta, *Carving Blocs*, p. 7.

which literally means no more than 'Hindu-ness' but has come to be the self-description, from the mid-1920s onwards, of a much more specific and narrow ideology.[10] And here extremes sometimes meet, for if secularism gets equated with anti-religion, the implication becomes that communalism can be countered only by exposing religion as 'superstitious' or 'irrational'. Once, again, in effect, 'communal' is being collapsed into 'religious community'. Operationally, such hostility to religion has been rare within Indian secularism, for here the term has really been synonymous with anti-communal policies and values rather than being anti-religious or even particularly rationalist. Anti-secularist polemic, however, frequently makes such an equation for its own purposes. Paradoxically, when combined with a rejection of Hindutva (as within an influential current intellectual trend), 'communal' and 'community' once again tend to get collapsed into each other, except that then a sharp disjunction is postulated between 'modern' and 'pre-modern' communities, 'religion-as-ideology' as contrasted to a somewhat romanticised 'religion-as-faith'.[11]

The sense of outrage evoked by religious conversion can be greatly intensified and made to appear much more legitimate if the loss can be given a 'patriotic' or 'national' colour. This, of course, has been the special advantage enjoyed by Hindu majoritarianism, particularly after 1947. Sangh Parivar justifications of recent outrages against Chris-tians are replete with instances of such an equation.

[10] I find unsatisfactory also the very common definition of communalism in terms of phrases like 'politicisation of religious identity', or 'political use of religion'. Politicisation can take many different forms. In the Non-Cooperation–Khilafat movement of 1919–22 there was intense mobilisation of both Muslims and Hindus through what may be crudely called 'political use of religion', and yet that was the highest level of Hindu–Muslim unity ever achieved in the anti-colonial struggle. The crucial distinction lies in the assumption of inevitable conflict.

[11] The ablest statement of such views, which have become a prominent trend also within late Subaltern Studies, is Ashis Nandy, 'The Politics of Secularism and the Recovery of Religious Tolerance', in Veena Das, ed., Mirrors of Violence: Riots and Survivors in South Asia (Delhi, 1990). For a fuller exposition of my views on this and related themes, see Sumit Sarkar, 'The Anti-Secularist Critique of Hindutva: Problems of a Shared Discursive Space', Germinal, Journal of Department of Germanic and Romance Studies, Delhi University, volume I, 1994, as well as my Writing Social History (Delhi, 1997), chapters 1 and 3.

One needs to note also the very effective semantic ploy through which it has come to be widely assumed that Hinduism is near-unique among religious traditions in being non-proselytising: conversion to other faiths therefore is a loss that cannot be recuperated, and so is made to seem particularly unfair. This at first sight seems to fit in well with the commonsense view that one can become a Hindu by birth alone, since caste (whether in the varna or the jati sense) is crucial to Hinduism, and your caste status is hereditary. But certain ticklish questions arise as soon as we enlarge the time perspective: where did all the Buddhists of ancient India go, for instance? And how did Hindu icons and myths spill over into large parts of South East Asia? More crucially, one needs to recognise that, across centuries but in an accelerated manner with modernised communications, Brahmanical Hindu rituals, beliefs, and caste disciplines have spread across the sub-continent and penetrated and sought to transform communities with initially very different practices and faiths. It has somehow become conventional to describe the processes here by anodyne terms like 'sanskritisation' or 'cultural integration', but they really amount nevertheless to what with other religious traditions would have been termed 'conversion'. There is also much historical data about the spread of specific varieties of Hindu traditions, like for instance Chaitanya bhakti from Central and Western Bengal into Orissa and the uplands of Jharkhand. A whole battery of terms was developed, in fact, from the late nineteenth century onwards as the expansion directed towards marginal groups and tribals became more organised: 'reclamation', *shuddhi* ('purification'), 'reconversion', '*paravartan*' ('turning back'—the term preferred by the VHP today). Common to all these labels is an insistence that all that is being attempted is to bring people back to their 'natural' state: which, for all the targeted groups, is always assumed to be being Hindu in a more-or-less sanskritised manner. Semantic aggression can hardly go further.

But if shifts in religious allegiance are obviously nothing new, their forms are likely to have changed over time. The precise meanings of 'conversion' need to be historicised.

The thrust of much recent historical work has been towards the destabilisation of assumptions of continuous, firmly-bounded identities. This is in significant contrast to the bulk of earlier historiography, which had tended to essentialise terms like Hindu or Muslim and gone on to emphasise either the moments of synthesis, or (in the communal variant) perennial conflict.[12] One need not go as far in the questioning of pre-colonial identities as some colonial discourse analysts would want, to agree that the absence of modern communicational networks (developed roads, railways, telegraph lines, the printing press, etc.) must have greatly hindered the formation of stable and tight countrywide religious blocs. Trends in medieval Indian scholarship seem to be moving in a similar direction, through a more rigorous probing of the rhetorical aspects and precise implications of texts that at first sight seem to indicate a high level of religious conflict and persecution. (Selective nineteenth-century translations from some of these, notably by Elliot and Dowson, had greatly contributed to communalisation.) Thus Persian chronicles boasting of wars against infidels and the desecration of temples—or for that matter a text like the Vilasa copper-plate grant describing in lurid but highly formulaic terms the Kali-yuga ushered in by Muhammad bin Tughlaq's destruction of the Kakatiya dynasty in Andhra—are being recognised to have been in part legitimising devices. (The same temples, for instance, seem to be getting destroyed again and again, as Romila Thapar has shown recently in an unpublished paper about Somnath.) Again, 'Hindu' texts, in Sanskrit or regional languages like Telugu, overwhelmingly use ethnic rather than religious terms (Turushka, most commonly) to describe the kingdoms and armies we have become accustomed since the nineteenth century to call 'Muslim'.[13] All this does not mean, of course, that there were not many instances

[12] See the perceptive criticism made by Richard Eaton of Dineshchandra Sen's interpretation of the Satya Pir cult of medieval Bengal in the latter's *History of Bengali Language and Literature* (Calcutta, 1954). Sen had described this cult to have been a synthesis produced by a situation where 'two communities mixed so closely, and were so greatly influenced by one another.' This, Eaton points out, 'postulated the more or less timeless existence of two separate and self-contained communities in Bengal, adhering to two separate and self-contained religious systems, "Hinduism" and "Islam".' Richard M. Eaton, *The Rise of Islam and the Bengal Frontier, 1204–1760* (Delhi, 1994), p. 280. A similar argument concerning fluid precolonial boundaries has been elaborated by Susan Bayly, *Saints, Goddesses and Kings: Muslims and Christians in South Indian Society 1700–1900* (Cambridge, 1989).

[13] Thus Cynthia Talbot states that the sample of *c.* 100 Telugu inscriptions (*c.* 14th–17th century) she has studied do not use religious labels at all while

of conflicts and acts of violence and persecution wholly or partly 'religious' (though even the meaning of that term is not entirely transparent, or impervious to change), amidst much everyday coexistence and the commingling of practices. But their generalisation into mass communal ideologies with a subcontinental reach was unlikely.

In an important discussion of processes of Islamisation in medieval Bengal, Eaton has tried to draw out the implications of this relative absence of firmly bounded communities for the question of religious conversions. Use of the term itself, he argues, becomes 'perhaps misleading—since it ordinarily connotes a sudden and total transformation', whereas the changes could have 'proceeded so gradually as to be nearly imperceptible.'[14] Like other secular-minded historians, Eaton rejects the theory of large-scale forcible conversion, since the regions that became massively Muslim—East Bengal and Western Punjab—were also those furthest away from major centres of Muslim politico-military power. He discounts also the view that Islam attracted converts from lower castes primarily by virtue of its egalitarian tenets, for these were also the areas where Brahmanical penetration, and therefore structures of caste oppression, had been relatively weak. By implication, Eaton's account draws attention to the possibility that in large parts of the subcontinent, certainly in medieval times and to a considerable extent even today, the great religious traditions have been expanding at the cost not so much of each other as in relation to a multitude of local cults and practices. Conflicts in pre-modern times would have been considerably reduced, further, by the slow, phased nature of the transition. Here Eaton distinguishes three heuristic moments: the 'inclusion' of Islamic cult figures within the local cosmologies, 'identification' of some of these with indigenous objects of worship, and finally (and perhaps often mainly in the nineteenth century) the 'displacement' through which Islam became 'purified' through reform or purging of non-Islamic beliefs and practices.[15] One might add that pre-colonial 'conversion' was probably

---

describing invasions and wars. Cynthia Talbot, 'Inscribing the Other, Inscribing the Self: Hindu–Muslim Identities in Pre-Colonial India', *Comparative Studies in Society and History*, volume 37, 1995. See also Brajadulal Chattopadhyaya, *Repre-senting the Other? Sanskrit Sources and the Muslims* (Delhi, 1998).

[14] Eaton, op. cit., p. 269.

[15] Eaton, pp. 113–19, 268–90.

not so much a matter of individual and one-shot choice, as of slow changes involving an entire group, family or kinship network, or local community—which would once again reduce the potentials for conflict.

Three major changes, starting roughly from the latter part of the nineteenth century, seem particularly relevant for understanding why conversions started becoming so much more controversial.

The first was the tightening of community boundaries: there has come into being a broad consensus about this among historians, despite continuing differences regarding the extent of novelty involved here, or in the precise weighing-up of causes.[16] Within the broader framework of developing politico-administrative, economic, and communicational integration, particularly important inputs probably came from colonial law, and from census operations. In matters of so-called 'personal' or 'family' law, the British had decided in the 1770s that they would administer according to Hindu or Islamic sacred texts and in consultation with Brahman pandits and Muslim ulema: differentially, in other words, for the two major religious traditions. In many everyday situations, therefore, one had to declare oneself a Hindu or Muslim (or a member of any of the other religious communities that were recognised to have 'personal' legal systems of their own). While superficially not dissimilar to Mughal practice, there was a significant change in so far as Mughal courts had never tried to penetrate deep into lower levels through the kind of systematic hierarchy of appellate jurisdictions that British rule developed over time. Disputes must have been often decided at local or village levels in accordance with diverse customary standards that would have had little to do with textual (or 'religious') principles. Colonial

---

[16] Chris Bayly's essay on the 'pre-history' of communalism which sought to question 'the facile assumption that intercommunal violence, specifically violence and contention between Hindus and Muslims, was a product of the colonial period alone' by drawing attention to many such clashes between c. 1700–1860, still rejected 'any unilinear or cumulative growth of communal identity before 1860. Indeed, one may very well doubt whether there was ever an identifiable "Muslim", "Hindu", or "Sikh" identity which could be abstracted from the particular circumstances of individual events or specific societies.' C.A.Bayly, *Origins of Nationality in South Asia: Patriotism and Ethical Government in the Making of Modern India* (Delhi, 1998), pp. 44, 233.

'personal' law centralised, textualised, and made operationally much sharper the boundaries between religious communities, and probably enhanced also to a significant extent the influence over the rest of society of high-caste and Muslim elites.

The impact of the census from the 1870s onwards is more obvious and has been repeatedly emphasised in recent academic discussions. Census operations necessitated the drawing of sharp distinctions, of religion, caste, language, or whatever else the administrators had decided on as worthy of being counted. Enumerated communities made for mutual competition, helped to produce complaints about unfair representation in education, jobs, administration or politics, and stimulated fears about being left behind in numbers games. That census procedures often involved the imposition of order, rather than a simple recording of realities on the ground, becomes clear, for instance, from the amusing instance in the 1911 census of a 35,000-strong community of 'Hindu–Muhammadans' in Gujarat, so termed by a Bombay census Superintendent confounded by the inextricable combination of multiple practices, beliefs, and even self-definitions. The latter was pulled up sharply by his superior, census Commissioner E.A. Gait, who ordered the location of 'the persons concerned to the one religion or the other as best he could.'[17]

Colonial modernity helped to tighten community bonds: it has been less often noticed, however, that it also stimulated forces that made them more fragile. What was coming into existence by the late-nineteenth- and early-twentieth century was a situation conducive to the growth of not one but many community-identities—religious, caste, linguistic-regional, anti-colonial 'national', class, gender, in interactive yet often conflictual relationships with each other.[18] Among the many merits of Datta's work is the way he has been able to bring together these interlocking narratives, in an effort to view 'communal

---

[17] *Census 1911, Volume I.i (India: Report)*, p. 118.

[18] The half century between *c.* 1875 and 1925 was marked by the formation of the Congress (1885), the Muslim League (1906) and the Hindu Mahasabha (*c.* 1915), a plethora of caste associations, the development of strong regional nationalisms in Bengal, Maharashtra, Andhra, Tamilnad and elsewhere, the foundation of the All India Trade Union Congress (1920), and of early women's organisations like the Bharat Stree Mahamandal (1910), the Women's Indian Association (1917), and the All India Women's Conference (1927).

formations . . . as part of a field in which they have to perforce relate to other collective identities (other than its binary in 'Hindu' or 'Muslim'), such as class, gender, or caste affiliations.'[19]

Signs can be discerned of the beginnings of a discourse of individual rights. The direct influence of Western liberal and radical ideologies, while not negligible, was no doubt confined to relatively few, but there was also the fall-out from certain institutional developments. Colonial justice, while shoring up religiously defined community norms in personal law, simultaneously enlarged up to a point 'the freedom of the individual in the market-place' in land and commercial transactions.[20] British Indian definitions of criminal liability, too, came to be theoretically based on notions of 'an equal abstract and universal legal subject'—though once again only to a partial extent, for there were many accommodations in practice with existing social hierarchies.[21] Equality before the law, promised in much-cited official documents like the Queen's Proclamation of 1858, was often severely tempered by white racial privilege. But then promises simultaneously held out and broken tend to whet appetites, and such a dialectic came to operate, though of course in widely different and at times even contradictory ways, both with respect to attitudes towards their foreign overlords of a growing number of Indians, and lower-caste (and/or class) resentments about indigenous hierarchies of privilege and exploitation.

Even more significant initially, perhaps, were developments relating to gender. It has been argued recently that the nineteenth-century legal reforms and debates around women (sati, women's education, widow remarriage, age of consent, polygamy) may have been significant above all for their unsettling effect. The concrete achievements of social reform were not very substantial, but, along with the intense debates around them that became possible through the coming of print, they did contribute to a 'destabilising and problematising [of]

[19] Datta, op. cit., p. 9.
[20] D.A. Washbrook, 'Law, State and Agrarian Society in Colonial India', in Baker, Johnson and Seal, eds, *Power, Profit and Politics* (Cambridge, 1981), p. 650, and *passim*.
[21] See Singha, *A Despotism of Law*, op. cit., p. viii.

the old order.' For legality now clashed with religious prescription,[22] a small but growing number of women took to education violating customary prohibitions, and even conservative defenders of the old rules and norms had to use, increasingly, a new language of the woman's own consent.[23] Indian reformist efforts at social change through colonial legislation, though much resented by many nationalists, helped constitute 'an excess that gave the woman, at least notionally, a sphere of personal rights *outside* the rule of the family and community.'[24] We also come across instances where notions of equal rights were counterposed directly to standard high-Hindu assumptions of community unity grounded in hierarchy (*adhikari-bheda*), as for instance in a debate about women in the pages of the Bengali monthly *Nabyabharat* in May–June 1884.[25]

I am arguing, then, that the heightened late- and postcolonial tensions around conversions have to be related to community borders becoming simultaneously harder and more vulnerable. Let me try to illustrate through a few sample instances of conflict (or its absence), relating in the main to Christian conversions.

[22] Sati, so long a supreme sign of Hindu womanly virtue even if operationally practised only by a few, became a crime, while widow marriage, condemned by respectable Hindu society, was made legal.

[23] The petition against Bentinck's banning of sati in 1829, along with scriptural exegesis, also argued that Hindu widows immolated themselves 'of their own accord and pleasure'.

[24] The above paragraph summarises the important argument recently put forward in several papers by Tanika Sarkar. See for instance 'The Feminine Discourse: A Candid Look at the Past and the Present', in Rukmini Sekhar, ed., *Making A Difference: A Collection of Essays* (New Delhi, 1998). Quotations are from this essay.

[25] Responding to a plea for gender equality made by Siddheswar Roy—with citations from John Stuart Mill, but also a rider that women have to be first carefully trained for freedom by men through proper education—Sadananda Tarkachanchu argued that men, women, and animals all have their respective claims, or *adhikar*, but these necessarily differ according to the specific qualities of each. A horse cannot sit at an emperor's table, women are made for motherhood and so need to remain housebound, and complete equality would mean that the bhadralok could not ride on the backs of palanquin-bearers. *Nabyabharat*, Jaishtha, Asar 1291/ 1884.

While Christian proselytisation generally tended to focus primarily on tribals and lower castes, the Scottish missionary Alexander Duff in the Bengal of the 1830s and 1840s tried out an alternative strategy of targeting elite Indians through higher education, public debates and individual contacts. There were some spectacular individual conversions in upper-caste households, like Krishnamohan Banerji and Madhusudan Dutta, and in 1845 a major controversy burst out in Calcutta around Umeshchandra Sarkar and his wife, aged 14 and 11, defying family elders to become Christians. The sharp differences in educated high-caste Calcutta society around social and religious reform (notably the ban on widow immolation) were suddenly forgotten as Radhakanta Deb (leader of the conservative Dharma Sabha), Debendranath Tagore (inheritor of Rammohan's Brahmo mantle), and even the Derozian Ramgopal Ghosh joined hands to float a Hindu Hitarthi Vidyalaya to rescue education from the clutches of missionaries. The terms of argument as defined by Akshoykumar Dutta, Brahmo editor of *Tattvabodhini Patrika* and possessing a considerable rationalist reputation, were particularly interesting: 'Even the women within the household have started to turn Christian! Will we not wake up even after this terrible event?'[26] Individual conversion was felt to be a threat to family order.[27] Resentment and fear among propertied Hindus was compounded in 1850 by the passage of the Disabilities Removal Act which sought to protect the right of inheritance of converts.

Throughout the nineteenth century there were numerous polemical encounters between missionaries and Hindu or Muslim spokesmen, in public debates as well as through the press. These could be full of theological rancour and verbal violence, and yet were not, perhaps, all that qualitatively different from what in today's perspective

[26] Ajitkumar Chakrabarti, *Maharshi Debendranath Tagore* (Calcutta, 1916, 1971), pp. 110–11, and *passim*.

[27] The conversion of mission-school-educated Narayan Sheshadri and his minor brother provoked a similar storm in Bombay city in 1843. Frank Conlon, 'The Polemical Process in Nineteenth-Century Maharashtra: Vishnubawa Brahmachari and Hindu Revival', in Kenneth W. Jones, ed., *Religious Controversy in British India: Dialogues in South Asian Languages* (New York, 1992), pp. 12–13.

would be termed intra-community debates: the *shastratha* of Brahman pandits, or the *bahas* among Bengal Muslims.[28] Unlike the bulk of twentieth-century communal discourses, such polemics had an intellectual content, turning around questions of religious doctrines or practices. They were not as yet mere appeals for unthinking community solidarity, whipped up through emotive enemy images. Instances would include Vishnubawa Brahmachari's anti-missionary lectures on Bombay Back Bay beach between January and May 1857, or the encounter between a particularly aggressive missionary, Carl Pfanzer, and Dr Wazir Khan, graduate of Calcutta Medical College, in Agra on the eve of the Mutiny.[29] But the polemic with the most far-reaching (and long-lasting) consequences was undoubtedly that launched by Dayananda Saraswati in Chapter 13 of *Satyartha Prakash* (1875). This combined serious logical argument (at their best, somewhat reminiscent of Rammohan's critique of Trinity and Original Sin) with an emergent anti-white, anti-colonial tone: 'if a white man kills a black man, he is for the most part declared not guilty and acquitted. The same must be the justice administered in paradise.' Dayananda also raised the question of what kind of face the personal God of the Christians has: 'White like European? Or Black like African Negroes?' Yet there was also a clear patriarchal-cum-class dimension to much of this polemic. Belief in immaculate conception, he

[28] Public religious debates continued an old practice, but with a significantly widening audience in the nineteenth century through the coming of print. For some accounts of such debates among or within diverse religious traditions, see J.T.F. Jordens, *Dayananda Saraswati: His Life and Ideas* (Delhi, 1978); Rafiuddin Ahmed, *The Bengal Muslims 1871–1906: A Quest for Identity* (Delhi, 1981); Kenneth W. Jones, ed., op. cit. Harjot Oberoi, *The Construction of Religious Boundaries: Culture, Identity, and Diversity in the Sikh Tradition* (Delhi, 1994) and Vasudha Dalmia, *The Nationalization of Hindu Traditions: Bharatendu Harishchandra and Nineteenth-century Banaras* (Delhi, 1997).

[29] Conlon, op. cit.; Avril Powell, 'Muslim–Christian Confrontation: Dr Wazir Khan in 19th century Agra', both in Kenneth Jones, ed., *Religious Controversies*, op. cit. Wazir Khan seems a particularly interesting instance, for his missionary contender complained that the doctor was using the arguments of European freethinkers to attack Christianity: Spinoza, Voltaire, Paine, even the Young Hegelian David Strauss' life of Jesus.

argued, could lead to loss of control over women—'Any virgin who happened to conceive would give out that she conceived through God.' Dayananda was angered both by the St Matthew passage predicting sons rebelling against fathers for the sake of Jesus, and even more by the image of the camel passing through the needle's eye.[30] Christ to him was a mere carpenter's son, living in a *junglee desh*, a wild and poor country: 'This is why he prays for the daily bread.'[31]

At a different and more obscure level, the spread of Christianity among peasants occasionally aroused zamindar hostility. Landlords seem to have felt that converted tenants became less amenable to their demands, for in missionaries they had found an alternative source of authority and patronage. Cultivators and fishermen of Rammakolchoke, a village to the south of Calcutta, were fined ten rupees each in the late 1820s and beaten with shoes by their zamindar for turning Christian. There were clashes in 1840 at Bohirgacchi near Krishnagar (Nadia), and in a Barisal village in 1846 Hindu zamindars seized the lands, implements, cattle and even clothes of 29 Christian families and destroyed their huts. The converts had to take shelter among Muslim neighbours.[32] Diligent work on missionary archives and local official records would probably reveal many other instances. The missionaries were no doubt motivated primarily—and in many cases perhaps solely—by the desire for conversion, and would not have been pro-peasant or socially radical on principle. Their presence could still be a resource for the underprivileged, as for instance when French Catholic missionaries of the Pondicherry-based Societe des Missions Etrangeres helped agricultural labourers beaten up by landlords in a court case at Alladhy in 1874–5, an incident which seems to have stimulated a wave of mass conversions in that area.[33] It needs to be

---

[30] 'Jesus was a poor man. . . . It is why he wrote this. But the principle is not correct. The rich and the poor both have good men as well as bad men. Whoever does a good action gets good fruit and whoever does a bad action bad.'

[31] Kenneth Jones, 'Swami Dayananda Saraswati's Critique of Christianity', in Jones, ed., op. cit. The quotations from *Satyartha Prakash* are taken from this essay, pp. 66, 69, 63–4.

[32] G.A. Oddie, *Social Protest in India: British Protestant Missionaries and Social Reforms, 1850–1900* (Delhi, 1979), pp. 114–16.

[33] Henriette Bugge, 'The French Mission and the Mass Movements', in G.A.Oddie, ed., *Religious Conversion Movements in South Asia: Continuities and Change* (Surrey, 1997), p. 105.

added that there were occasions when missionary lobbying provided important inputs in moves towards pro-tenant legal reform, as in the run-up to the Bengal Tenancy Amendment of 1859, or in early-twentieth-century Chhota Nagpur where, according to the Census Report of 1911, 'the agrarian legislation, which is the Magna Carta of the aboriginal, is largely due to their influence.'[34]

It is true that there can be a nationalist position, abstracted from considerations of social justice, which might find in such pro-peasant missionary interventions evidence only of efforts to consolidate colonial power through dividing Indians.[35] But then what are we to make of a substantial section of foreign missionaries in Bengal during the 1850s, headed by Reverend James Long, who took a public stand against fellow white indigo planters before and during the 'Blue Mutiny'? Long even went to jail, accepting responsibility for publication of the English version of Dinabandhu Mitra's play *Neel-Darpan* (exposing the horrors of indigo), which had been translated by another Christian, Michael Madhusudan Dutta. Long has been deservedly immortalised in Bengal folk memory by a popular ditty:

The indigo monkeys have been ruining golden Bengal
Harish died before his time, Long has been sent to jail.

Prior to around the turn of the century, Christian proselytisation among the poor—as distinct from the rare but spectacular conversion of prominent men—does not seem to have become a central upper-caste (or *ashraf*) intelligentsia concern. Much of the expansion, in the nineteenth century as well as often later, was in outlying areas, largely untouched by mainstream Hinduism and Islam. The element of competition and conflict entered much later, with Hindu 'reconversion' efforts. In an interesting analysis of Christian conversion in Nagaland, Richard Eaton suggested that this could even provide a 'paradigm of

---

[34] To cite one more instance: J.C. Jack's *Bakarganj Settlement Report* (Calcutta, 1915) mentioned Christian bargadars as particularly active in the struggle for commutation of produce-rents in 1908. See chapter III above, pp. 89–91.

[35] The Census passage I have just quoted, incidentally, figures in Arun Shourie's violent polemic against Christianity: *Missionaries in India: Continuities, Changes, Dilemmas* (New Delhi, 1994), p. 23. For him this is a telling argument proving that Christian conversion is motivated uniquely by 'worldly benefits', and forms part of a deep-rooted Western conspiracy.

how previous aboriginals of India might, in earlier epochs, have accul-
turated to Hinduism, Buddhism or Islam.' As he argued later about
medieval Bengal, the role of political coercion seems to have been
negligible, despite the racial affinity between missionaries and colonial rulers. The great leap in Naga conversions took place *after* Independence, and there is also a significant lack of correlation between
the presence of foreign missionaries and the spread of Christianity.[36]
Much more decisive was the association of Christianity with the
spread of literacy and effective modern medicine, processes that were
greatly accelerated starting with the Second World War and the
Kohima campaign. The missionaries came as 'emissaries of the high
culture of the plains bringing the written word to the forest'—a
region of shifting cultivation with no written script or town life—not
unlike, in other parts of the subcontinent earlier, Brahmins, Buddhist
monks, Muslim officials and holy men. There were, in addition, elements of skilfull adaptation of Christianity to indigenous traditions,
establishing links with existing Naga notions of a supreme divinity,
for instance: once again, a parallel suggests itself with processes of the
sanskritising kind.[37]

The last quarter of the nineteenth century was marked by a surge
in the number of Christian conversions, so much so that it has been
described in mission histories as the era of 'mass movements'. Whole
families, villages or sub-castes came over en masse in a manner that
possibly reduced the aspect of conflict at local levels, but heightened
fears elsewhere.[38] Repeated famines could have had something to do

[36] The proportion of Christians among Nagas was only 17.9% in 1941, but
rose to 66.7% in 1971, while 'The Semas . . . never had a missionary among
them until 1948, which was *after* the steepest climb of conversion had already
taken place for that group.' Richard Eaton, 'Conversion to Christianity among
the Nagas: 1876–1971', *Indian Economic and Social History Review*, xxi.i,
January–March 1984, pp. 17–19.

[37] Ibid., pp. 32, 43, and *passim*.

[38] The number of Protestants in Madras Presidency shot up from *c.* 75,000
in 1851 to 300,000 by 1891; while converts of the Jesuit Madurai Mission,
169,000 in 1880, had become 260,000 in 1901. There was a sharp upturn also
in North India, after a long period of very slow growth. 'Native' Christians in
the North West Provinces and the Punjab numbered only 2000 in 1852 and

with this—the phenomenon of 'rice Christians', relief work by missions accompanied by baptisms, at times of small children, which embarrassed many Christians at times. But, in some areas at least, there were also links with lower-caste/class discontent, as among the pariah agricultural labourers of Chingleput and North Arcot in the early 1890s, where Methodist and Free Church of Scotland missionaries actively fostered efforts at empowerment directed against oppressive *mirasidars*.[39] Developments like these may have had something to do with Vivekananda's powerful pleas, in course of and after his travels in South India, for the upliftment of Untouchables—with which he often linked up the danger otherwise of Christian conversion.

Three processes began coming together from around the turn of the century to raise high-caste Hindu fears about conversion to a qualitatively higher level. The competitive logic of numbers made possible by census enumeration acquired greater salience through the gradual spread of representative institutions. In regions where the major religious communities had been revealed by census operations to have roughly equal numbers (like, notably, Bengal and Punjab), even small changes through conversion came to be perceived as ominous. There were in addition clear signs of a rapid growth in lower-caste affirmations, in part stimulated by the census bid in 1901 to fix caste rankings. There was a quantum leap in the number of caste associations and of publications by or on behalf of lower-caste groups, seeking in the main upward mobility of a sanskritising kind, but also going in at times for quite a lot of anti-Brahmanical and anti-caste rhetoric. An additional imput was provided by British divide-and-rule moves like Gait's abortive suggestion in 1910 to list separately in the coming census lower castes denied Brahman services and entry to temples. The compound of resentment and anxiety stimulated by census discourse was best articulated by U.N. Mukherji's very influential text, *Hindus: A Dying Race* (Calcutta, 1909), which skilfully

---

5000 ten years later, but 40,000 in Punjab alone in 1901. Bugge, op. cit.; Avril Powell, 'Processes of Conversion to Christianity in Nineteenth-century North-Western India': both articles in Oddie, ed., *Religious Conversion Movements*, pp. 97, 17.

[39] Oddie, *Social Protest*, op. cit., pp.128–46.

used some census data and predictions to develop a horrific vision of Hindu decline as contrasted to Muslim growth and strength.[40]

Mukherji pinpointed subordinated castes as the Achilles' heel of Hindu society, and his suggested remedies amounted therefore to a kind of organised and limited sanskritisation from the top at Brahmanical initiative. In practice, particularly in northern India as spearheaded by the Arya Samaj, the concrete response to the fear of declining numbers so vividly expressed by Mukherji took the form of the *shuddhi* movement to 'purify' or 'reconvert' marginal groups. Social upliftment efforts, which in strict logic could have been directed towards all subordinated lower castes and Untouchables, became in practice exercises in policing and modifying the borders between religious communities. The major targets of shuddhi—the Rahtia Sikhs around 1899–1900, the Malkana Rajputs of the Mathura-Farrukhabad region immediately after the collapse of the Non-Cooperation–Khilafat movement in 1922—were precisely those among whom syncretistic practices had been most prominent.[41] *Shuddhi-sangathan*, in tandem with their Muslim counterparts, *tabligh* and *tanzim*, became a principal source of acute Hindu–Muslim tension and violence in the mid-1920s.

If Sikhs, initially, and then on a far more intensive scale Muslims, were the dominant 'Others' of shuddhi, Christians were not being entirely forgotten in this fast-developing Hindu communalist discourse which was simultaneously tending to build bridges between reform-oriented Aryas and their old—at one time very bitter—Sanatanist rivals. The danger of Christian conversion in the wake of missionary famine-relief work had been one factor behind the Arya interest in the Rahtias, treated as virtual outcastes by other Sikhs.[42] A central text of the mid-1920s shuddhi movement, Swami Shraddhananda's *Hindu Sangathan: The Saviour of the Dying Race* (1926), while fulsomely acknowledging indebtedness to Mukherji in title and initial chapter,

[40] Dutta, *Carving Blocs*, op. cit., chapter I; Sumit Sarkar, 'Identity and Difference: Caste in the Formation of the Ideologies of Nationalism and Hindutva', *Writing Social History*, chapter 9. See also chapter II above.

[41] Thus the 1911 census described the Malkana Rajputs as a group that claimed 'that they are neither Hindus nor Muhammadans, but a mixture of both. Of late some of them have definitely abjured Islam.' Op. cit., p. 118.

[42] J.T.F. Jordens, *Swami Shraddhananda* (Delhi, 1981), pp. 52–3.

modified the latter's thesis by giving far greater centrality to conversion as a central cause of Hindu decline, and by somewhat unexpectedly giving almost as much space to Christians as to Muslims in its polemic. Conversion in any case had to be made into the key grievance in a movement directed towards 'reconverting' through purification, and Shraddhananda's chapter entitled 'The Causes of Decline in Number' announced, in bold headlines, 'the first cause' to be the 'conversion to other religious faiths'. Sections followed about Muslim and Christian conversions by 'force' and 'means other than force', with the author trying to use a bit of intra-Christian polemic (a German Protestant diatribe against Jesuits and the Inquisition) to establish his argument about Christian coercion and trickery—not too convincingly, it has to be said, because all the instances are confined to sixteenth-century Goa.[43]

Anti-conversion sentiments received a major stimulus from Savarkar's very far-reaching and influential definition of 'Hindu' in 1923 as those who uniquely combined *pitribhumi* and *punyabhumi*, fatherland with holyland. Through a very effective appropriation of nationalism by Hindu majoritarianism, indigenous origin of religious (or by extension, other) beliefs, practices, or institutions was made into the supreme criterion of value. It became easy to brand Muslims and Christians as somehow alien, unpatriotic by definition—a charge particularly effective against Christians in the colonial era due to their religious affinity with the foreign rulers.

The aggressive Hindu-nationalist ideological-political bloc that had come to be constituted by the mid-1920s (Savarkar's 1923 text and the foundation of the RSS in 1925 providing the obvious benchmarks) also tended to be socially conservative, even though reformist strands had contributed significantly to its making at times. The point can be made clearer through a glance at the precise ways and extent to which much-hated conversion—or more generally the presence of alternative proselytising religious structures—could contribute towards an empowerment of the downtrodden in Hindu society.

[43] Shraddhananda Sanyasi, *Hindu Sangathan: Saviour of the Dying Race* (n.p., March 1926), pp. 14–20, and *passim*. The once-standard Arya-reformist themes of 'perversion of the Aryan social polity' and 'child marriage and degradation of women' are mentioned, but only as second and third causes of Hindu decline, well after conversions.

Here it is easy to both exaggerate and downplay. Proselytisation, most of the time, seeks new adherents, not social justice—except perhaps as a means towards that end, and it would be absurd to portray Christianity (or Islam or Buddhism) as having been consistently egalitarian in its this-wordly impact. Conversion again seldom guaranteed equal treatment, for it is well known that caste prejudices and hierarchies have often persisted among converts to Christianity or Islam despite theoretical principles of equality in the eyes of God and Allah. Yet an instance from the history of the lower-caste Namasudra movement in Central and South Bengal in the early twentieth century suggests that a degree of empowerment was possible through missionary presence—even where that presence did not lead to significant conversions. As we have seen earlier, the metrical biography of Guruchand Thakur (1847–1937), leader of the dissident Vaishnava Matua sect which constituted the core of the Namasudra upthrust, explains in vivid detail the circumstances that led the Matuas to seek the assistance of the Australian Baptist missionary C.S. Mead—striking an alliance that proved very fruitful for the Namasudras in their quest for educational facilities, service jobs, and, eventually, political advantages. The Namasudras wanted to start a high school at Orakandi, Faridpur (the centre of their movement), the poem explains, because landlords and moneylenders constantly tricked illiterate peasants like them in everyday matters of rent or debt-payment receipts. They encountered stiff opposition from the local high-caste Kayasthas, who were afraid that their sharecroppers and servants would no longer work for them if they became educated. That, as we saw they argued, would disrupt the age-old principles of adhikari-bheda as enshrined notably in the *Ramayana*. The biography explains that it was such bhadralok hostility that made Guruchand accept the offer of financial and other assistance from Mead, and it is also very careful to emphasise that the motives were entirely pragmatic—to get money for the school and obtain access to British officials. The Namasudras were quite satisfied with their Matua faith founded by Guruchand's father Harichand Thakur, and very few of them turned Christian.[44]

There is no evidence that Mead himself had been directly interested in peasant questions, but a generation later Reverend Victor J.

---

[44] *Guruchand-Charit, passim.* For more detail, see chapter II above.

White of the same Australian Baptist Mission, working in the Netra-
kona region of Mymensingh, presented a most remarkable exposure
of the oppression of tribal and Muslim sharecroppers (under the local
tanka system of produce-rent) to the Floud Commission investigat-
ing land relations in Bengal. A few years later, the Communist-led
Kisan Sabha organised a powerful movement of Hajong sharecroppers in that region. The well-known Kisan Sabha memorandum to
the Floud Commission in 1939, however, had been much less concrete about the bargadar issue than had the now totally forgotten
Reverend White.[45]

The Christian conversions issue fell somewhat into the back-
ground in the 1930s and 1940s, with communalism turned into an
obsessively Hindu–Muslim affair, culminating in the bloodbaths of
1946–7. That it had not vanished, however, was suddenly revealed
by a near-explosion on the floor of the Constituent Assembly on 1
May 1947, in the course of debates on the fundamental right to religious freedom. Many members objected to freedom of religion extending to the right to propagate, with Purushottamdas Tandon even
declaring that 'most Congressmen are opposed to this idea of "propagation". But we agreed to keep the word "propagate" out of regard
for our own Christian friends.' And once again the social dimensions
of the issue got exposed, particularly in a speech by Algurai Shastri,
who listed among the 'unfair means' adopted by Christian missionaries the utilisation of 'bhangis and chamars': 'disputes between members of such castes as the sweepers or the chamars on the one side and
the landlords or some other influential members on the other have
been exploited to create bitterness among them. No effort has been
made to effect a compromise. This crooked policy has been adopted
to bring about the conversion of the former.'[46] Eventually the right
to propagate—in effect, to convert—was not rejected, but, if the
memory of the already cited Gandhian opponent of conversions is
to be trusted, this was because such a ban 'would make reconversion
difficult'.[47]

[45] Government of Bengal, *Report of the Land Revenue (Floud) Commission*
(Alipur, 1940), volume II, pp. 394–407 (White), 1–72 (Bengal Provincial Kisan
Sabha).

[46] *Constituent Assembly of India Debates, Volume II*, pp. 483, 492.

[47] *The Indian Express*, 7 January 1999.

It is worth recalling also that, along with the promotion of highly sanskritised Hindi and cow-protection, the fight against Christian missions was made into an early plank of Jan Sangh activity in the early 1950s as Hindutva forces sought to regain the ground lost after the murder of the Mahatma. In November 1954 the Jan Sangh organised an Anti-Foreign Missionary Week in Madhya Pradesh. Much had started being made of insurgency in largely Christian Nagaland: then, as often now, what was conveniently forgotten is that many so-called 'secessionist' and/or 'terrorist' movements have had nothing to do with religious minorities (e.g., the predominantly high-caste Hindu ULFA in Assam), while relatively little can be understood about the deeper reasons behind such movements by simplistic 'foreign hand 'explanations. The Madhya Pradesh Congress reacted to the Jan Sangh agitation in what had already become a strong base of the Hindu Right in a manner quite characteristic—and always in the long run disastrous. It tried to outflank its rival by becoming more 'Hindu', a move conditioned also by the strong presence of very similar elements within its own members and leaders. (The Mahakoshal Congress was the one provincial unit which had supported Tandon against Nehru in 1951.) The Niyogi Commission it set up to enquire into Christian missionary activity is still repeatedly and reverentially cited by Sangh Parivar spokesmen and publications, for it suggested a ban on conversions unless explicitly proved to have been entirely voluntary—passing the onus of proof in effect on missionaries and converts. The Jan Sangh-led Madhya Pradesh government of 1967–8 did actually implement some of these recommendations, and imposed a strict test for proving voluntary choice on Christian converts. Under the post-Emergency Janata government with a strong Jan Sangh component, the destruction of some churches in what was then the Union Territory of Arunachal became the occasion for a law (1978) which made the erection of places of worship subject to administrative permission in that region. A private bill to ban conversions was also moved in December 1978 and supported by Prime Minister Morarji Desai, but it had to be dropped in the face of Christian and other opposition.[48] Vajpayee's suggestion now for a

[48] Christophe Jaffrelot, *The Hindu Nationalist Movement and Indian Politics, 1925 to the 1990s: Strategies of Identity-Building, Implementation and Mobilisation* (*with special reference to Central India*) (Paris, 1993; Delhi, 1996), pp. 163–5,

'national debate' on conversions is therefore not a liberal proposal put forward by a good man fallen among unfortunate associates but part of a well-thought-out Sangh Parivar strategy.

Till the recent anti-Christian campaign, the VHP may have been associated in the public mind primarily with Ramjanmabhumi and the onslaught on Muslims, culminating in the destruction of the Babri Masjid. But at the time of its foundation in 1964, and for quite some time after it, its main thrust had been directed primarily against Christian proselytisation in tribal areas (the North-East, Madhya Pradesh, South Bihar). Significantly, those who figured prominently at the inaugural meeting of the VHP at Bombay included—along with the RSS boss Golwalkar and RSS *pracharak* S.S. Apte (who became the first general secretary of this new affiliate of the Sangh Parivar)—Brahmachari Dattamurti of the Masurasram, which had been carrying on shuddhi-sangathana work with a pronounced anti-Christian slant ever since its foundation in 1920.[49] The *achara samhita* drawn up by the VHP in 1968 included *paravartan* (turning back, i.e. reconversion) among the basic samskaras of the Hinduism it was trying to redefine—which amounted really to a major innovation, and indicated once again the centrality of this motif for this branch of Hindutva. There was thus a continuity with early-twentieth-century shuddhi, but also some departures. Early Arya shuddhi had had a measure of reformist, anti-caste (or at least anti-untouchability) thrust critical of orthodox practices, and had at times served as a channel for upward mobility among subordinated groups irrespective of the question of reconversion. But paravartan is intended solely 'for those who have left Hinduism for foreign creeds like Islam and Christianity', and is not envisaged 'as a means of removing untouchability'.[50]

Jaffrelot gives some details of VHP anti-Christian work among tribals of the Chhattisgarh region of Madhya Pradesh, which has been channelled through the Vanavasi Kalyan Ashrama, set up already in

---

224, 287. A virulently anti-Christian pamphlet entitled *Seva ki aur me church ki sharayantra* (Delhi, Sivaratri, 1999) ends with an extract from the Niyogi Commission Recommendations of 1956.

[49] Eva Hellman, *Political Hinduism: The Challenge of the Visva Hindu Parishad* (Uppsala, 1993), pp. 70–1.

[50] Ibid., pp. 110–11.

1952 by an ex-official of the government tribal welfare department with RSS affiliations. The class linkages are particularly interesting: the major patrons of the organisation have included the Maharaja of Jashpur; his son Dilip Singh Judeo, who combines landed property with industrial entrepreneurship and became a RSS full-timer in 1992; and tendu-leaf magnate Lakhi Ram Aggarwal, RSS activist since 1946. More recently Judeo has extended his activities to Chhota Nagpur, organising a 'Ghar Vapsi' (home-return) movement there. A *Times of India* report dated 21 December 1997 described some of the fall-outs of the intense anti-Christian activities headed by men like Judeo in South Bihar: 17 cases of murder or assaults upon priests between 1992 and 1997, including the stripping of the principal of a Dumka missionary school, with the SDO a benign spectator of the scene (2 September 1997), and the beheading in a Hazaribagh forest of a priest who had been helping tribals in land ceiling cases.

The Meenakshipuram (Tirunelveli) mass conversions to Islam of thousands of Dalits in February 1981 inaugurated an era during which there was an intense targeting of Muslims for well over a decade. But it is clear that the Sangh Parivar has always also had the anti-Christian arrow in its armoury, and a quick switch in emphasis proved no problem at all after the formation of the BJP-led coalition in Delhi.

III

But why target the Christians? They are after all only a tiny minority, stagnating in number—despite many dire Hindu predictions of their proliferation—at around 2.5% of India's population?

Part of the explanation could be crudely pragmatic. Central Government responsibility would be difficult to reconcile with wholesale campaigns against Muslims, a minority numbering well over a hundred million. There would be the possibility of large-scale violence, difficulties with coalition partners (for some of whom Muslim electoral support remains important), and international repercussions. There is also, obviously, the desire to target and embarrass Congress President Sonia Gandhi as foreign-born and Christian.

But there might be two deeper and more significant reasons. Despite swadeshi rhetoric, concessions to multinationals have been going ahead at unprecedented speed under BJP rule. Yet many aspects of globalisation remain uncomfortable for a political tradition reared on crudely nationalist and indigenist values. There is a need for surrogate enemies to reconfirm nationalist credentials without seriously disturbing the liberalisation agenda. Both Pokhran, and anti-Christian campaigns, it might be suggested, fulfil this need. What could be more convenient for the Sangh Parivar than giving to residual anti-imperialist sentiments a purely religious-cum-culturalist twist, targeting Christians, and not—at least not with any real seriousness—multi-nationals?

And the foreign origin charge does carry a certain plausibility among many with respect to Christians, despite the absurdity of characterising thus a religion which, in parts of the South, is almost 2000 years old, older in fact than most living varieties of Hinduism. The plausibility derives in large part from fairly deep-rooted traditions, quite common also on the Left, of seeing Christianity and white missionaries as invariably agents of Western imperialism and Indian Christians as always collaborators with colonial rule.

No doubt there have been numerous instances of such linkages and complicities. But this needs to be considered in relation to the significant fact that British rule in India depended to a much greater extent on a far larger number of non-Christian Indian collaborators and dependent allies: notably, the bulk of princes, zamindars, and government officials, most of whom were of high-caste Hindu origin. In more general terms, Christianity, like any major tradition, has included within its fold any number of diverse, quite often mutually conflicting, tendencies. One remembers the Inquisition, the many iniquities condoned or committed in the name of converting 'heathens' in the colonial world, numerous instances of crude cultural arrogance and Eurocentrism, the bitter hostility displayed towards so many progressive causes from the French Revolution down to the Spanish Civil War. Nor should one forget the lunatic-fringe Christian fundamentalists of the USA today. But dissident readings of Christianity have also been central to innumerable movements of the oppressed. Two obvious examples would be late-medieval European peasant movements, and Black slave culture in the USA. Even the ideals of modern democracy, and socialism of a kind, originated in signi-ficant part through a 'Puritan' revolution in seventeenth-century England.

Today, in particular, the churches have been changing in quite striking ways, above all through the spread of 'liberation theologies' that have contributed substantially to movements for radical change in Latin America and elsewhere. Christian groups have been prominent in many anti-war and anti-nuclear protests, and numerous other undeniably progressive initiatives. Small gains in the direction of somewhat greater social justice may earlier have been the largely unintended fallout of Christian proselytisation efforts in India. Today, there is ample evidence of a far greater awareness of such issues among many—though of course very far from all—Christian activists in India. There is also a welcome tendency, in face of brutal attack, not to retreat into sectarian or fundamentalist shells but to build bridges through dialogue and joint work with secular, liberal, and Left formations.

Let me suggest in conclusion that it is precisely these aspects of contemporary Christianity that arouse the greatest anger and fear among adherents of Hindutva. I cannot think of more convincing evidence for this assertion than that provided unwittingly by Arun Shourie in his *Missionaries in India*, the publication of which in 1994 preceded the large-scale campaign against Christians by just a few years. Shourie might seek to frighten his readers by citing the occasional grandiose plans of some conservative or fundamentalist Christian groups to evangelise the globe in honour of the new millennium, but he is surely intelligent enough to realise that this is no more than absurdly arrogant tall-talk. (It has been been denounced as a 'residual Western colonial mind-set' by a devout Christian like the Rev. Valson Thampu, who has also demanded the elimination from mission work of 'Western triumphalist notions'.[51] Shourie's book however provides ample signs that what has really worried him are developments like Liberation Theology. 'Today, spurred by the new 'Liberation Theology',

> the Church is spurring movements among so-called Dalits, etc. But many
> of the leaders . . . patronised by way of helping 'Dalits' speak with poison

[51] Rev. Valson Thampu, 'Read the Scriptures, Mr Shourie', *Asian Age*, 11 April 1999.

in their tongue. They advocate hatred . . . encouraging, projecting, assisting 'Dalit leaders' . . . would certainly disrupt Hindu society.[52]

At the beginning of his book Shourie states his central assumption:

I believe that the interests of India as a whole must take precedence—overwhelming precedence—over the supposed interests of any part or group, religious, linguistic or secular . . . the movements which are currently afoot ostensibly to 'liberate' and 'empower' those groups may well break India . . . those who foment them . . . ought to be dealt with using the full might of the State.'[53]

What Shourie does not explain is how and by whom 'the interests of India as a whole' are to be determined; whether, given the anti-democratic measures he clearly envisages, such alleged 'interests' could not become an ideological cover for the special interests of a dominant minority of high-caste Hindus.

[52] Shourie, op. cit., pp. 201, 235.
[53] Ibid., p. 3.

CHAPTER IX

Hindutva and History

I PLAN TO read the title of my essay both ways. 'Hindutva and History': it is impossible today for this not to refer primarily to the very numerous efforts of the Sangh Parivar, whenever and wherever they are near or in power, to bring history and historians under their control. Attacks on National Council of Educational Research and Training (NCERT) textbooks in the Janata regime in 1977–8; the projection with considerable success of views on Babur and Ayodhya totally at variance with scholarly history during the Ramjanmabhoomi movement; the wholesale communalisation of school textbooks in the states ruled by the BJP; the packing of academic funding bodies—starting significantly with the Indian Council of Historical Research (ICHR)—within a few weeks of coming into power at Delhi in 1998; the campaign to depict Christians as alien, dangerous and somehow uniformly guilty of Inquisition atrocities; the move to impose pre-censorship on the Towards Freedom collection of documents; and a recent attempt to stop the Left historian K.N. Panikkar speaking at a Montreal conference—the list is long and ever-growing. But my intent here is not primarily polemical. I want, rather, to pose two questions which I find interesting. Why, first, is history so exceptionally important for Hindutva? And second, reversing the order in the title to 'History and Hindutva'—what implications can be teased out about the nature of the Hindutva movement from this unusual centrality?

Let me define this exceptionality a bit more closely, for some might consider it to be exaggerated. Authoritarian regimes of very different kinds, as well as governments moving that way, have restricted the freedom of historical scholarship often enough: Hitler, Stalin, McCarthy immediately come to mind. But usually attacks on history have been a part, and often a rather minor one, of overall onslaughts on intellectual and cultural freedom. What does seem rather exceptional is the prioritisation of history as prime target, repeatedly, by the Sangh Parivar. Government efforts to influence history-writing, and intellectual life in general, through the giving and the withholding of patronage, is again common practice. It is not at all difficult to think of numerous instances of nepotism under Congress regimes, or for that matter under CPI(M) governments—and there was also that absurdity of the 'time capsule' during the Emergency. Yet the fairly common cynical stance—all governments interfere, so why get excited—is not really tenable, for what does distinguish the BJP is the systematic, consistent, and generalised level at which it has been operating. Two sets of appointments made in the 1980s, under Rajiv Gandhi, can help to illustrate my argument. The Congress government then made Irfan Habib, India's top Marxist historian—who is also a member of the CPI(M)—Chairman of the ICHR. This was not, as might be assumed by some today, an instance of Congress–Left collusion, for the CPI(M) then was bitterly opposed to Rajiv Gandhi, and in fact in 1989–90 virtually allied with the BJP, with both parties supporting the non-Congress ministry of V.P. Singh from the outside. Under that same Congress government, scholars with very different political affiliations who were close to the Sangh Parivar, including some who later went on to acclaim the destruction of the Babri Masjid, remained the dominant group in the Archaeological Survey of India. My point is that under non-BJP regimes there has been, on the whole, some degree of correspondence between academic stature and appointments: for Irfan Habib happens to be perhaps India's best living historian, while men like B.B. Lal and S.P. Gupta combine their Sangh Parivar affinities with considerable reputation as archaeologists. The academic credentials of the members of the present ICHR—with a few exceptions—would not stand overmuch scrutiny, while the review committee set up to go through the 'Towards Freedom' volumes edited by K.N. Panikkar and myself, publication of which has been arbitrarily halted, consists of one reasonably well-known medieval historian (the volumes concern only the calendar years of 1940 and 1946), and two others, supposedly teachers of modern Indian history, about whom the only information available is that they are *pracharaks* of the RSS.

Constructions of histories or lineages as morale-booster, for legitimacy, to link up present aspirations with more-or-less imagined pasts in efforts to move towards specific kinds of futures—have all been a standard feature of modern political movements. Thus, in twentieth-century South Asia, anti-colonial nationalists have imagined glorious pasts shattered by foreign rule and exploitation; the Left has sought sustenance from narratives of past tribal, peasant, or labour protest; movements of subordinated castes and Dalits have constructed histories of continuous Brahmanical oppression and occasional protest; feminists and gay or lesbian groups have also searched for predecessors. Yet one can think of several reasons why the relative weight of imagined histories has been qualitatively greater in the formation of what Indian English since the 1920s has appropriately termed 'communal' ideologies.[1]

The movements I have just referred to were all based primarily on perceptions of present-day tensions and conflicts. Colonial rule and mass poverty, exploitation by landlords or capitalists, caste oppression, the manifold burdens of patriarchy old or new, the opprobrium attached to unconventional sexual behaviour: all these have been, and

---

[1] Terms like 'religious nationalism', 'Hindu nationalism', 'Muslim nationalism', that have been frequently used to indicate communal ideologies and movements in a large number of valuable works, suffer from being insufficiently precise. Tilak, Gandhi and Savarkar can all be described as in some (but very different) senses, 'Hindu nationalists', and it becomes difficult under such rubrics to categories the distinctions between, say, Khilafatists and the politics of the Muslim League in the 1940s, or for that matter between the earlier and the later Savarkar. The crucial differentia of communalism is not a developed sense of religious community or identity, not even its 'politicisation', but a further assumption of conflict with a similarly imagined communal Other as both inevitable, and over-riding—in the sense of being more crucial than other tensions or projects (such as ending colonial rule, national economic development, social transformation). I have tried to elaborate these distinctions in my 'Indian Nationalism and the Politics of Hindutva', in David Ludden, ed., *Contesting the Nation: Religion, Community, and the Politics of Democracy in India* (Pennsylvania, 1996), chapter 12, as well as in *Writing Social History* (Delhi, 1997), chapter. 9.

in most cases continue to be, palpable and undeniable. History could help, though sometimes also harm:[2] it has not been, at least in sheer logic, indispensable. Twentieth-century communalism no doubt also drew some sustenance from specific conflicts between groups that could be religiously defined, and above all from memories of riot violence as such clashes became more and more common from the 1890s—and particularly from the mid-1920s. But as generalised ideologies, Hindu or Muslim communalism has had to run counter to the enormous counter-evidence of everyday shared living, fairly fuzzy boundaries, the relative absence of obvious physical markers.[3] In post-1947 India, particularly, it is surely far from obvious or 'natural' to brand Muslims (or the tiny Christian minority) as the most important threat or problem before the 'nation'. That so many have come to internalise such myths has been largely due to sustained ideological work, above all by the RSS, and in that 'history' has been quite indispensable. This is a history that assumes a tripartite framework, with the medieval as marked by 'Muslim' invasions, conquest, 'Muslim rule', destroying an age of alleged 'Hindu' ancient glory and characterised by tyranny, forced conversions, and the destruction of

[2] Nationalist evocations of an India somehow 'fundamentally' united across the centuries by 'culture' or 'civilisation' have often slided towards Brahmanical-Hindu, as well as North India-oriented, assumptions. I am tempted to recall Marx's warning, in his *Eighteenth Brumaire of Louis Napoleon*, that it could be dangerous for transformative movements to take their poetry from the past. It is seldom remembered that the much-quoted passage about the tradition of dead generations weighing like a nightmare on the brains of the living (with which that famous text began) referred, in its immediate context, not to conservative but to radical traditions: the Jacobin revolutionary heritage. Bolshevik leaders after 1917 paid a heavy price for ignoring that warning: obsessed by the fear of a Bonaparte, they took little notice of the quiet amassing of power by Stalin.

[3] Here there is some difference between communal conflict and 'racial' or 'ethnic' tensions between dominant whites and indigenous, Afro-American or recent immigrants in the contemporary West, even though all such distinctions are of course primarily historical and not 'natural' constructs. I do not find the efforts to equate Hindu–Muslim conflicts with race or ethnic difference, as made for instance by Dipesh Chakrabarty, helpful: see his 'Modernity and Ethnicity in India', in David Bennet, ed., *Multicultural States: Rethinking Difference and Identity* (London/New York, 1998), pp. 94–5.

temples. No one can know of such things from first-hand, unlike, say, instances of racist injustice under colonial rule, landlords evicting peasants, Dalits facing discrimination, or familial oppression: 'history' of a special kind is indispensable.

To this one needs to add the paradox of a movement replete with nationalist rhetoric which historically remained absent from every type or phase of anti-colonial nationalism. The two key organisations of the Hindu Right in pre-Independence India, the Rashtriya Swayamsevak Sangh and the Hindu Mahasabha, share with the Muslim League the distinction of never becoming targets of British repression at any time. Communists are still often denounced as traitors for staying out of the Quit India struggle as part of their anti-Fascist Peoples' War line, even though their party had been almost continuously persecuted and illegal under British rule down to 1943. That Savarkar as Hindu Mahasabha leader had ordered his followers to 'stick to their posts' in August 1942,[4] and that Shyamaprasad Mukherji, the future founder of the Jan Sangh, had actually been a member of the Bengal government while the Midnapur movement was being brutally suppressed, are facts that somehow are seldom remembered. More significant to my mind than physical participation or absence from direct anti-British struggle, however, is the ideological absence. What makes anti-colonial nationalism in India really significant is not so much that the British eventually had to leave (their formal empire ended virtually everywhere, even where effective movements had not really developed much), but that both an exceptional level of mass participation, and a rich gamut of ideas regarding the kind of society and polity that should replace colonialism, did emerge in South Asia. This deepening of the content of anti-colonial struggles had as its roots an abiding concern with mass poverty, with the fact that, in the words of a leading Indian economic historian, 'In 1900, India, the "brightest

---

[4] In a message dated 3 September 1942, Savarkar instructed 'all Hindu Sabhaites . . . in municipalities and other local bodies, legislatures, councils, committees, serving in the army, navy, airforce or working in ammunition factories of . . . holding any post or position of vantage in the Government services' to 'stick to them and continue to perform their regular duties in the various capacities.' V.D. Savarkar, 'Stick to Your Post', 3 September 1942, in *Historic Statements*, ed. S.S. Savarkar and G.M. Joshi (Bombay, May 1967), pp. 78–9.

jewel in the British Crown" was one of the poorest countries in the world.'[5] The question was sought to be tackled in an enormous variety of often conflicting ways. Moderate Congress reform of specific British policies and economic development on capitalistic lines; the Gandhian dream of wiping the tears from the eyes of every Indian through village-based Ram Rajya; Nehruvian and Left perspectives of egalitarian change, planning, some kind of socialism; Ambedkarite prioritisation of high-caste oppression—what all these had in common, across all differences, was a recognition of mass poverty and the need for one or other type of social justice. It is impossible to include Hindutva in this list: there is only an enormous silence.

This twofold absence has generated a need to endlessly invoke a specific kind of 'history' that could transfer nationalist rhetoric back into pre-colonial times, through the depiction, often in the most lurid colours, of a mythical continuous struggle of 'Hindus' against 'Muslim' invaders and rulers throughout the 'medieval' centuries as the true 'national' history. Let me cite two instances, from texts crucial in the evolution of Hindutva: V.D. Savarkar's *Hindutva/Who Is A Hindu?* (1923), the foundation-text, if there is any, of this entire political-cultural formation; and the tract by M.S. Golwalkar, top leader of the RSS after the death of its founder Hegdewar, entitled *We, or Our Nationhood Defined* (1939; 3rd edn, Nagpur: Bharat Prakashan, 1945).

Savarkar begins with the claim that 'Hindutva is not a word but a history—a history in full',[6] and indeed around half of his 140-odd pages do attempt a kind of historical narrative. There is some evocation, predictably, of ancient Hindu glory, tarnished by the harm caused to 'national virility' by Buddhism's 'mealy-mouthed formulas of Ahimsa and spiritual brotherhood',[7] recuperated through a succeeding era dominated by Rajput princes. But Savarkar's language and imagination catches fire only with Mahmud of Ghazni and the coming of the Muslims:

---

[5] Amiya Kumar Bagchi, *Private Investment in India, 1900–1939* (Cambridge, 1972), p. 1.

[6] Savarkar, p. 3. I am using the 6th edition of *Hindutva/Who is Hindu?* (New Delhi, 1989).

[7] Ibid., p. 19.

That day the conflict of life and death began. Nothing makes Self con-
scious of itself so much as a conflict with non-Self. Nothing can weld peoples into a nation and nations into a state as the pressure of a common
foe . . . Day after day, decade after decade, century after century, the
ghastly conflict continued . . .[8]

The historical narrative culminates with a long and ecstatic account
of Shivaji and Maratha glory. It then comes to an abrupt halt with
'the fall of the last of our Hindu empire[s] in AD 1818'. Savarkar turns
'to the main task of determining the essentials of Hindutva',[9] and
somehow manages the remarkable feat of writing another 70 pages
without referring at all to British rule, its consequences, in terms of
exploitation, poverty, racism—any of the standard anti-colonial nationalist themes, or to the many movements against colonialism. Not even
1857 finds a mention, though Savarkar little more than a decade back
had written the first major account of it from the Indian side as the
'first national war of independence.' The author of Hindutva had
been a notable revolutionary-nationalist, had spent years in the Andamans under atrocious prison conditions—and yet he does not mention
the Jallianwalabag massacre of 1919, or the Non-Cooperation–
Khilafat upsurge of 1919–22, the point of greatest Hindu–Muslim
unity in the entire history of anti-colonial struggle. The silence is of
course not accidental: it is bound up with the central thrust of the
entire tract, which is the proposition of an indispensable and unique
linkage between *pitribhumi* and *punyabhumi*, fatherland and holy
land, with the latter again immediately equated with the land of origin
of one's religion and culture. Indians who happen to be Muslims or
Christians therefore cannot be as patriotic or genuinely nationalist as
Hindus, in whom, according to Savarkar, these two are uniquely
combined. The edge of the argument is clearly directed against Indian
Muslims, Christians, or anyone else who might not like to be termed
Hindu: the British are irrelevant here, for they never thought of India
being either fatherland or holy land.[10]

[8] Ibid., pp. 42–3, 44.

[9] Ibid., p. 70.

[10] For some further discussion of the implications of Savarkar's very influential
definition of 'Hindu', see Tapan Basu *et. al.*, *Khaki Shorts and Saffron Flags: A
Critique of the Hindu Right* (Delhi, 1993), pp. 8–9.

Golwalkar's *We, or Our Nationhood Defined* follows a very similar pattern of argument, but with certain distinct nuances and at times a greater clarity following from a blunter and cruder logic. There is much more about ancient Hindu glory, for he is clearly more of a social conservative than Savarkar, and has no hesitation at one point in defining the normative 'Hindu Nation' as 'a people characterised by Varnas and Ashramas', learning their 'duties at the feet of the "Eldest-born" Brahmans of this land.'[11] But, once again, the real national struggle has been against the Muslims: 'Ever since that evil day, when Moslems first landed in Hindustan, right up to the present moment, the Hindu Nation has been gallantly fighting on to shake off the despoilers.' Muslims are made responsible even for the British conquest, which could happen only because the strength of the Hindu Nation had been 'greatly sapped' by 'this 800-year's war.'[12] Writing at a time of dominant anti-colonial nationalist moods, Golwalkar could not avoid all reference to anti-British movements, but he tucked away these within half a page of a 77-page tract, where there is even a mention of 'M. Gandhi and others, too recent to be named.'[13]

As with Savarkar, the stresses and omissions are perfectly logical, given the basic premise of Golwalkar, that a nation must be characterised by unity of religion-cum-culture. He dismissed as an 'amazing doctrine', a 'serai theory', the view that 'the Nation is composed of all those who, for one reason or the other happen to live . . . in the country'. Rather, 'in Hindustan exists and must exist the ancient Hindu nation and nought else but the Hindu Nation. All those not belonging to the national, i.e. Hindu Race, Religion, Culture and Language naturally fall out of the pale of real "national" life.'[14] And the fate other communities could expect was spelt out with enviable clarity: 'the non-Hindu peoples in Hindusthan must learn to respect and hold in reverence Hindu religion, must entertain no idea but those of glorification of the Hindu race and culture—must cease to be foreigners, or [they] may stay in the country wholly subordinated

[11] Golwalkar, pp. 15, 16.

[12] Ibid.

[13] Ibid., p. 16.

[14] Ibid., pp. 48–9. By language, the same passage explained, is meant Sanskrit, and the 'local tongues' derived from it, above all Hindi.

to the Hindu nation, claiming nothing, deserving no privileges, far less any preferential treatment—not even citizen's rights.'[15]

Golwalkar gave two examples, as models, of the way 'old nations ought to, and do deal, with the foreign races, who have chosen to live' in their countries. The first is Nazi Germany.

> German race-pride has now become the topic of the day. To keep up the purity of the Race and its culture, Germany shocked the world by her purging the country of the semitic races—the Jews. Race pride at its highest has been manifested here. Germany has also shown how well-nigh impossible it is for Races and cultures, having differences going to the root, to be assimilated into one united whole, a good lesson for us in Hindustan to learn and profit by.

It may be mentioned here that the preface to the first edition stated that the manuscript had been completed in November 1938. Its composition thus coincided almost exactly with Kristallnacht.[16]

The second exemplar is also not without interest: it is the United States of America, written of course much before the rhetoric, or limited practice, of multiculturalism. There, according to Golwalkar, 'Emigrants have to get themselves naturally assimilated in the principal mass of population, the national Race, by adopting its culture and language and sharing in its aspirations . . . forgetting their foreign origin . . . That is the only logical and correct solution.'[17] The numerous present-day admirers of Hindutva among Indians resident in the USA or other Western countries might ponder over the implications of these words.

But let us return to conceptions of history.

Down to the 1950s, there would have been a considerable degree of overlap—rhetorical flourishes and extreme statements apart—

[15] Ibid., pp. 42–3.

[16] Ibid., pp. 40–1. The passage, it has often been argued by interested persons, is spurious, or was a quickly removed aberration. It is very much present in the third, 1945, edition of the book, which is why I thought it worthwhile to quote it *in extenso*. Along with some other exceptionally blunt passages, it probably explains why *We, or Our Nationhood Defined* found no place in Golwalkar's *Bunch of Thoughts*, published in 1966. But the earlier tract has never been disowned, or to the best of my knowledge criticised in public, either by the RSS or any constituent of the Sangh Parivar.

[17] Ibid., p. 52.

between the assumptions of a Savarkar or a Golwalkar and much professional history-writing. Affinities would be even more evident with a widespread 'historical' commonsense embodied in, and largely moulded by, a very considerable volume of literature from the mid-nineteenth century onwards. The tripartite division of Indian history into ancient/Hindu, medieval/Muslim, and modern/British periods, first made by James Mill, quickly became standard. It was accepted, with only the value-judgements regarding the 'medieval' inverted, by educated high-caste Hindu, and Muslim literati alike.[18] Why this happened is a subject worthy of much more exploration than has been attempted so far. Terming it a 'derivative discourse' at best only describes the problem, and internalisation of colonial discourse was selective, not total (the condemnations of Hindu tradition by Mill and other utilitarians or evangelists were emphatically not accepted). Perhaps there could have been a subconscious search for an alibi. If British rule had been preceded by an equally alien and more oppressive domination, that might justify the general acceptance of colonial rule by the new, predominantly Hindu, intelligentsia for much of the nineteenth century, particularly in regions like Bengal which had remained demonstratively loyal during the anti-British upsurge of 1857. The same intelligentsia was eagerly learning a language of patriotism from contemporary Western culture, and its projection back into the past could constitute a safer, 'surrogate' form of nationalism. With the rise of mass anti-colonial nationalism in the twentieth century, however, images of medieval Hindu–Muslim harmony or 'syncretism' also became quite common, at times in exaggerated, counter-mythical form, seeking to deny any instance of pre-colonial tensions—with British divide-and-rule held solely responsible for all subsequent conflict. It is noticeable, though, that as history became a professional discipline in the first half of the twentieth century, surrogate nationalism still seemed to characterise a fair amount of

[18] Bankimchandra's novels and essays, to cite one striking example, are replete with references to seven hundred years of foreign rule in Bengal, beginning with the coming of the Muslims. For two contrasting readings of Bankim, see Sudipta Kaviraj, *The Unhappy Consciousness: Bankimchandra Chattopadhyay and the Formation of Nationalist Discourse in India* (Delhi, 1995), and Tanika Sarkar, 'Imagining Hindu Rashtra: The Hindu and the Muslim in Bankimchandra's Writings', in *Hindu Wife, Hindu Nation* (Delhi, 2000).

academic research. Rajput, Maratha, or Sikh struggles against Mughal rulers remained favourite themes for research or teaching, while twentieth-century mass nationalism was generally avoided, ostensibly because the archives would not be available, but also no doubt from some considerations of prudence.[19] There was, perhaps, a more fundamental, methodological reason, too, for the long persistence of Mill's tripartite periodisation along with its corollaries. History was still looked at, in the main, from the 'top' downwards, in terms of rulers, their policies, and consequently their religions, too. As elsewhere, the professionalisation of the discipline had helped to strengthen such tendencies, given the nature of most conventional sources, their inevitable derivation from centres of political authority.

It is here that the big change came about in the 1960s and 1970s, at the level of methods and perspectives, a transformation in which Marxism was one major, but far from only, input. It needs to be emphasised that today, for state-of-the-art historical understanding anywhere in the world where South Asia is being studied, the assumptions of Savarkar or Golwalkar would appear so absurd as hardly worth refutation or debate.[20] Irrespective of their other differences, historians of all trends, liberal, nationalist, the erstwhile 'Cambridge' school, Marxists of diverse kinds, late-Subalterns, feminists, post- or anti-modernists—would all agree that the essentialised assumptions of Hindus and Muslims being homogeneous, continuous blocs across time and subcontinental space, with Muslims as a community ruling Hindus in the medieval centuries, are totally unacceptable. There is no way that the masses of Muslim peasants or artisans of medieval times can be considered part of the ruling elite, whereas a large number of Hindus, particularly Rajput princes, held very high posts in the

---

[19] The habit died hard. I remember several among my senior teachers at Calcutta University expressing doubts whether the Swadeshi movement in Bengal was not too 'recent' a subject for research, when I decided to choose that for my doctoral work in 1961. And in a way it has persisted: 'modern' history for the bulk of Indian teaching and research still seems to end around 1947!

[20] I remember the distinguished medieval historian Sanjay Subrahmanyam writing in a Delhi newspaper, for instance, that the view that there had been massacres of Hindus by Muslims under 'Muslim rule' comparable to the Holocaust deserves to be 'laughed out of court'.

Mughal mansabdari bureaucracy, with the proportion of Hindus actually rising in the reign of Aurangzeb. The question, really, is not how bigoted an Aurangzeb had been or how tolerant an Akbar, but why, despite the occasional destruction of temples and other sporadic instances of tensions, there is virtually no evidence of mass communal riots in pre-colonial times on anything like the regional or subcontinental scale that would become increasingly common from the 1890s. There is no reason here to assume any perfect amity or happy 'syncretism' between religious traditions, or to argue that what appears to have been religious persecution was 'really' spurred by mundane, financial or political motives.[21] One needs only to imagine how long it would have taken for news of, say, a clash that could be construed as between Hindus and Muslims in Kerala to have reached Punjab or Bengal to recognise the difference between those times and ours.

Historians nowadays also try to look at their sources in more critical and less positivistic ways. The claims in some medieval court chronicles about the destruction of temples by devout Muslim rulers appear quite often to have been rhetorical devices for legitimacy rather than literal truth: thus the recent work of Romila Thapar on Somnath indicates how the same shrine is claimed to have been destroyed again and again. To cite one more instance: through a meticulous study of medieval Sanskrit texts, including some that seem at first glance quite violently anti-'Muslim', Brajadulal Chattopadhyaya has shown that the 'Other' against whom the 'Hindu' rulers were fighting is hardly ever described in religious terms—the preferred categories are ethnic or dynastic, not 'Muslim'.[22]

One can now begin to understand the real anger in Hindutva circles, directed ostensibly against 'Marxist' (or what they like to call 'pseudo-secularist') historians, but actually against the whole state-of-the-art historical scholarship. Arriving at the threshold of countrywide power, they are in danger of finding the crucial 'historical' weapon being struck out of their hands. Recuperation, a rolling-back of history to its earlier digits, is needed, and it must be added that the

[21] Two arguments often used in anti-communal, secular discourses that I do not find particularly convincing.

[22] Brajadulal Chattopadhyaya, *Representing the Other? Sanskrit Sources and the Muslims* (Delhi, 1998).

danger of this happening is extremely grave. For the reach of the new kinds of history has remained quite limited, and the old stereotypes still keep getting reproduced in the bulk of school and undergraduate teaching in most parts of the country. Even the notable effort in the early 1970s to commission more advanced level and up-to-date high school texts, commissioned by the National Council of Educational Research and Training, was somewhat unimaginatively planned and implemented. The textbooks, even though written by some of the country's best historians, were seldom written with due regard for the specific pedagogic needs of schoolchildren. And now these texts are again under attack, while in BJP-ruled states new syllabi and books are being enforced steeped in the ideological assumptions of Hindutva.

Anger is combined with fear, nevertheless, for what the 'Towards Freedom' controversy of 2000 indicates is that the Sangh Parivar is afraid even of historical documents. The volumes attacked, or, in the case of those edited by K.N. Panikkar and myself, arbitrarily withdrawn from the publishers and placed under pre-censorship, consist, not of the personal views of any of the editors, but of masses of archival and other contemporary documents of the last decade before Independence-cum-Partition. It had been collectively agreed that editorial views and comments would be kept to a minimum, and located mainly in the Introductions to each volume. The volumes are bulky and bound to be extremely expensive, meant primarily for libraries, geared to a limited, scholarly and research audience.

Why be afraid of such volumes? What the RSS probably is afraid of is not the presence but an absence, the absence of Hindutva form-ations from any and every confrontation with British rule, above all during the Quit India movement as well as the post-War upsurge during the winter of 1945-6 in major Indian cities that culminated in the Royal Indian Navy mutiny of February 1946. Absence also from the rich history of debates and discussions about the content and meanings of freedom, apart from the narrowly communal.

It may be noted that one charge that has not been made about the editors of these volumes is that they have suppressed data about the RSS or the Hindu Mahasabha. This is not surprising, for the material that is there is often embarrassing enough—not because of some secular bias, but because such reference is there in the archives, and a meticulous, liberal, non-Marxist scholar like the late Partha Sarathi Gupta saw no reason why it should be suppressed. Let me cite a few instances from his massive and enormously impressive volumes covering 1943-4, which have been filthily abused after the editor was safely dead.

* Here is V.D. Savarkar, at Nagpur on 15 August 1943, declaring, with reference to Jinnah's Pakistan demand, that 'There can be two Nations but only One State'.

> 'I have no quarrel with Mr Jinnah's two nation theory. We Hindus are a nation and it is a historical fact that Hindus and Muslims are two na-tions,' said Mr Savarkar, replying to a question at a press conference. (*Hindu*, 17 August 1943)

The documents presented by Gupta indicate a certain embarrass-ment among other Hindu Mahasabha leaders about such excessive frank speaking by their leader, which could in addition seem to contradict the Mahasabha's trenchant demand for Akhand Bharat, a single, unitary India. Eventually a clarificatory statement was worked out: the readers can be left to decide as to how much it improved matters, from any non-communal or liberal point of view:

> Muslims are not a separate Nation by themselves, as they are part of 'the same unitarian [sic!] and homogeneous community recognised as Hindus . . . The Muslim of India are real Hindus in blood and bones, being born of Hindu parents but otherwise converted by force, fraud, or willingness to Islam. . . . (V.B. Gogte to B.S. Moonje, n.d., Moonje Papers File 67)[23]

In the wake of the 1942 upsurge, the Indian government seems to have had a brief moment of doubt about what the disciplined, secretive, and paramilitary RSS might be really up to. It circular-ised all provincial governments on 10 August 1943, requesting up-to-date information about RSS functioning and activities. Partha Sarathi Gupta has presented copious extracts detailing the replies

[23] Partha Sarathi Gupta, *Towards Freedom 1943–44, Part III* (Delhi, 1997), chapter XVIII, document nos 53, 61, pp. 2976, 2986.

from district and provincial levels, and they do make very interesting reading. For from district after district came back police and Home Department reports testifying to the sterling loyalism of the RSS. Perhaps most striking is the report from Bombay city, a storm-centre of the Quit India movement.

> The Commissioner of Police, Bombay, and the Deputy Inspector-General of Police, Criminal Investigation Department report that the RSSS [Rashtriya Swyam Sevak Sangh] had not in any way infringed Government orders and that it has always shown willingness to comply with the law. (9 October 1943)

The same report recalled that way back in December 1940, the RSS in the city had given an assurance 'that it had no intention of offending against the orders of the Government', and that 'orders had been issued to the RSSS leaders throughout the province to desist from any activity that Government considers to be objectionable.'[24] That was at a time when every section within the Congress, including the Communists, were bitterly opposing the war, into which India had been dragged without asking for the consent of any of its political leaders, and when Communists in particular were being arrested in large number for their campaign of '*na ek pai, na ek bhai*' (Not a pice, not a single brother, for the war).

The 1943–4 reports on the RSS also give extracts from speeches allegedly made by Golwalkar and other leaders to their cadres. One sample among many:

> M.S. Golwalkar (Guruji), Nagpur, on 2 May 1944, at a RSS OTC (Officers' Training Camp) at Thalakwadi, Belgaum: 'Hindus are the only Nationals of Hindustan. One ideal, one way, one heart, one expression, and all at the disposal of one leader.'[25]

It is this insistence on a homogenised, unitary, and aggressive Hindu bloc that demands the imposition of a specific kind of history.

[24] Ibid., document no. 66, Government of Bombay to Government of India regarding Volunteer Organisations. 9 October 1943, Home Political (I) 28/3/43, pp. 3058–9.

[25] Report on activities of the RSS, Government of Madras, File Number 56/1943, Tamilnadu Archives. Gupta, op. cit., document no. 167, p. 3182.

But what underlies such insistence, whose interests and values are being voiced through the project of tight community-unity? This is hardly the place for a full exploration of a theme evidently full of complexities, for the appeal of Hindutva has waxed and waned across times and territorial and social spaces, and cannot be reduced to any single, formulaic explanation. But let me try to make two points, in conclusion.

It is widely recognised today that the late colonial era, and more specifically the fifty years or so from the 1870s to the 1920s or 1930s, was characterised by a marked 'hardening', if not sometimes the very constitution or 'invention', of a wide range of identities: anti-colonial 'national', 'regional', religious, caste, class, gender, diverse 'tribal' 'ethnicities'. Groups or organisations claiming to represent such solidarities, and clearly seeking to constitute them, all emerged during this half-century,[26] and the necessary backdrop for all these projects was the tightening of subcontinental economic, administrative-political, and—in the broadest sense—communica-tional grids. The role in particular here of census enumeration and classification has been highlighted very often in recent research, as counting depended on the invention of neat boundaries, and stimulated comparison and competition. What is less often noticed is that if identities were being hardened, they were also becoming in a way more fragile: for the simultaneous development of a multitude of possible and intersecting identities could undercut or undermine the putative unity or solidarity of any particular formation. Thus a project that postulated as its supreme value the unity of all Hindus could come up against lower-caste affirmations, as well, sometimes, cross-cutting solidarities of anti-colonial nationalism, class, or gender. More pertinently, in the context of the overwhelmingly high-caste (and exclusively male) composition of the core organisation of Hindutva, the RSS, such a programme could be implicitly geared towards a displacement of

[26] A few relevant dates: the Indian Association was founded in 1876, and the Indian National Congress in 1885. Provincial Conferences began meeting from around the late-1880s or 1890s. The Muslim League began in 1906, the Hindu Mahasabha from around 1915. The All India Trade Union Congress started in 1920, the All India Kisan Sabha in 1936, the All India Women's Conference in 1927.

lower-caste resentments through constructing powerful images of hostile Others. I have presented in another chapter some evidence of an early manifestation of this syndrome in post-Swadeshi Bengal.[27] The hypothesis requires much more rigorous empirical testing, but the puzzle about the emergence of both the ideology and the core organisation of Hindutva in Maharashtra—and more precisely, the Nagpur region—during the mid-1920s seems to demand an explanation in similar terms. The Muslims there were a small, and in the words of a strongly pro-Hindu newspaper 'very nervous and terror-stricken' community. But Mahars—the community of Ambedkar—constituted one-sixth of the population of Nagpur district, and 40% of the city's textile workers, and among them Phule's anti-Brahmanical Aryan conquest theme had been propagated by Kisan Faguji from around 1909 onwards. The 1925 Berar Non-Brahman Conference of 1925 aroused violent high-caste hostility, with B.S. Moonje's diary next year using the language of contagion to refer to the 'virus of the non-Brahmin controversy.' (2 April, 1926)[28] The RSS, it may be recalled, was founded in Nagpur on Vijay Dashami day, 1925, and Moonje was one of its five founding members.

There still seems a bit of a mystery as to why an ideological formation claiming to speak for the majority community in British-ruled India should have remained so aloof from anti-colonial movements of all kinds. Perhaps a clue lies in the potential logic of mass struggle, particularly as inspired by a man who was a devout Hindu, but who had made, right from the beginning of his political life, Hindu–Muslim unity a basic credo. Savarkar's reminiscences of his years in prison provide some illuminating data here. In his last years in the Andamans, and then in Ratnagiri and Yeravda prisons in 1921–3, the man who around the same time was getting down to writing *Hindutva* repeatedly encountered prisoners of the Non-Cooperation–Khilafat movement. He was horrified by their 'jejune politics', 'disease of insanity, an epidemic of megalomania.' For here were people who did not seem worried even by Mappila atrocities, and dared to suggest that 'whatever had happened should be treated as dead past; Hindus

[27] See chapter III above.
[28] John Zavos, *The Emergence of Hindu Nationalism in India* (Delhi, 2000), pp. 153–4.

may convert themselves to Islam; what mattered most was Swaraj, and it must be won.' Savarkar claims, in two sections entitled 'The trouble of the Khilafat' and 'the confusion of Gandhism', that eventually he was able to win them over, through lectures about the Malabar events, 'dealing at large with the whole history of the question.' 'Their politics changed from non-cooperation into responsive cooperation [with British rule]. . . . Winning Swaraj by Charkha, supporting the Khilafat movement as the duty of the Hindus, and ridiculous definitions of non-violence, I exploded them all by invincible logic and by an appeal to history.'[29] 'History' again, one notes.

It is in this pattern of silences and displacements that we can discern most clearly the fundamentally Right-wing nature of the Hindutva movement. It seems to have something of the nature of a roll-back operation, or more often perhaps a pre-emptive strike against possible advances by lower-caste groups, women, and oppressed people in general. The utter silence in the writings of ideologues like Savarkar or Golwalkar about questions of mass poverty could not have been accidental. That, in divergent ways, had been a central theme in every other strand of national politics—till the coming of the ideologies of 'globalisation' and 'liberalisation'. Here we have a coincidence in time with the spectacular advance of Hindutva which requires much further explication, but once again is unlikely to have been merely fortuitous.

At the heart of Hindutva, finally, lies an authoritarian frame of mind the appeal of which might well grow among the more privileged sections as economic disparities get sharpened through the policies inaugurated under Rajiv Gandhi and Narasimha Rao but speeded up enormously, despite all the 'swadeshi' talk, under Vajpayee. The RSS organisational principle, one must remember, has always been '*ek chalak anuvartita*', following one leader. Despite the limitations imposed by coalition politics, the preparatory work for the fulfilment of this fundamentally authoritarian, anti-democratic dream is very much in progress. In the same speech at Staten Island recently that aroused some controversy through the declaration that he would always remain a 'swayamsevak', Vajpayee, the BJP's allegedly moderate

[29] V.D. Savarkar, *The Story of My Transportation For Life* (Marathi original, 1927; Eng. trans. 1st edn, Bombay, 1950), pp. 521, 544, 556.

or 'human' face, promised to his wealthy NRI supporters 'the India of our dreams' if given a two-thirds majority. Some of the contours of that dream might have been outlined, if only for the moment as a kind of testing of the waters, by the draft of a new Constitution circulated by an activist of the Akhil Bharatiya Vidyarthi Parishad. (*The Times of India*, 9 August 2000). This would subordinate Parliament, elected by universal franchise still, to a 'Guru Sabha' chosen by the highly-educated alone. The Guru Sabha would oversee defence and even the Supreme Court, and federalism would be restricted by changing the definition of the country from 'an union of states' to 'union of citizens of Bharat.' Predictably, the right to 'propagate' would be removed from the Fundamental Rights definition of religious freedom. The 1950 Preamble, quite strikingly, and in interesting contrast to other bourgeois-democratic constitutions, had placed Justice first among the proclaimed ideas of 'We, the people of India.' Now Justice will be pushed down to third place in the Preamble, below Security (i.e. no doubt, the Bomb) and Prosperity. One could not wish for greater clarity or frankness.

Index